Praise for *Home and Away*:

'Excellent.'
The Sun

'A glowing testament to the camaraderie and inclusiveness
of supporting a team lower down the football pyramid.
Everyone is welcome in this uplifting book that celebrates
the happiness to be found in reconnecting with your
friends, your team and your home.'
When Saturday Comes

'Pure gold . . . A brilliant book that all football
fans can relate to.'
Late Tackle

'A wonderfully warm-hearted book, which gives
the beautiful game a good name.'
Saga

'Endearing and engrossing . . . what this book does
beautifully is affirm that the enjoyment of football isn't so
much about the game or the result, it's about the journey
we, as supporters, take in the process.'
FourFourTwo

'A timely celebration of non-league football . . . provides
a great antidote to sport as big business.'
The Bookseller

Home and Away

Round Britain in Search of
Non-League Football Nirvana

Dave Roberts

BANTAM BOOKS

LONDON • TORONTO • SYDNEY • AUCKLAND • JOHANNESBURG

TRANSWORLD PUBLISHERS
61–63 Uxbridge Road, London W5 5SA
www.penguin.co.uk

Transworld is part of the Penguin Random House group of companies
whose addresses can be found at global.penguinrandomhouse.com

Penguin
Random House
UK

First published in Great Britain in 2016 by Bantam Press
an imprint of Transworld Publishers
Bantam edition published 2017

A CIP catalogue record for this book
is available from the British Library.

ISBN
9780857503435

Typeset in Ehrhardt by Falcon Oast Graphic Art Ltd.
Printed and bound by Clays Ltd, Bungay, Suffolk.

Penguin Random House is committed to a sustainable
future for our business, our readers and our planet. This book
is made from Forest Stewardship Council® certified paper.

1 3 5 7 9 10 8 6 4 2

For my dad

Home and Away

Prologue

It was a gorgeous sun-drenched day in the early part of the warmest May since records began. The sun was beating down from a cloudless sky. Summer had arrived and it felt good to be alive.

That was Connecticut on the day I left to move back to England after thirty-three years. Ten hours later I was standing, shivering, on Platform 3 of Gatwick station, a bitingly cold wind tearing through my flimsy Bromley FC polo shirt. My American wife, Liz, was sitting a few yards away on a bench. Her expression and body language were not saying 'I'm really glad you talked me into moving over here'.

At least things improved slightly when we got on the train. And since we were about to spend the best part of three hours travelling to our new home town of Leeds, there was plenty of time to warm up. It was great to be home.

Liz and I were both full of optimism as the train sped us from Gatwick towards London. Inspired by a few flying visits in the previous ten years, we'd decided to make the move across the Atlantic. We'd been saving as much money as we could, and had got enough − or at least we thought so − to keep us going for a year. After that, we'd decide whether to make the move permanent or go back to the US.

I was so wrapped up in the prospects of the next twelve months that I almost failed to notice that while some things change, others stay the same. The train (my first since the days of British Rail) had come to a complete standstill, and this was followed by an announcement that following a signal failure at Clapham Junction, it would now be terminating at East Croydon.

Dodging between grumpy passengers on the platform, we were told that there were unlikely to be any further trains to Victoria for at least an hour. Which would mean we'd miss our connection.

Since desperate times call for desperate measures, we dragged our suitcases out of the station and found a taxi. Could he get us to King's Cross in time for the 1.35 train to Leeds?

As it turned out, no. But that didn't stop him charging £50 for trying. And how much did Virgin Rail want for two one-way tickets to Leeds? Just £230. We decided to get a coach instead.

The coach crawled through London, and I couldn't wait to get on the motorway. Once we did, things got even worse. There were roadworks almost the entire way, with traffic jams every few minutes.

We finally pulled into Leeds bus station over an hour late, tired and hungry. And the drama hadn't finished. Our driver was starting to unload luggage from the narrow compartment under the coach when a discussion with a passenger, who blamed him for the late arrival, got a bit heated. As things escalated, and threats were exchanged, the driver dropped the bag he was holding and began to chase the man, vaulting a barrier to narrow the gap between them. As they disappeared on to the vast concourse, still screaming at each other, it became apparent that we'd need a Plan B.

And that was how I found myself, after travelling for eight hours, crawling through a sea of suitcases and backpacks collecting our luggage. As well as a few items belonging to several other passengers.

When we at last got to the hotel, Liz fell asleep straight away. But I couldn't. There were so many unanswered questions running through my mind. Like, what on earth is a chevron? And why is the M1 suddenly full of them? What is the red button on the TV remote, and what happens if I press it? How come everyone suddenly has a beard? Why do people keep asking me if I have a Nectar card?

But there was one change in England since I'd left in 1982 that was more dramatic than the rest put together. We had arrived just as my football team, the perennially underachieving Bromley of my youth, had transformed into an elite non-league side that had recently been promoted to the vertigo-inducing fifth tier of English football.

It was by far the greatest achievement in the club's 123-year history.

And while it would be a stretch to say that my little team would now be playing the giants of English football, it was true that they'd be playing teams that had *beaten* the giants of English football. There was Wrexham, who famously knocked Arsenal out of the Cup in the early nineties; Halifax, who beat Manchester United in front of the *Match of the Day* cameras when I was fifteen; and Tranmere, who'd beaten Everton fifteen years previously. At Goodison Park.

My dream was for Liz to travel the country with me, falling in love with England and falling in love with Bromley FC during the forthcoming 2015/16 football season. And by glorious coincidence, the year we'd given ourselves to make a decision would finish just after the last game.

The last – and only – time we'd gone to a game together had not provided cause for optimism. We were sat together in the John Fiorini Stand at Bromley's home ground, Hayes Lane, and following a superb defence-splitting pass from Tutu Henriques I glanced over at her in a 'See? Told you this was going to be brilliant' way, only to see that she was engrossed in a game of Angry Birds on her phone.

Still, we were both keen to discover – or rediscover in my case – Britain. And what better way than through the Vanarama National League, building trips around away fixtures? Or at least that was my pitch to Liz. We'd be able to explore the majestic beauty of the Lake District when visiting Barrow, the timeless charm of the Cotswolds (Forest Green) and industrial towns steeped in history (Kidderminster). Together we'd explore the west coast's rugged coastlines (Southport), the golden beaches of the British Riviera (Torquay), and eat the finest fish and chips money could buy (Grimsby). We'd visit the home of one of the world's most famous film studios (Borehamwood), and make pilgrimages to the birth-places of The Jam (Woking) and Joy Division (Macclesfield).

All of this made me realize how little of my country I'd seen in my twenty-five years here before heading overseas in an ultimately futile search for fame and fortune. And now we had the chance to explore some of the United Kingdom's biggest attractions, each time with a Bromley game thrown in. It was like the ultimate package holiday.

There was another reason for wanting to cram in as many games (and collect as many programmes) as possible. I think long-term fans of all but the biggest teams are conditioned to expect disappointment and I was already thinking that this season could be a one-off, forever talked about in hushed tones as the high point in the club's history.

My biggest worry – apart from Bromley finishing with no points whatsoever – was how easy it would be to adjust to the changes that recent success had brought with it. After all, the club I'd fallen in love with wasn't one that attracted gates of 3,000 plus. Or played in front of TV cameras. Or one that was planning to tear out the benches behind one of the goals and replace them with executive boxes.

The club I'd fallen in love with had been an alternative to this. You could stand or sit where you liked, and it felt like being part of a family. The queue for a half-time cup of tea was made up of the people you were watching the game with. Players recognized you, but still didn't mind giving you their autograph for the thirtieth time.

While these worries continued to surface occasionally, Liz and I gradually settled into our new home. We instantly fell in love with Leeds and met up with my sons again, who both lived there, having made the move to Yorkshire some years previously. My daughter Hazel and grandchildren came up from Burntwood, in Staffordshire, and I went down to see my dad in London. It felt as though the family was back together.

We'd got ourselves an apartment (in the time I'd been away, it seemed flats had become apartments), which was great, although the estate agent had somehow forgotten to mention that it was directly above a bay where recycling was collected at 5.50 in the morning. As I'd unpacked my suitcase, it became clear what a huge part Bromley FC still played in my life, even though I'd been living 3,368 miles away from Hayes Lane (people like me tend to know details like this). On top was a selection of programmes wrapped in my red and black Bromley scarf for protection, and a T-shirt commemorating promotion to the Conference South in 2006. Towards the bottom came my BROMLEY FC mug, a car sticker (we didn't own a car, so no idea why I got this), my well-worn copy of *Bromley Football Club 1892–1992: A Centenary History* by Muriel V. Searle, and finally a small brass lapel badge which had been a present from Roy, a friend since we first met at Hayes Lane in the 1960s.

With these scattered around the place I was soon feeling more at home. I found out what the red button was for and loved the difference it brought to my TV watching.

Our cable supplier had been an easy choice. We got BT. Their main selling point was that they covered the Vanarama National League. They didn't need any other selling points.

Every day I was discovering exciting new things about the country I thought I knew. One of the best was finding out that Marks & Spencer sold food. Food so good that our fridge, which was the size of a hotel-room minibar, was permanently stuffed with M&S ready meals, M&S salads and M&S fruit jellies. Another thrilling discovery was that bus shelters now had electronic displays, telling you how long you'd have to wait for a bus.

The more we found out about modern-day Britain, the better it felt.

Everything was in place. I was now ready for the pre-season build-up.

In many ways, this is my favourite time of the year. There's a feeling of blind optimism, without any pesky evidence to cloud it. Fantasies run free. It wasn't totally impossible that Bromley would be a Football League club this time next year. Unlikely, but not impossible. It was a time to dream.

The first major summer landmark came when season tickets went on sale. They would cost £300 according to the announcement on the club website. I seriously thought of getting one, but then reminded myself that my plan was to travel the length of the land watching Bromley play away, and taking those exorbitant Virgin trains down to London every other weekend I'd end up paying about £75 for every home game I went to. Even Arsenal fans would baulk at that.

Despite the fact that £300 seemed a lot for a non-league team, the likes of Tranmere and Grimsby were charging a fair bit more. Only moneybags Eastleigh in the Vanarama National League had season tickets for less – and bizarrely, moneybags Manchester City in the Premier League did as well.

But there was no time to dwell on such matters, because the next major event on the pre-season calendar was soon upon us. The betting odds for 2015/16 appeared online, and when I saw them I felt a warm glow of pride and satisfaction: we were eighteenth favourite at 66-1. Sensing a shrewd investment, I put a tenner on Bromley to win the League. The smart money (unlike mine) was on Tranmere, Grimsby and Wrexham.

The Bromley odds, however, represented more than just an opportunity to idiotically throw money away. They meant that the bookies were confident that six teams would finish below my team. Which meant Bromley would avoid the relegation zone, and that was all I wanted from the season. Even twentieth would be a massive achievement.

Favourites for the drop were the nearest club to my new Leeds home, Guiseley, who were fourteen minutes away by train. If it ever looked like a battle between them and us to avoid relegation, I'd be able to go along and support whomever they were playing.

A few days later came the highlight of the summer, Vanarama National League-wise: the release of the fixtures – the time when planning for the season can begin in earnest.

The fixture gods were extremely kind to me. Part of my reasoning for not investing in a Hayes Lane season ticket was that I wouldn't be able to afford to go to every game unless I managed to get more work. For August, I showed remarkable restraint by pencilling in just three of the seven matches on offer – the opener against Wrexham on 8 August and away to Grimsby and Halifax on the following Saturdays.

An hour later, this remarkable restraint had slipped and I'd added the home game with Dover and the trip to Forest Green Rovers. I was now planning on watching five games in the first three weeks. At that rate, my football budget wouldn't come close to lasting until Christmas.

Hopefully these games would be enough for me to adjust to the new, successful Bromley FC. Not only did I need to get used to the rarefied level of the Vanarama National League, I would also have to get acquainted with the players. I'd hardly seen any of them play apart from on YouTube.

This newfound status was rammed home in early July when I had my first experience of big-club problems: trying to arrange travel for the season opener at home to Wrexham when there was a possibility that the game might be moved to Friday night because of TV coverage. Bromley Football Club on live TV nationwide? The thought still seemed like some kind of weird dream. I couldn't book a train until I knew when the game was. And while I waited, the fare could well go up. Plus, if it was on the Friday night, I would have to find a place to stay. Supporting a football team was getting a lot more complicated.

A few weeks later, as I checked my Twitter feed in bed (I followed seven Bromley players; excitingly, one of them, Jack Holland, followed me back), I finally saw the announcement I'd been waiting for. The League tweeted that no game in the opening round of matches would be televised, which meant Bromley would be playing Wrexham on the Saturday.

I was slightly baffled when Liz showed no interest in a ten-hour round trip to witness history being made, but she was happy for me to go. Fearing a sudden overnight rush for Leeds-to-London tickets for 8 August, I leapt out of bed just after midnight and booked my same-day return trip.

The next few weeks were busy. There were important matters to take care of, such as booking a car for our just-the-two-of-us getaway bank holiday weekend, which also included finding a romantic B&B within easy walking distance of the Forest Green Rovers ground.

Soon it was time for the pre-season friendlies, and I nervously kept an eye on updates on Twitter. The games attained huge significance. A draw with a strong Millwall side (League One) was proof that we were in for a brilliant season; a 2-1 loss to Gillingham (also League One) was proof we were in for a disappointing season. A draw with Cambridge United (League Two) was, on balance, a good sign. And then, on 30 July, came the ultimate test: a full-strength Premier League squad, Crystal Palace, came to Hayes Lane. The last time this had happened, as far as I knew, was just before the disastrous 1969/70 season, when Palace scored six times before easing off and Bromley's season went downhill from there.

This time, when Palace again scored six times before easing off, I tried not to read too much into it.

A couple of days later came a satisfying 2–0 win against Sutton, from the Vanarama Conference South, and the pre-season was finally over. It was time to get on with the proper football, starting with Wrexham at home.

Being a Saturday, the recycling truck didn't wake me early on the morning of the match. Instead it was the truck delivering laundry at 6.15 to the hotel attached to our building, the words 'Stand well clear – vehicle reversing' playing over and over again as it manoeuvred into a tiny gap. Anticipation of the day ahead made it impossible to get back to sleep and I was ready to go with several hours to spare.

As I was leaving, Liz looked a little worried.

'Are you sure you're going to be OK?' she said. 'It's a long day at your age.'

I laughed it off, not wanting to acknowledge that she probably had a point. Ageing was another thing I was having to adapt to, and I'd noticed that at sixty I was finding getting around a little harder. The last time I'd followed the Ravens (Bromley's nickname, after the three birds that can be found on the club badge) for an entire season I'd briskly walk a couple of miles just to see them train. Those days were gone.

Perhaps with that in mind, I took a leisurely stroll to Leeds station and boarded the train just half an hour before it was due to depart.

I sat down in an aisle seat and put a bag of the M&S version of classic Pick'n'Mix sweets on to the table. I then took out an old but perfectly preserved programme from my backpack. It was from Bromley's home game with Newport in early 2010, the last time a Welsh team had played at Hayes Lane. I could think of no better way to get in the mood.

I was full of nervous excitement. The nervousness came from my previous experiences with trains and not actually knowing whether we'd make it as far as King's Cross, the excitement from knowing that if we did, I would soon be back home – standing behind the Wrexham goal at Hayes Lane.

Watching the biggest League game in my team's 123-year history.

HOME
AND
AWAY

One

I first started feeling really worried on the Victoria to Bromley South train. Not because of any concerns over another signal failure drama, but because the carriage was absolutely packed with red-shirted Wrexham fans. If there were this many of them just under two hours before kick-off, there had to be a good chance they'd outnumber the Bromley fans.

This thought added to the growing feeling that we were out of our depth. We were about to play a famous and very well-supported club that had played at Wembley in each of the last two seasons in the FA Trophy final.

As a way of avoiding eye contact with my fellow travellers, whose songs indicated that they didn't much like (a) Bromley or (b) the English, I studied the paper intently.

And that was when I saw something that gave me hope.

The Vanarama National League table, which was alongside the fixtures, showed Bromley to be on the edge of the play-offs while Wrexham were right at the bottom. This was, of course, because the season hadn't yet started and the teams were listed in alphabetical order, but I clung to the possibility that this would give us some sort of psychological advantage.

Sometimes I love alphabetical order.

When we arrived at Bromley South there was no question in my mind as to what I was going to do to pass the nearly one and a half hours before the game started. I'd head straight to the ground.

This was something I'd been wanting to do since the day we arrived in the country. I had even suggested it to Liz when we were stranded in East Croydon, my argument being that it was less than half an hour away and we'd probably miss the Leeds train anyway.

'Who are they playing?' she'd asked.

'There isn't a game on – I just want to go to the ground.'

'What, and watch training?'

'No, I doubt there'll be any training this time of year.'

'So you want us to drag these bags halfway across London just so you can go and stand around in an empty football stadium on a freezing cold day?'

Well, obviously. Sometimes the cultural gap between us felt like a gaping chasm.

Needless to say, we didn't make the trip that day; but here I was, three months later, on the familiar route down Hayes Lane. The sun was out and a steady stream of people were making their way into the ground. Most were wandering around in a kind of happy daze – like me, wanting to make the most of this historic occasion.

Once I'd paid my £15 and got in, I looked around and recognized a few faces, some from previous visits, some from Facebook. It was still well over an hour before kick-off but there were already more people than I'd ever seen packed into the ground.

The away end was almost completely full – a sea of scarlet. It looked spectacular. This was something Bromley would never be able to match. When your team plays in white and black, you're never going to make the same visual impact.

As I approached the programme stand, I made a painful and

difficult decision. In order to economize and maybe squeeze an extra game in, I'd buy only one programme instead of my usual two. Two would cost me a fiver. I could get two melon-free fruit salads from M&S for that.

Having made the decision, the obvious dilemma was this: do I use the programme throughout the game and risk damage, or put it in the bag I'd brought, keeping it in pristine condition for my collection? Taking the latter course would make it redundant in terms of its core function, which is to help identify players.

And that was when the Vanarama National League intervened. The back of the programme revealed that squad numbers would now be used, with each player's name on the back of his shirt. I wouldn't need the programme during the match. I felt the stress melt away.

Another innovation demonstrated that Bromley were now literally playing in a different league. It was 2.30 p.m. and both sides were warming up when, directly in front of me, the referee and his linesmen appeared from the tunnel, wearing pristine black uniforms, complete with headphones and mouthpieces. They looked immaculate. And very, very fit. They faced one another and had an intense motivational discussion. They then carried out an elaborate set of perfectly synchronized stretching exercises before running around the pitch together.

This left me with a slight hankering for the Isthmian League days, when you could witness a linesman strolling out on to the pitch, taking one last drag of his cigarette as he took up his position then reluctantly grinding it into the turf with the studs of his boot.

There was something familiar about today's referee. I was sure I'd seen him before. And then I remembered.

In the sort of incredible coincidence that only a programme obsessive would find exciting, the same referee had officiated on one of my last visits to Hayes Lane, seven years earlier. Mr Nigel

Lugg had been in charge for our Cup loss to AFC Hornchurch, and seeing him brought back all the feelings of injustice over the blatantly unfair penalty he'd given our opponents.

As I watched Mr Lugg (I knew he came from Chipstead – which was just as well, since programmes apparently no longer consider officials' home towns important) and his colleagues run off into the distance, I realized that the ground was filling fast and I needed to take up my seat.

I tentatively made my way behind the goal that Bromley were attacking. It had taken me several visits over the years to get around to sitting on the fringes of the supporters behind the goal. This was down to a mix of shyness and feeling like an impostor. I wasn't even sure I could call myself a real supporter, as I'd only seen a handful of games in the past thirty-five years. These were the hardcore Bromley fans. The ones who'd sat behind the same goal, week in week out, for decades.

I singled out a few I'd spoken to before or talked to on Facebook and asked them which players I should look out for. One name was trotted out by all. Rob Swaine. He was the definition of the modern-day captain, keeping in touch with fans via social media and email, a tough defender who was great in the air. Anthony Cook, a powerful winger, got a few mentions. And the goalkeeper, Alan Julian, seemed to be highly rated as well.

All I knew about Wrexham was what I'd seen on the news the previous night. A fan was saying that there was a real buzz about the place, and that the arrival of manager Gary Mills had brought a feeling of hope to the club as well as a host of new players. And a lot of these players had Football League experience.

I looked around, taking in the atmosphere. The stand was packed and the noise was shockingly loud for Hayes Lane, with each set of supporters trying to drown the other out.

As Chipstead's most prominent football official got the game – and the biggest season in Bromley's history – under way, a pattern soon emerged. Bromley sat back, while Wrexham moved the ball around, finding space with ease. We really were looking out of our depth, and the only surprise when Wrexham scored after twenty or so minutes was how long it had taken them.

I was just glad Liz wasn't here to witness the inevitable carnage.

A couple of minutes later, a Bromley free kick was floated into the area. After a scramble, Rob Swaine, still on the ground after a collision, pushed the ball into the path of centre-back Sean Francis. His first touch took the ball wide on to the corner of the six-yard box, before he struck it sweetly past the keeper into the roof of the net.

There's always that split second when a goal goes in and you can't quite believe what's just happened.

But then I felt an explosion of uncontrollable joy coursing through me as I rushed forward, punching the air. This answered any questions I might have had over whether Bromley would still mean as much to me at sixty as they had when I was fourteen.

Now I was wishing Liz was by my side. I was sure she would have finally understood.

We were level. With Wrexham. The day had taken on a dream-like quality. And before my heart rate had even got back to anything like normal, Bromley added a second. Alex Wall, the sort of player normally described as 'a big unit', finished the sort of chance most Bromley strikers from the past would have missed. An Anthony Cook pass found him ten yards out and he struck a superb first-time shot past the Wrexham keeper.

Once again, I leapt out of my seat.

But the best was yet to come. Minutes later, Cook went on a long run from his own half, leaving defenders in his wake. His pass to Wall on the edge of the area was played into the path of fellow striker Moses Emmanuel, who made it 3-1 to Bromley.

It was a hugely unlikely scoreline. I don't think anyone had expected this – certainly not the bookies, who'd had the visitors as hot favourites.

The second half felt as though time had stood still. Bromley packed their defence and Wrexham just couldn't find a way through. And when they finally did, Alan Julian made one of the best saves I'd seen at Hayes Lane, diving full length to prevent what had looked to be a certain goal.

It felt as though it might, just possibly, be Bromley's day.

As the fourth official held up his board to indicate three minutes of added time, I noticed Graeme, a man in his forties I knew from Facebook, pacing aimlessly around behind the goal, looking absolutely petrified. He was pale and breathing rapidly, beads of sweat on his forehead.

'They're going to score,' he said. 'I just know it.'

Even though I barely knew him, I put a consoling arm around his shoulder.

'Don't worry,' I said with a confidence that surprised me. 'We're going to win this.'

When the final whistle went, there was a huge, spontaneous roar from the home fans. All the suffering Bromley teams of the past had put us through was forgotten. It was one of the best results in the club's history. And as someone who has pored over every single page of *Bromley Football Club 1892-1992: A Centenary History* by Muriel V. Searle, I feel suitably qualified to make that claim.

My instinct was to stick around, soaking up the atmosphere and reliving the goals, but I had a train to catch – and I knew from experience that missing it would be costly. Luckily, I made it to King's Cross in plenty of time, took my seat on the 6.35 to Leeds and managed to find a wifi signal.

One of the biggest benefits of the internet to mankind is that match reports are now available not long after the final whistle. On the journey home I was able to read the North Wales media's view of the game. They were, on the whole, generous in their praise of Bromley and disappointed in their team's performance.

One of the reports included an interview with the Wrexham manager, Gary Mills, whose explanation as to why his team conceded the first two goals was an outstanding example of football manager-speak. 'Manny Smith has tried to win a ball,' he said, 'which he could never win and gives away a free kick and we don't deal with it, it goes in the box, then we are still dictating play straight after that, and the full-back is too far on because we were dictating play that much, so it is a tough one.'

I think he was saying that Wrexham lost because they were a much better side and therefore too much in control of the game.

It was time to move on to reading the programme, and I spent a happy ten minutes looking at a double-page spread showing all the players and the names of their kit sponsors. It was a great way to learn to recognize Bromley's squad, even though only captain Rob Swaine actually had a kit sponsor, Universa Law.

When I finally put it down, just before Grantham, I reflected on events. It had been a day I'd never forget. I'd loved sitting with the Bromley fans, celebrating with them. If this was what success felt like, I'd happily take a season of it. Were Bromley any good? I thought so. Their counter-attacking looked impressive and they definitely had the ability to shut up shop.

Bromley were now third in the table, just behind Boreham Wood on alphabetical order. Sometimes I hate alphabetical order. Despite that, we were officially in the play-off places.

We were on our way to League football. And this was more or less a fact.

The *Sun* that morning had carried a story on how a Norwegian fan had run *Football Manager* for fifty-six days non-stop and this revealed that the Premier League table for 3015 would have

Bromley in fifth place. Which raised the tantalizing, if distant, promise of Europa League football at Hayes Lane. For now, though, third in the Vanarama National League would do just fine.

The chance to climb the ladder even higher came just three days later. Bromley, who for some reason would be playing in an all-yellow kit, were making the short trip to Woking. I couldn't afford it, although in a cruel twist Liz, who still had her US job at the time (the company allowed her to work overseas for six months), had spent the morning in a meeting not far from the ground. She came straight back to Leeds afterwards.

Last time I followed Bromley for an entire season, I'd ring the ground for score updates every few minutes, making such a nuisance of myself that they eventually stopped answering. Now, there was no need. I had my headphones on, plugged into the BBC Radio Surrey commentary on the laptop. In my right hand was my phone, which was showing the official Bromley FC Twitter feed, and in my left was Liz's phone with live Vanarama National League scores. The iPad was propped up against a box of tissues, showing an up-to-the-minute League table.

The evening got off to a quiet start. The 'big unit' Alex Wall was causing a few problems but it really didn't sound as though much was happening. This was perfect. A draw would be a great result.

My hopes dimmed slightly when defensive midfielder Lee Minshull, who had impressed on Saturday, was carried off the field and replaced by Reece Prestedge. A quick Google search revealed little about him, apart from the fact that he was born on Christmas Day.

The highlight of the opening half hour came when the commentator was momentarily drowned out by the travelling fans singing 'Come on, Bromley', reminding me of Saturday and making me wish I was there. 'Good support coming from supporters who have made the journey from Kent,' he noted, through gritted teeth.

But as Bromley clung on, our next opponents Grimsby had gone two up against Barrow and leapfrogged above us in the table. We were now fourth.

The bad news continued when captain and personal trainer Rob Swaine went down injured and had to be substituted. According to Google, his replacement, Jack Holland, had the same birthday as me. No wonder we had already made a Twitter connection.

The next news came from Tranmere. They had gone a goal up, sending Bromley down to fifth.

Then things went from bad to catastrophic. Woking scored and Bromley's freefall down the table continued. The live update now showed them in ninth place.

By the time Woking's second goal went in, following a goalmouth scramble, Bromley had dropped to eleventh – one place behind Wrexham. Saturday suddenly seemed a distant, if still happy, memory.

As I stared in miserable disbelief at the table, long after the full-time whistle had blown, I acknowledged that there were still plenty of positives. Even the commentator had been impressed with Anthony Cook, who would have had Player of the Season wrapped up if it was awarded after two games, while goalkeeper Alan Julian and 'big unit' Alex Wall continued to impress.

On the evidence so far, Bromley weren't out of place playing at this level and could well survive. There were huge games nearly every week and I felt lucky that I was back home so that I could see as many as was humanly possible. We now had a run of fixtures which included consecutive games against teams yet to get a point this season – Halifax away and Dover at home. But before that there was the small matter of Grimsby away. Which I was

particularly excited about because I'd arranged a pre-match chat
with my Grimsby equivalent – a sixty-year-old non-league fanatic
who followed his team around the country, having supported
them from an early age.

His name was Dave Roberts.

HOME
AND
AWAY

Two

I was sitting at Doncaster station waiting for the train to Cleethorpes, which was already ten minutes late. To pass the time I sat on a bench, writing down questions to ask Dave Roberts.

I'd read about Dave in the *Guardian*, just before the season started. He wasn't just a Grimsby fan, he'd also helped crowdfund over £100,000 for their manager to spend on players, after the disappointment of losing in the play-off final on penalties the previous season.

As I was making a note to ask him about his role on the club's board, I slowly became aware of some noise coming from a small group of Scunthorpe fans standing on the platform opposite. 'Train-spot-ter, train-spot-ter, train-spot-ter,' they were chanting, and they were pointing at me and laughing. At first, I had no idea why. But it didn't take long for me to work it out. There I was, an old bloke with glasses in a khaki combat jacket, pens sticking out of my top pocket, sitting at a railway station with my packed lunch beside me, jotting things down in a notebook.

I wanted to reassure them that I was a genuine football fan, just like them, but instead settled for waving weakly. It was a relief when their train (a Virgin Rail EMU Class 390 390044) arrived and took them away.

My train arrived a few minutes later. A couple of Bromley fans, one from Cardiff, the other from Manchester, were on board and I sat down with them.

As we talked about the game ahead, I checked Twitter and saw that Rob Swaine, who had gone off injured on Tuesday night, had tweeted that his room-mate, Jack Holland, had forced him to take the single bed at the hotel last night. This was exciting and unexpected news – it meant that he'd made the journey and was therefore fit enough to play.

We arrived in Cleethorpes with a renewed sense of optimism.

Cleethorpes station is on the seafront, so I decided to have a quick look around. The seaside was another piece of England that I'd missed; the salty smell and squawking seagulls, weather-worn B&Bs and bright-pink candyfloss, slot machines and sandcastles. The only things missing from the picture were the fishing trawlers. They'd disappeared a long time ago.

On the way to the ground, which was a brisk twenty-minute walk past an endless row of nail bars, tattoo parlours and chip shops, I got talking to a few Grimsby fans. They were easy to identify on account of the fact they were all wearing black-and-white-striped replica shirts. This was an unusual sight. Unusual for me, anyway. The last time I'd been to any English football ground other than Hayes Lane was in 1986, when scarves were the most common way of showing which team you supported.

The atmosphere around football grounds seemed a lot less threatening than in the eighties too, although admittedly I was basing this on a sample of one. Despite the warm welcome, I was still worried about being attacked as I emerged from the Mariners fish and chip shop, clutching a bag of chips.

The danger came from above, in the form of hungry seagulls. After co-existing with humans for thousands of years, there had recently been reports from a number of resorts of these birds assaulting people and flying off with their chips. The problem had become so serious that the Prime Minister waded in, saying, 'I think a big conversation needs to happen about this and frankly the people we need to listen to are people who really understand this issue.'

But although a few gulls flapped around noisily overhead, none swooped and I finished my chips just as I arrived at Blundell Park, using the time-honoured method of following the floodlights.

Compared to Hayes Lane, it was a massive stadium. It was also the first all-seater I'd ever seen, and I couldn't stop taking pictures on my phone. There were a number of other firsts, too, including a £3 programme and a sighting of huge plastic inflatable fishes at a football match. The thought of Bromley playing here in a League match was ridiculous. It felt more like a cup tie.

I went into the bar for away fans (another first) and told the barman that I was here to see Dave Roberts. He took me through to the other bar, which was absolutely packed with mainly bald middle-aged men wearing Grimsby Town shirts.

It was there that I was introduced to Dave Roberts.

He was an amiable, no-nonsense kind of man, so passionate about his team that his pint glass sat on the bar untouched for the full fifteen minutes he spoke to me about them. Dave was rightly proud of 'Operation Promotion'. It had allowed Grimsby not only to sign a couple of players, but also to take on the goalkeeping coach that manager Paul Hurst had always wanted.

One thing was clear. Unlike the higher levels, non-league football still belonged to the fans.

I finished by asking him who I should look out for today. He mentioned a couple of names, and then said, 'Keep an eye on Padraig Amond.'

After a souvenir selfie, Dave Roberts left the bar, walked on to the pitch in front of nearly 5,000 people and presented the club he loved with a cheque for £110,000. It was a surprisingly powerful moment.

The teams came out not long after, Grimsby in shirts I was already very familiar with and Bromley all in yellow. As I watched Bromley warm up, from behind the goal where the Bromley fans had been put, I had a feeling of impending doom. Neither Rob Swaine nor Lee Minshull, two key defensive players, were in the starting line-up – although Swaine was on the bench.

There was also a mystery player on the pitch. Despite Bromley's squad numbers only going up to 20, there now seemed to be a number 27. I say seemed to be, because the number on his yellow shirt was white, unlike the rest of the team who had black numbers, and it was almost impossible to read from a distance.

After the game had been going for a couple of minutes, I looked around for Padraig Amond and soon saw him. He was right in front of me, slipping the ball past Alan Julian for Grimsby's opening goal. Dave Roberts had been right.

He was also right about Omar Bogle, who made the most of a Jack Holland tackle by theatrically sprawling over the defender's outstretched leg, prompting one of the linesmen, whose names were Smith and Jones, to wave his flag furiously. Bogle converted the penalty and it was 2-0 with barely ten minutes gone.

I don't think any of the Bromley fans were expecting their team to win. But I also don't think any were expecting it to be this bad. Grimsby had complete control of the midfield and our defence looked disorganized.

When Amond added a third after twenty or so minutes, it was becoming painful to watch. Refreshingly, the travelling fans were as upbeat as ever, making more noise than I'd ever thought possible from eighty-seven people. When the cry of 'Up the Mariners, fish, fish, fish!' rang out from several thousand Grimsby voices, the small army of Bromley fans responded loudly with 'Is this all you get at home?'

Making more noise than anyone else was Naughty Nigel. I'd heard about Naughty Nigel from several people, but this was the first time I'd seen him. He was of an indeterminate age, with long, unruly hair. He had a Bromley flag draped around his neck, an inflatable pink flamingo in his hand, and a glazed expression on his face. His encouragement was often incoherent, but he did seem to be starting most of the songs and chants. Occasionally a fellow supporter had to urge him to calm down, even though there was little to get excited about on the pitch.

That is, until just before half-time. This was when our mysterious number 27 rose high to head a perfect Joe Anderson cross into the corner of the net to make it 3-1, giving the travelling fans real hope for a second-half fightback.

'We're gonna win 4-3, we're gonna win 4-3!' sang a delirious Naughty Nigel. And this time everyone – including me – joined in.

During the break the announcer read out the Premier League scores, and I noticed that very few people were paying attention. I had also found myself caring less and less over the years. The cheque that Dave Roberts had handed over before the game represented the loyalty and passion of over two thousand fans in an area of high unemployment, and had taken months to collect. Meanwhile, in the Premier League, a twenty-year-old winger who'd won nothing in his short career had just switched teams for nearly double that amount. In wages. Every week.

Half-time was also an opportunity to watch the highlights of the first half on the big screen – something else I'd never seen at a football ground. Watching the penalty decision again fuelled my feeling of injustice. I hadn't yet forgiven Mr Lugg of Chipstead for his terrible decision against AFC Hornchurch in 2008 and had a feeling this one might also take me a while to get over.

When Bromley came out for the second half, they'd made a change. There was no number 27. I later found out that his name was Callum Davies, who had signed on loan from Gillingham the day before. The reason for the white numbers was because they'd been acquired from the Grimsby club shop as soon as it opened, and hurriedly ironed on before kick-off. His debut had lasted forty-five minutes.

He had been replaced by Louis Dennis, a more attacking option. Bromley had reorganized and looked much more effective. This was either brilliant tactical awareness from Mark Goldberg (the Bromley manager, best known for losing £40 million when he bought Crystal Palace FC), or Grimsby easing off, feeling that they'd already done enough.

As the clock on the screen ticked towards ninety minutes, I felt as though we were on the verge of a huge victory. Bromley drawing a half with the mighty Grimsby Town would be a massive achievement, proving beyond doubt that we belonged at this level.

Half a dozen stewards took up their position behind the goal, looking bored.

'Running-on-pitch stewards get ready,' boomed Mash, a Jamaican-born teacher and one of the more eccentric Bromley fans, sounding like a particularly evil Bond villain. 'You will not be able to handle us.'

Even the hard-faced stewards burst out laughing at this.

Soon after that came heartbreak when a clever passing move cut open a tired Bromley defence, and Craig Clay made it 4-1 from close range. Last-minute goals always hurt more, but this one was extra painful. It ruined our second-half clean sheet.

Seconds later, the final whistle went, and I took one last look around, taking in the scene. The Bromley fans had stayed behind to applaud their team, who had come over to thank them for making the journey. Naughty Nigel had fallen between a couple of benches, still clutching on to his inflatable flamingo and making no effort to get up. He had avoided injury and seemed happy enough.

A cheerful middle-aged security woman said 'See you again' to a couple of departing Bromley boys.

'I doubt it,' one responded, ruefully. I wasn't sure if he was saying we were going down or they were going up, but you wouldn't have bet against at least one of those things happening.

As I walked back to the station, I realized Grimsby Town were a Football League club in every sense apart from the literal one. Their stadium was superb, the state of the pitch brilliant, and the fans turned out in big numbers. They'll beat a lot of teams this season, I thought.

When you're looking for a place to persuade you that modern Britain is somewhere you want to call home, you probably wouldn't start at Cleethorpes, but I'd enjoyed it. I was starting to recognize the Bromley players and getting to know some of the fans. We had lost 4-1 and were in twentieth place in the table, but apart from that it had been a good day.

But if Grimsby away was a game we were expected to lose, Braintree at home the following Tuesday was a game we had to win if we were going to survive in the Vanarama National League.

On the morning of the Braintree game, I thought seriously about going down for it, but decided that I needed to preserve my fast-dwindling Bromley-watching budget and follow it from home.

Ian, a former GB international cyclist whom I'd met at Grimsby, had set up a helpful Twitter service for fans unable to make the game. He called it Naughty Nigel Watch, and this was where he posted photos and updates on Naughty Nigel's activities. The pre-kick-off tweet reported 'No sign of Naughty Nigel yet. Situation Calm.'

The first sighting of the evening came at 7.35, simply entitled 'First Beer', with a picture that didn't really convince me that the pint in Naughty Nigel's hand was the first of the evening. But with kick-off approaching it was time to put Naughty Nigel aside and focus on the game, courtesy of BBC Radio Essex. In an attempt to build Sky Sports levels of hype into the game, the commentator repeated, at every possible opportunity, that Braintree playing at Bromley was some kind of massive show-down between Essex and Kent.

As opposed to a Tuesday night fixture between two of the League's lesser lights.

Having seen them twice now, it seemed obvious that the first quarter of a game was Bromley's weakness. Against Wrexham they'd barely touched the ball during that time, and at Grimsby they'd gone three down.

Listening to the commentary, it was clear that this game was no different. The first twenty minutes were tense, with Braintree looking dangerous and Bromley unable to get started. But as the stopwatch app on my phone ticked past the 20:01 mark, I started to relax.

After twenty-three minutes, Braintree scored. From the description, it sounded as though once again the Bromley defence had switched off, failing to clear the ball after an excellent save by Julian.

Braintree scored again just after half-time – again, poor defensive work. Apart from a shot by the manager's son, Bradley Goldberg, that hit the post, we didn't look like scoring.

As the game went into the closing stages, and since nothing much was happening, I checked in on Naughty Nigel Watch. The latest news had him 'leading a group of 12-year-olds in chants abusing the Braintree keeper'.

But then, much to the dismay of the commentary team, Bromley scored what sounded like the goal of the season so far. A miracle pass from Anthony Cook and a brilliant first touch from Moses Emmanuel, who then finished coolly. It was, as the commentator put it, game on.

His co-commentator went a step further, saying that he felt Bromley could get a draw. It seemed he could be right as Bromley mounted attack after attack, with Cook leading the way. But Braintree held out. It was another disappointing finish. When the co-commentator had said he thought Bromley could snatch a draw, I'd taken his word for it. But all he'd done was give me false hope.

Bromley were on the cusp of the relegation places. If we lost again on Saturday, any of the four teams below (Aldershot, Kidderminster, Southport and Halifax) could overtake us by winning.

That game was the visit to Halifax, who were bottom of the table with no points. Liz would be coming along for her first match of the season. I wondered what she'd make of Bromley FC. I wondered what she'd make of the fans. Most of all I wondered what she'd make of Naughty Nigel.

HOME
AND
AWAY

Three

Halifax is a small West Yorkshire town steeped in history. Famously, back in 1972 the local football team, then in Division Four, beat a full-strength Manchester United in the Watney Cup.

It's also a town of great unspoilt natural beauty. I know this because it was the setting for cosy Sunday night BBC drama *Last Tango in Halifax*. Liz and I couldn't wait to visit the idyllic dales, and see the beautiful Victorian architecture, cherry trees and old-world country pubs in real life.

The only cloud on the horizon was the weather forecast for 22 August which included rain, lightning, thunderstorms and possible tornadoes. Not ideal conditions when you're trying to convince your wife that the UK is a brilliant place to live and Bromley are a brilliant team to watch.

From the moment the laundry delivery truck woke us at 7.20 a.m. we were eagerly anticipating the day ahead, and it got off to a perfect start with lunch with Steve and Sheila, friends who lived in a village overlooking Halifax in the valley below.

The first shock of the day came as we drove to the ground. Real-life Halifax wasn't quite the same as the Halifax on TV. *Last Tango* hadn't featured the concrete tower blocks or run-down shops.

Still, the football ground was in a lovely leafy setting, and that's what really matters.

It was a measure of Bromley's pulling power that there was a huge row of empty parking spaces on the road outside the stadium. This was unusual: since I'd been back I'd noticed that cars were everywhere. Streets that used to be tree-lined were now car-lined – bumper to bumper, the tiniest of gaps between them. When I lived here before, you could park pretty much anywhere, even in central London.

Everywhere also seemed more crowded. Well, everywhere apart from Shay Stadium. There were a few hundred scattered around the huge stand and behind one of the goals. This was disappointing for a ground with so much history. George Best had played here, as had Denis Law. And I still remember Halifax's winning goal from *Match of the Day*. Dave 'Little Chaddy' Chadwick was pulled down in the box, in a tackle with 'timing so late it belonged to last season', according to excitable commentator Barry Davies. Bobby Wallace converted.

The memory added to the thrill of being there. It also made me feel proud of what Bromley had achieved. They'd earned the right to play at venues like this.

Liz's first question was not about Rob Swaine's injury or whether Moses Emmanuel (last season's top scorer, albeit under the name Moses Ademola) would be starting up front. She wanted to know where the bar was. When she saw it, she perked up, and we wandered over to get her a bottle of cider. We were about to climb the stairs into the stand when a steward told her that bottles weren't allowed in the ground and she was sent off to the naughty step, at the edge of the bar area, to finish it. She seemed perfectly happy with that.

Someone missing from the naughty step, and indeed the Shay Stadium, was Naughty Nigel. It seemed he'd decided not to come. The place would be a lot quieter without him.

Other familiar faces turned up. I wished I had the social skills
to go up and talk to them. Instead, I read one of my copies of the
programme (I was predictably back to buying two), which was
called *Shaymen Shout*. Or at least stared at the part of the cover
that said 'FC Halifax Town v. Bromley', as though I couldn't quite
believe it was really happening. At the dawn of the 1970s when I
was watching Bromley play teams like Corinthian Casuals,
Dulwich Hamlet and Walthamstow Avenue, Halifax Town, managed by Alan Ball's dad, were playing teams like Aston Villa,
Swansea City and Fulham in the old Third Division.

This was just one of the reasons I was determined to collect
each programme from the biggest season in Bromley's history.
Someone I knew from Facebook but had never met had got me
the programmes from Woking away and Braintree at home, which
would complete the set to date. I'd arranged to meet up with him
at the Forest Green Rovers game to collect them. He told me he'd
be wearing a yellow Adidas rucksack.

As I read through *Shaymen Shout* (and Liz got through
another bottle of cider fifty yards away) I came across the most
poignant line I've ever seen in a programme. 'Jordan Burrow,' it
read, 'is still The Shaymen's top scorer, and only scorer, with
three goals.' So if we could keep him out, we should get at least a
point.

In recent days I'd felt my old obsession with Bromley FC creep-
ing back. It had been growing stronger with each game, as I started
to identify the players and pick out my favourites (currently goalkeeper Alan Julian and mercurial winger Anthony Cook). The
signs were all there: anxiously checking the time every few minutes before leaving; re-reading the previous week's programme
from cover to cover; checking the weather forecast to make sure
there was no possibility of postponement. I was hugely excited
about this game. I knew we weren't as bad as the table suggested.
There was a run of home games coming up in early September,

which I'd decided to miss for financial reasons. I wondered if I'd be able to stick to this.

The Bromley contingent (seventy-three, officially) were in good voice, going through their vocal but, in all honesty, limited array of songs. There wasn't a lot of variety. And that was why when a post headed 'New Chant' had appeared on the Bromley FC forum before the game, it felt like potentially very good news. It had been posted by first-timer speediej, and read:

> My mate told me a chant that he thought would be good at Bromley:
>
> B-R-O
> B-R-O
> B-R-O-M-L-E-Y
> WITH A G-double E-Z-E-R-S
> BROMLEY GEEZERS ARE THE BEST!
>
> Thoughts?

Thoughts were unanimous, ranging from 'This wins for the funniest post on here . . . Song sounds fully rubbish to be honest' to the slightly ironic 'One of the best maiden posts on a football forum I've ever seen'. My view was that it was on roughly the same level as the trainspotter chant dreamed up by those Scunthorpe supporters. I was glad I'd only had to read speediej's song and not hear it.

I'd invented a song for the terraces once. Or rather, adapted it. As a young Bromley fan forever trying to get in with the school skinheads, I penned the following, to the tune of 'Fortune's Always Hiding':

Woking's always running,
Sutton's running too,
So's the Bench End, Bromley
Running after you.

The only thing that watered down the intimidation factor somewhat was the knowledge that the Bench End usually consisted of just me, my peace-loving hippie friend The Grubby, and a couple of pensioners.

It was probably just as well that no one ever heard it.

But it meant I understood the hope that must have been present in the creator of 'Bromley Geezers Are the Best' – presumably about the same age now as I was then – when he released his composition, imagining it being chanted by hundreds if not thousands of Bromley fans.

I felt sorry for him and hoped it wouldn't put him off trying again.

It seemed we'd be stuck with the usual chants today when a burst of 'You are my Bromley, my only Bromley, you make me happy, when skies are grey' greeted the players as they ran out on to the pitch. As I'm sure you've worked out, 'You Are My Bromley' is essentially 'You Are My Sunshine', but with 'Bromley' replacing every 'sunshine'.

They were playing in all red, which was better than last week's all yellow. As I told a fascinated Liz who had finally taken up her seat, I'd seen Bromley three times this season and each time they'd worn a completely different strip.

There was still no sign of Rob Swaine (whose latest tweet had him asking the staff at a Manchester Premier Inn if they could replace his TV remote) or Lee Minshull, but manager Mark Goldberg had made a few changes. Number 27 from last week had been replaced by last season's Portsmouth captain, Ben Chorley, who would now partner Sean Francis in central defence. Max Porter came into midfield.

As the game got under way, I was expecting Halifax to prove that their position at the bottom of the table, like ours, was a false one. This was a big club. But it was soon clear that Bromley would comfortably survive those troublesome first twenty minutes. A scrappy first half was scoreless only because of the ineptness of the finishing and the brilliance of both goal-keepers. Jordan Burrow, 'The Shaymen's top scorer, and only scorer', was particularly busy, hitting the bar as well as bursting clean through, only to have his shot spectacularly saved by Julian.

For me, the most interesting thing was that the stand opposite us, which was home to the TV gantry, had just one person sitting in it. And the terraces behind the goal at the North End? Completely empty.

I was in the process of settling for a draw when Moses Emmanuel put Bromley ahead from a sitting-down position, swinging his foot at the ball which rolled, almost in slow motion, past Matt Glennon and into the corner of the net.

This set off wild celebrations. The singing and chanting, which had hardly let up all day, went into overdrive. After another burst of 'You Are My Bromley', a lone and unidentified voice sang out three letters to the tune of 'This Old Man'.

'B-R-O!'

A few others quickly worked out what was going on and joined in as he sang 'B-R-O' again.

At least ten people sang the next line, 'B-R-O-M-L-E-Y'.

By that point, just about every one of the travelling fans knew what was going on. Speediej's mate would have been proud as at least three dozen voices, including mine, belted out the words 'WITH A G-double E-Z-E-R-S, BROMLEY GEEZERS ARE THE BEST!' It finished a bit weakly as most seemed to be laugh-ing too much to sing. But this was turning into the best day out for ages. The sun was out, the predicted torrential conditions having never materialized. Even Liz seemed to be enjoying herself.

In the ninetieth minute it got even better when the two substitutes combined to wrap it up. A nice through ball from Alex Wall found winger Pierre-Joseph Dubois who confidently finished with a quality sorely lacking until then.

These are the moments you watch football for.

It was great for Bromley finally to score a last-minute goal instead of being on the receiving end of one. It felt fantastic to witness one that didn't cause pain and anguish, and 2-0 at Halifax was a fine achievement. As the game drifted into added time – the fourth official had indicated five more minutes – I suggested to Liz that we go out for dinner to celebrate a result that should be enough to lift us into a mid-table spot.

Deep into injury time, Connor Hughes, one of Halifax's better players on the day, tried his luck from thirty yards with a powerful swerving effort that barely gave Julian time to move. The ball rocketed over him and into the net. As consolation goals go, you don't see many better. I could afford to be generous in my praise. It was surely just about the last kick of the match.

In the remaining seconds, Bromley gave the ball away from the restart and Halifax took it forward, but lost it. After a botched clearance from Alex Wall, the ball was launched back into the area. The alarm bells started clanging in my head. 'Nooooooooo,' I heard myself whimpering softly, sensing disaster unfolding in front of me. 'Please, noooooooooooooooo.'

But I was powerless to stop it. A mistimed header from Jack Holland, a clash of heads, a collapsing striker and a referee pointing to the spot were the images that flashed in front of my eyes in rapid succession.

It felt like a terrible decision, but then again it always does. I can never accept that any penalty given against Bromley is either justified or fair. And when they're given two games running, it's clearly a conspiracy. So even though Holland clattering Andy Bishop to the ground and almost knocking him unconscious in the process might have looked bad, I preferred to think an inexperienced referee (Martin Coy from Durham) had been intimidated by home crowd pressure. Despite the fact that most of the home crowd had already gone.

The penalty was converted, as every single Bromley fan in the ground knew it would be, and Halifax were level. The final whistle went literally five seconds after the restart.

I was filled with rage. In the end, six minutes had been added – where had they come from? And what about the minutes when Holland's victim was being treated? Why no added time for that?

This was clearly a referee favouring the establishment big club.

Support for my theory came from a not entirely unexpected source. Mark Goldberg said afterwards, 'It was as if he was giving as much time as necessary for Halifax to get back into the game.'

Unlike Goldberg, I couldn't speak. I didn't just have one last-minute goal to deal with, but two. The pain was intense. I looked at the pale, shell-shocked faces around me, all of them going through the same thing. We had gone from mid-table safety to nineteenth in the space of ninety horrible seconds.

After leaving the ground, Liz and I had to take what is officially the most depressing walk in football. Or maybe the result just made it feel that way. The route from Shay Stadium to Halifax station felt like a post-apocalyptic wasteland, taking in a derelict shell of a building, scattered debris, broken bricks, concrete and graffiti.

'It's not the end of the world,' said Liz.

I think she was referring to my reaction to the result, but couldn't be sure.

We both just wanted to get out of town – me to escape what had just happened, Liz to have that promised meal.

Naturally, the train back got stuck in the middle of nowhere due to an unspecified 'incident at Bradford Interchange'. By the time we arrived in Leeds most of the good restaurants were full. Eventually we found a pub that had recently opened and wasn't completely packed. Pub food had improved vastly in the time I'd been away. You used to be lucky if you got a soggy pasty or steak and kidney pie, kept warm all day in a heated glass display unit on the counter. Now every pub in town boasted a restaurant-quality menu, and this place was no different.

After we'd ordered, I noticed a concerned expression on Liz's face as she sipped her cider.

'Did you see that kid at the football in the red and black check shirt?' she asked.

'Which one?'

'He was on his knees in the aisle, face down against the step, hitting the concrete with his fists after that last goal. It was bizarre.'

Bizarre? I thought. Surely such behaviour is understandable? The only difference between me and him was that I'd resisted the urge.

The food wasn't that great, and as we walked home the heavens opened as the predicted torrential downpour finally arrived. Why hadn't I followed Liz's example and worn a raincoat? My shirt and jeans got completely soaked. But that wasn't the worst part. That came later when I went to bed and couldn't get to sleep because I had a song stuck in my head, playing over and over.

B-R-O
B-R-O
B-R-O-M-L-E-Y
WITH A G-double E-Z-E-R-S
BROMLEY GEEZERS ARE THE BEST!

Despite these low points, what kept me going was knowing that by next weekend I'd be revitalized, with a renewed sense of hope, optimism and anticipation. It's nature's way of ensuring the survival of the football fan.

Which was just as well considering Bromley had two games coming up in three days. Including a visit to the runaway League leaders.

HOME
AND
AWAY

Four

'Bromley are in the Champions League, right?' asked Liz as we set off in our rented car for the five-hour drive from Leeds to Hayes Lane.

This was greatly encouraging. It was the first time she'd ever asked a non-cider-related football question.

'No, it's the Vanarama National League.'

'So why do the Bromley pictures on Instagram have the hashtag "Champions"?'

'They won the Conference South last season.'

'Really?'

Not a normal conversation to have at the start of a honeymoon, but then this was no normal honeymoon. For a start, we'd already been married fifteen years. For another thing, it was a romantic bank holiday weekend break taking in two Bromley matches.

At the time of our wedding in 2000 we'd been so broke that we got married in someone's back garden and promised ourselves a honeymoon when we could afford it. That time had come.

The deal was that if we went to the two matches, one at home to Dover, the other away to Forest Green Rovers, Liz got to choose what we did the rest of the time.

'Go on, we'll do whatever you want – just name it,' I'd said.

'We should go horse riding in the Cotswolds.'

'Pardon?'

'Horse riding. Hacking they call it over here. I've been reading about a place near where we're staying. We could go the morning before the match.'

And so we'd booked a one-hour hacking session. I tried not to think about it, because I could think of few things more terrifying than sitting on a horse that was moving. But I kept my fear to myself and tried to concentrate on the game against Dover.

We arrived at the ground with plenty of time to spare, and, as always, my priority was to get a couple of programmes. As I approached the seller, I felt a familiar stab of envy. It was a job I'd dreamed of doing since my early teens and the desire hadn't faded. In fact it had got even stronger: my heart raced at the thought of selling programmes at the highest level the club had ever reached.

When I confessed these thoughts to Liz, she looked at me a bit pityingly, but said that I should ask the club if I could do it. 'What's the worst that could happen?' she reasoned. 'They could only say no.'

She was right. It's never too late to live your dreams. I decided to send an email when I got back to Leeds rather than risk face-to-face rejection. I would even offer to volunteer. As a writer, I was used to working for no money.

My other motivation was that I wasn't sure how much longer programmes would exist. I was having to fight the suspicion that they were becoming redundant; I feared for a future without them. Now that squad numbers had been introduced, team line-ups had disappeared from programmes. Instead the entire squad was listed and you were meant to tick the boxes next to the names of the players in the starting eleven, thus disfiguring your pristine programme. I'm generally a fan of progress, but you have to draw the line somewhere.

We sat down behind the goal on one of the hundred or so white plastic seats bought from the London Aquatics Centre after the 2012 Games. These had been incongruously placed among the wooden benches, which probably dated back to at least the 1950s, presumably to meet League regulations.

As the match got under way, I noticed an unfamiliar feeling of optimism. Bromley had started well, building on the improvement seen at Halifax. The team were beginning to gel and players who had looked off the pace were coming right. Even the defence was looking more solid.

Dover were a good side, not far from the play-off places, and the game was so even that the teams were cancelling each other out. There were few chances in the opening forty-five minutes and 0-0 was a fair reflection of the play.

We couldn't change ends at half-time, as we were used to doing at the level Bromley traditionally played at. In a high-tech segregation operation, a yellow plastic ribbon had been draped across the terraces, dividing the fans. So we stayed where we were, quietly seething. It wasn't just that we were being denied standing behind the Dover goal in the second half, but that we were being denied access to the chip van, which lay tantalizingly just beyond the yellow ribbon.

I'd promised Liz chips and been unable to deliver. And then the mood soured even further.

Midway through the second half, Dover scored right in front of me. I instinctively shut my eyes as I couldn't stand the thought of watching happy Dover players prancing around, celebrating scoring against Bromley. It was too much to take.

I felt distraught. I'd really started to believe that my team had turned the corner.

After the goal went in it registered that the man in front of me was wearing a grey 'Fortress Hayes Lane' T-shirt. This was a remnant from the previous season when the club's new management ambitiously renamed the ground 'The Fortress Stadium'. Home form had subsequently dipped – so much so that 'The Help-Yourself-To-Three-Points-Stadium' would have been more accurate. A few months later the name was quietly dropped, the new management vanished, and Bromley got back on the promotion track. All that remained of those Fortress days was this T-shirt.

There were only minutes left on the clock when Bromley, who were routinely denied two or three clear-cut penalties every game as far as I was concerned, were finally given one. Anthony Cook, who was having another strong game, was blatantly brought down in the box. As the Bromley fans around me went through a list of possible penalty takers, one name was absent: Bradley Goldberg, the son of the manager.

But it was Goldberg, a striker who hadn't scored in any of the season's five games, who took the ball and placed it on the spot. This was either very gutsy or career suicide. I wanted him to score for more than the obvious reason that it would give Bromley a point. He was a player who never stopped running, and was unselfish and skilful. I was convinced that he'd soon come right. He was clearly low on confidence and that was affecting his game.

His penalty wasn't a good one and the Dover keeper saved with ease, pushing the ball out. But Goldberg reacted quickest, stabbing the ball home. I went from hope to despair to euphoria in the space of one and a half seconds.

It finished 1-1, Bromley just about deserving the point that kept them in nineteenth place. The improvement, which had started at Halifax, had continued and I was happy with the result. I'm not convinced that the Dover players felt the same way. As soon as Mr Hicks (home town Sutton) blew the whistle for full time, a huge row had erupted between some of the visitors' defenders, with plenty of pointing fingers and shoving going on.

Behind the Bromley goal, where I was still sitting, Alan Julian, who'd had his usual blinder, stayed around to chat to fans. To my horror, I saw that none of them were handing him a programme to sign – another symptom of their impending obsolescence.

They wanted selfies with him instead.

The ever-obliging Julian, who had already endeared himself to the supporters by applauding them after (and during) each game, was the last to leave the pitch. As he walked towards the dressing room, Liz and I made our way back to the car. On the way, Liz stopped off at the club shop and came out clutching a Bromley scarf.

This gave me hope that the draw had ignited a passion in her. Either that or she was just cold. I think it was the latter, as she wore it all the way to Gloucestershire.

We'd both been looking forward to this leg of the trip for a long time. Forest Green Rovers lay in a part of England, the Cotswolds, that tourists came from around the world to visit.

British roads had changed since I'd last driven on them. I noticed that there were no hitchhikers any more. Nor did I see any police cars on motorways, whose chevrons I still wasn't convinced by: the markings were designed to keep cars a safe distance apart, but most people seemed to ignore them. It was also obvious that drivers were a lot less patient these days, as evidenced by our getting at least one blaring horn and angry look per hour.

And then there were the cows. Big brown ones, standing on the Minchinhampton to Nailsworth road. They only moved when they were good and ready, after which we drove down a steep, winding road known as The Ladder (it was confusing to hear the satnav say 'continue on the ladder for 800 yards'). Just minutes later, we had reached our destination: Axpill House – officially the fourth best B&B (out of five) in Nailsworth.

Because I'd left booking until the last moment, this was the only one that had a vacancy. Expectations were not high. And then we went inside. Now, how often do you look around a B&B and think 'they've spared no expense here'? That's right. Never. But this place was unexpectedly brilliant. Huge beds and luxurious leather armchairs into which you could sink and sip upmarket Clipper tea accompanied by top-of-the-range Belgian chocolate and ginger biscuits. There was Pellegrino water. The bathroom was furnished with big fluffy cotton towels and extravagant soaps and lotions. Even the taps were high end, water cascading out of them like a miniature waterfall.

If this is only the fourth best, I thought, I'd love to see the others.

After unpacking we walked around the town, exploring. There were wheaten stone cottages with tiled roofs, a bench overlooking the village square, and a proper old-fashioned cast-iron red phone box (the first one Liz had ever seen). There was a pub, but something was missing. I soon worked out what it was: there was no blackboard sign outside announcing to the world that they had Sky and BT, and which games they'd be showing. There were no pizza delivery drivers either. No taxis. No one with a clipboard asking if you had a minute to talk about the plight of dolphins. No free wifi in shops to lure in the customers. In fact this was something they seemed proud of. An organic food shop even had a sign in the window reading WIFI FREE ZONE. The streets were filled with small independent butchers, grocers, DIY retailers and the like. None of the names you see on every high street, just local businesses.

And to complete the picture of England circa 1979, every single shop was shut for the entire bank holiday weekend.

We were starting to like Nailsworth.

The next morning, we woke to a rare sound. The sound of silence. Over breakfast, we enjoyed the church bells and birdsong, a pleasant change from sirens and bottles smashing into recycling bins.

The disappointment of realizing there was no Bromley game that day was partially offset by half looking forward to spending time with horses. I certainly loved to see Liz doing the things she loved. I think she felt the same way about me, which was why she came along to football.

Although I'd only ever been on a horse once in my life, they had featured in my teenage years. A couple of them lived in a field outside the Bromley ground, and I used to feed them Weetabix on the way in.

Another football connection was revealed as we filled in the forms at the stables (which was going fine until I saw they wanted to know my next of kin). We were told that Ady Pennock, the Forest Green Rovers manager, had brought his family there earlier that morning.

With that spurring me on, I warily climbed aboard the horse I'd been given. He was a two-year-old cream and beige shire called Alan, which Liz thought was a rubbish name, but I disagreed. My favourite Bromley players throughout the Weetabix horse-feeding years were both Alans – Stonebridge and Soper. And my favourite of the current players? Alan Julian. I saw riding Alan the horse as a sign, although its meaning wasn't yet clear.

Being a bank holiday weekend, it was a damp, overcast morning with a steady drizzle of rain. The kind of weather I really missed when living abroad, but not ideal for my second time on a horse.

It felt like a long way to the ground and I kept telling myself not to look down. Alan seemed a giant of a beast, but I saw a photo afterwards and it looked as though I was sitting on an undersized donkey.

After the initial nerves had faded, I actually started to enjoy it. Hannah, our instructor, was a real pro and the scenery was spectacular: golden fields, stone cottages and huge overhanging willows, all experienced at walking pace. And in the distance, rolling green hills draped in mist.

This was an England I'd never bothered to see before.

It was leisurely, but never boring. I even found myself thinking about how I'd like to do this again some time. Even if it didn't coincide with a football match. That was how much I enjoyed it. And by the time we'd completed the one-hour circuit I was convinced I was an expert horseman.

'That was easier than I thought,' I said to Hannah back at the stables when it was time to dismount. As instructed, I lifted my right leg over the saddle and began slowly to slide down Alan's side. It was then that I got my belt caught in the stirrup. As a result I found myself dangling horizontally just inches above the ground with my face pressed against the underside of Alan's belly, until Hannah heard my muffled pleas for help and I was rescued.

Apart from that, I'd had a great day. It felt good to do something Liz wanted to do, and to see more of England. The rest of the day was spent exploring Nailsworth and its surrounding villages, this time not on horseback. It was a beautiful part of the world.

The next day, after a quick lunch at the pub-with-no-TV, it was time to go and watch football. As we were walking out, I noticed someone in a Bromley polo shirt but didn't think any more about it.

David, our host at the B&B, had said the ground was just a twenty-minute walk away. What he'd failed to mention was that it was twenty minutes of struggling up an Everest-gradient hill. In the pouring rain.

As we began the ascent, I decided to try some expectation-lowering psychology on Liz, saying that anything less than a 4-0 defeat would be seen as an outstanding result for Bromley. But I was unable to develop the argument as I ran out of breath. This was one of the steepest hills I'd ever climbed and it just seemed to go on and on and on. It didn't bode well for our plan to hike up

England's highest mountain in March, when we'd be in the Lake District for the Barrow match.

After several stops along the way, we finally reached the summit. And as the Forest Green floodlights came into view and our breathing returned to normal, it was time to concentrate on the match.

A staple of every boys' comic is the eccentric millionaire who buys a football team and fills it with really good players. Dale Vince, owner of Forest Green Rovers, had done just that. He had impeccable eccentric millionaire credentials, which included (a) living in a commune, (b) banning meat pies from the stadium, and (c) not watching TV or owning a mobile phone.

I knew that bringing Liz here was a high-risk strategy. She was a vegetarian with a keen interest in the environment so might well have her head turned by Forest Green Rovers. There were football reasons, too. They were hugely successful – top of the table, having won every one of their games so far and conceded only one goal in the process – and when you first discover football, there is nothing more seductive than a winning team. I just hoped she'd see beyond the superficial (obviously something she hadn't needed to do when she first met me) and realize that Bromley were the team for her.

Still, it was too late to worry about that now. Once inside the stadium, I looked around. It wasn't as imposing as Halifax and Grimsby, just a good old-fashioned non-league ground, no different from the hundreds scattered across Britain. Apart from the giant solar panels. And vegan tofu pies. And biodegradable goal nets. The playing surface looked great, a rich, vibrant green, which was testament to the work of cow manure (no chemical fertilizer here) and the mowbot (a solar-powered lawn-mowing robot). And in probably the only football ground in Britain without a single meat pie to be found, it was no surprise to see a sign urging people to 'give meat the red card'.

The crowd wasn't huge – around 1,700, with plenty of spare seats. There were seventy or so Bromley fans, most of whom I now recognized but was still too shy to approach. Naughty Nigel hadn't made the trip, but Roy, my old friend who could be easily identified by the well-worn Tesco plastic bag that he carried everywhere, had. The bag was rumoured to contain, amongst other things, sandwiches, keys, a bus pass, spare glasses and a transistor radio. But no one had yet managed to look inside.

After greeting him, I had a quick look at the programme, which was probably printed on recycled paper. The first thing I learned was that pretty much all of the Forest Green players had found a kit sponsor. This was in contrast to Bromley, where Rob Swaine was still the only player to have one. And he hadn't played for several weeks. He wouldn't be featuring today, although he was on the bench. Which meant yet another patched-up defence.

As I was thinking about this, a roar went up as the Forest Green players ran out. This was when I saw the familiar portly figure of Jon 'The Beast' Parkin, formerly of Stoke City, Cardiff and Preston. The last time I'd seen him was on TV, when he was scoring a hat trick against Leeds. At Elland Road. And now he was playing Bromley.

I was suddenly very, very nervous.

FOOD

HOME
AND
AWAY

Five

Picking the Bromley team to counter Jon Parkin had been hard. It had kept me up the previous night, pen and notepad in hand, until Liz reminded me that this was meant to be our honeymoon. But now I'd got to know the players and seen them a few times, I could finally settle on my ideal starting eleven.

Like most fans, I felt sure I could do a better job than the manager. Which is why I was genuinely shocked when I saw the line-up Mark Goldberg had chosen. Apart from ex-Portsmouth captain Ben Chorley missing out to someone called Paul Rodgers, it was exactly the same line-up I'd finalized at my desk at Axpill House that morning.

Alan Julian picked himself. I'd been impressed with Joe Anderson at left-back. Apart from one slip against Grimsby, he'd been steady. Jack Holland and Sean Francis had also caught my eye in defence. Ali Fuseini and Reece Prestedge were outstanding in midfield, together with exciting wingers Anthony Cook and Pierre Joseph-Dubois, while Alex Wall and Moses Emmanuel were a handful up front. The bonus was having Swaine, Chorley and Goldberg to come off the bench.

Before now, there had always been a possibility that we'd lose because the manager got it wrong. Now that excuse was gone. It appeared that he'd got it right this week.

Goldberg's counterpart at Forest Green, Ady Pennock, was having a far more comfortable season, with six wins out of six. And if Dale Vince was an eccentric owner, Pennock was an equally eccentric manager. My fellow horseman had got heat stroke the previous week by refusing to remove his jumper (it was a superstition thing) during their win against Lincoln in searing temperatures. This scenario was unlikely to be repeated today. A week is a long time as far as the British weather is concerned, and today, the last day of August, felt like an early taste of autumn.

As the North Stand slowly filled, I noticed the man I had seen in the pub earlier unfolding a large BROMLEY GEEZERS banner, and draping it across the railings. I also noticed a yellow Adidas bag by his side. It was Rich, the man who had been kind enough to get me programmes from the games I'd listened to on the radio. He handed them over while I took a picture of his banner.

The first few minutes were surprisingly even. Bromley looked confident and were spraying the ball around. Forest Green's tactic seemed to be to get the ball to Parkin as often as possible, even though it was clear he wasn't in peak physical condition; in fact he moved with all the speed and grace of Alan the horse. Yet his value was obvious: he provided positional sense, touch and pure power. Plus, you couldn't really knock him off the ball.

After six minutes, Bromley, being Bromley, conceded a soft goal, even though it was genuinely against the run of play. A mishit shot from the full-back wrong-footed Julian and it was 1-0. But then, just a minute later, Alex Wall equalized with a looping header from a Fuseini free kick, which somehow went over the head of Jonny Maxted in the Forest Green goal.

It was a goal that put Bromley fans in good spirits.

'We know where all the meat pies went – Parkin ate them!'

shouted one of our seventy-strong contingent scattered across the terraces.

And then the B-R-O song broke out. I'm pretty sure Rich started it, but at least half of the North Stand joined in. It's really hard to sing, especially the 'G-double E-Z' part, which requires total concentration, otherwise it comes out horribly wrong. But amazingly, it sounded sort of all right.

It certainly got the attention of the ball boy, who spent the next few minutes staring open-mouthed at the Bromley fans behind the goal, which probably broke every rule in the ball-boy book. And when some of the fans noticed, they sang 'Ball boy, ball boy, give us a wave', and he responded with a bashful flutter of the hand.

He was still looking in our direction when Dubois came off injured after around the half-hour mark. This meant Brad Goldberg's spell on the sidelines was over. His coming on as a replacement provided one of the comedy highlights of the season when he stood next to Jon Parkin, who must have been twice his size.

'Watch out he doesn't eat you, Brad,' advised someone behind me.

Towards the end of the half, James Jennings swung his leg and put the ball into the Bromley net. The trouble was, he was sitting on the goal line in an offside position. It was so blatant that I don't think anyone was that worried. But referee Adam Hopkins (Plymouth – thanks, Google) looked at his linesman, who was nodding furiously. Astonishingly, the goal was allowed to stand.

It really was clearly offside. Have a look if you don't believe me – I'm sure it's on the internet somewhere.

I was in shock, together with most of the others. Jim, who ran the Bromley club shop, adopted a disappointed-more-than-angry tone. 'We are not happy with you, linesman,' he scolded. Mash settled for a reminder of the official's mortality: 'Death will get you in the end, Lino.'

Just before the interval, a wild shot from Parkin cleared the bar and bounced into the North Stand. The ball boy, perhaps eager to impress his new fans, tried to vault the railings to collect it, and ended up flat on his back. Alan Julian was first to react, rushing over to see if he was all right – he was – and helping him to his feet. When the half-time whistle went, Julian checked up on him again.

During half-time, I glanced through the programme and found more evidence of their decline when Forest Green's Rob Sinclair answered a few questions. Did they want to know his favourite meal – something asked in programmes since programmes began and a perfect opportunity to impress the boss by saying 'tofu burgers'? No. The first thing the interviewer wanted to know was 'What shampoo do you use?'

With a feeling of genuine sadness, I put the programme away.

Liz, to my surprise, said that she was really enjoying the game. 'Much better than the others' was her verdict. Her favourite players were Julian and centre-back Sean Francis, who, coincidentally, were also the best-looking.

The second half was probably Bromley's best of the season, more than matching their high-flying opponents. The whole team looked confident and, despite being behind, my relegation anxiety was at its lowest level of the season so far.

The ball boy was much busier in this half, with Bromley attacking the goal at his end. When a Goldberg shot went just wide, into the stand, he sensibly waited for someone to throw the ball back rather than going after it himself.

The best chant of the half was a version of the Grimsby Town 'Fish, Fish, Fish' one, which went 'Meat, Meat, Meat', a reminder of what the home fans were missing.

Towards the end we were treated to the bizarre sight of the League leaders timewasting and panicking to clear the ball before the final whistle went. To me this was confirmation that Bromley were improving rapidly. They could hold their own against the superpowers of the Vanarama National League.

The ultimate Bromley compliment came from the Coventry Building Society. They were match sponsors, and had given Player of the Day to the Forest Green goalkeeper, Jonny Maxted (kit sponsor: Amberley Bisley Bouncy Castles). Personally, I felt that the linesman had probably done more to help them win, but the award was acknowledgement that Forest Green had needed an outstanding defensive effort to scrape home.

I looked up at the partially solar-powered scoreboard, which shone through the darkening gloom. It read FOREST GREEN 2 BROMLEY 1, but I felt almost satisfied. It was a loss that felt like a win, which was a massive turnaround from the draw that had felt like a loss at Halifax.

I was more than ready for a win that felt like a win.

As we walked down the hill, Liz remarked that it was going to be sad leaving the Cotswolds behind. And I knew what she meant.

'Don't worry,' I said reassuringly, 'we'll be back.'

'Promise?'

'I promise.'

'But when?'

'January the thirtieth,' I said. 'Bromley are playing at Cheltenham.'

When we got back to Leeds, I filed four programmes away – the two from the trip and the two Rich had got me – and while Liz caught up with her work, I sat down to compose one of the most important emails of my football-watching life.

It might sound easy, asking a football club if you can be a programme seller for one match, but it's not. I couldn't say that it was one of my life's ambitions, because that would have sounded plain tragic. In the end, I just asked the question.

'This might sound a little weird,' I wrote, 'but do you think it might be possible to arrange for me to be a programme seller (voluntary, of course) for one game towards the end of the season?'

I clicked send and tried not to get my hopes up too high. It was now time to catch up with the Bromley FC forum.

Crucially, there had been a development on the increasingly popular B-R-O chant. Speediej reappeared, for only his second ever post, and seemed to be changing his story about its origin. After seeing how successful it had become, with a BROMLEY GEEZERS banner on the terraces and the song being sung regularly, he was now claiming ownership – or at least part ownership – of the lyrics. 'It was a joint effort between me and my mate,' he stated.

His young mate (if he existed and hadn't been invented as a scapegoat in case the song bombed) was about to learn a harsh fact of life – that success has many fathers, but failure is an orphan. It would only be a matter of time before he was erased from the history books completely.

It took a few days to get over all the travelling. Another harsh fact of life is that the older you get, the less stamina you have. But as Saturday came around, I found myself anticipating the next game, at home to high-flying Gateshead, with real excitement.

I wouldn't be going to Hayes Lane. I couldn't afford it, especially with some expensive trips coming up, so I settled for listening to it on the radio.

At lunchtime, still several hours before kick-off, a game was taking place at Welling that could dramatically change Bromley's season. Welling were at home to Tranmere in front of the BT cameras. This sort of thing still took some getting used to. Only top games used to be on live TV, but this was important in its own way. There was plenty at stake. If Welling won, Bromley would slip into the relegation zone.

I had never wanted Tranmere to win so much. In fact, I had never had any feelings at all about Tranmere, apart from an irrational hatred for the weedy moustache John Aldridge sported when he played for them. But they could do Bromley a huge favour here. Another justification for watching was that we'd be playing both teams in the next month, so I needed to have a look at them.

Generally, I thought Tranmere looked good without being terrifying. They were a goal up with minutes left on the clock, but down to ten men – someone had been sent off for being in the vicinity of a Welling defender who'd decided to collapse to the ground clutching his face. It was a decision that probably would have pushed me over the outer edges of rage had I been a proper Tranmere fan instead of just a temporary one.

But then, as the camera was focusing on the Welling owner sitting in the stands, BT's commentator started screaming about a goal that had just been scored. The replay showed a stunning long-distance strike by Welling's nineteen-year-old captain, Sam Corne.

And then the game ended.

'Let's talk to Sam Corne, scorer of the match-winning equalizer,' said the commentator, getting a little confused in all the excitement. But I couldn't watch the interview. Corne's goal had brought Welling level on points with Bromley and I had no interest in hearing what he had to say.

Bromley were now precariously perched on the precipice of the relegation zone. A loss today would tip us into the bottom four.

Just one point and one place clear of the relegation zone. And yet, despite Bromley v. Gateshead being an absolutely vital game, I discovered that there would be *no* TV *or* radio coverage. In fact it was the only Vanarama National League game that wasn't being covered that day. This was too much to take. First that Corne goal, now this.

The BBC didn't reply when I asked them for an explanation. I had to go with Plan B and follow the game on Twitter.

When I saw the team, I was pleasantly surprised to see that Rob Swaine was back. Also notable was Brad Goldberg starting, which meant Moses Emmanuel playing out of position, on the wing.

The game got under way – at least I assumed it had. This was followed by a period of prolonged Twitter silence from everyone at the ground. Even the normally reliable official Bromley FC feed was having a quiet day. 'Just under half an hour gone' was the first from them. 'Very even.' It was as if there was a news blackout, and my mind began playing strange tricks on me. What was *really* going on at Hayes Lane? There wasn't even any word on Naughty Nigel.

I decided I'd happily settle for a draw and congratulated myself on picking such an uneventful game to miss. We were twentieth, they were fourth. If it finished even, it would stretch our unbeaten run to four games (if you wiped Forest Green's blatantly offside 'goal' on Bank Holiday Monday).

Then the game came to life. And it was left to the official Gateshead feed to tell the waiting world about it.

GATESHEAD FC @Gateshead FC
75: Goal: Bromley 1 (Emmanuel) Gateshead 0

It was dry, just the facts, but the upset was on. I allowed myself the most muted of celebrations – a gripped fist and a satisfied nod of the head, tempered by the knowledge that there was still work to be done. The Halifax injury-time wounds were still raw. We'd taken the lead there after seventy-five minutes too. There was still plenty of time for more goals.

Sure enough, news soon came through from the Bromley FC feed which was a little less understated:

Bromley FC @bromleyfc
GOOOOOOALLLLLLL!!!! 2-0 BROMLEY! Louis Dennis
nicks the ball, beats one, fires shot bottom corner! IN
THERE!!!!! #WeAreBromley

This was now the same lead we'd thrown away at Halifax. But I didn't have time to worry about history repeating itself because minutes later, the game was safe.

GATESHEAD FC @Gateshead FC
90: Goal: Bromley 3 (Emmanuel) Gateshead 0

Over the last few games I'd started to believe that Bromley belonged at this level, and here was further evidence. We were now in eighteenth place – not all *that* far from the play-off places.

It was a bittersweet feeling because I was left regretting not making the trip to Hayes Lane. I felt a bit empty, remembering the high I was on after the Wrexham game and feeling a part of it, proudly watching the celebrations and lapping up the atmosphere. Why did I have to miss this of all games? I could only imagine what it must be like to be as rich as someone like Dale Vince and go to every game, wherever your team is playing. I wasn't greedy. I didn't want enough to buy a football club – just enough to watch one.

And this stunningly brilliant game against Gateshead wasn't the only one I was going to miss. There'd be no Bromley games for me for three more weeks. I had no choice since my football fund was dwindling, especially after already buying train tickets for October's visits to Tranmere, Aldershot and Lincoln. If I spent any more it could mean missing out on games at the end of the season – and those could be the most important of the lot.

Besides, there were good reasons for skipping the next four

games, even though they could see Bromley climb towards the play-offs. Torquay, a very long round trip, was a no-no, as was a Tuesday night at Boreham Wood FC, which would have meant staying in a hotel. In Borehamwood. On a Tuesday night.

This left a couple of home games which, according to the overall project of discovering Britain, were always less important. There was little my home town had to offer the tourist anyway, apart from a blue plaque outside Primark commemorating the birthplace of H. G. Wells.

Still, missing five games in a row, if you included the win against Gateshead, was going to be tough. I could feel the grip of the old obsession. But it had to be done.

Luckily, one of the few advantages of being sixty was that I was now mature enough to resist temptation.

HOME
AND
AWAY

Six

A pile of train tickets lay on the table in front of me. There was one to Torquay (a day trip which included over fourteen hours of travel, ninety minutes of football and barely enough time there to get Liz a stick of rock), one to Elstree and Borehamwood (an overnight trip which meant spending twenty hours in Borehamwood), and one to Bromley South, for Bromley v. Altrincham in November (just the six hours on trains that day).

Financially, the damage wasn't quite as bad as it could have been. I'd managed to get a refund from the journey to Leeds that was cut short at East Croydon when we first arrived, and had also been given a small job writing an advertising copy line for the front of a pack of dog food. This had boosted my Bromley-watching fund by enough almost to cover the cost of an off-peak return to Torquay.

I saw these added games as a reward for staying away from the home game against Macclesfield on 12 September, which was next up, and which meant I was depriving myself of two games in a row. That alone was going to be difficult. Three, I had decided, would have been impossible.

Besides, I had good reason to celebrate. I'd had an email from Nicola in the office at Bromley FC: astonishingly, they were happy

71

to let me sell programmes at the Woking game in February. This was brilliant news and put me in the perfect mood for following the Macclesfield game from 218 miles away.

I had a bit of a soft spot for Macclesfield. Their Twitter account is one of the more entertaining ones around, as demonstrated here, during the pre-season friendly at Nantwich Town:

> Macclesfield Town @thesilkmen Jul 14
> 64 | Great work between Trialist and Trialist who plays in Trialist down the right, his ball in just misses Trialist. Still 3-0.

When a slightly irate fan took exception to this, asking, 'Any chance of getting some names?', this was the official response:

> Macclesfield Town @thesilkmen Jul 14
> What do you mean? The Trialist family are in town.

The club had also got plenty of attention in the media by bidding for the 2026 World Cup, arguing that with 'free wifi at nearby Macclesfield library' and constant temperatures of 14.1°C (possibly a dig at Qatar) it was well placed to vie with the world's greatest cities to host the contest. They also showed a commendable understanding of how these things work by saying that a budget of £40 had been 'set aside for gifts to the FIFA family'. The proposal ended by dangling the enticing prospect of the opening and closing ceremonies taking place at the Moss Rose Stadium, with entertainment provided by manager John Askey and TV antiques expert David Dickinson.

Despite all this, the USA were inexplicably made favourites to host the event; Macclesfield never even made the long list. Well, they might have missed out on hosting the World Cup, but at least they wouldn't be deprived of glory altogether. They still had the honour of playing at Hayes Lane during Bromley's greatest ever season.

As kick-off approached, I uncovered clear evidence of a BBC anti-Bromley bias. It was hard to come to any other conclusion when *once again* there was no radio commentary, despite all but two other Vanarama National League games being covered. Clearly the BBC could no longer be relied upon, which added further justification to my decision to go to more games than I'd originally planned.

It also meant that my Bromley v. Macclesfield options were severely limited, boiling down to two choices: following it on Twitter or avoiding all match updates and watching the two minutes of highlights on BT the following night. It would be like watching the game live, apart from missing eighty-eight minutes or so.

I decided on the latter, which meant a day of media blackout and carefully avoiding websites that might break news of historic victories in the Vanarama National League.

The agonizing twenty-six-hour wait was extended by the fact that Bromley v. Macclesfield was the last game shown on the highlights package. This, together with Bromley not featuring in any of the live games announced so far, was clear evidence of a BT anti-Bromley bias.

From the evidence provided by the highlights it looked like Bradley Goldberg had been involved in everything, setting up a chance Alex Wall should've scored, then making a very well-taken goal by striker Ben May, which looked as good on the tenth viewing as it did on the first.

It was the only goal of the match.

'So Bromley have managed two wins on the bounce for the first time this season and move up to thirteenth in the table,' said the host. This was something that should have prompted a feeling of pride, but instead it led to a sense of dread. It was hard to escape the feeling that I might be a jinx. I miss two games, Bromley win both; I watch the previous three, Bromley win none. I had previous history with jinxing the club I loved. In my first full season of watching them, they managed just ten points. On my last-but-one visit back, I saw them play Didcot from a couple of divisions below, and we lost 1-0. The test of this season's evolving theory would come on Tuesday night. I didn't just want a win. I needed one.

The reason I had originally planned to give Boreham Wood a miss (apart from lack of funds) was that it was on a Tuesday night and I'd have to spend the night there. After changing my mind about going, this negative became a positive. I loved floodlit football and hadn't seen any since the 1980s.

Although I'd booked the train well in advance, I'd left accommodation to the last minute, as usual. I soon discovered this was a big mistake. One of the hotels told me that there was an Arms Fair at the ExCel Centre in London and most hotels had been booked out for months. I frantically rang around, and it did indeed seem that every room was taken. How could it be right that arms dealers and people wanting to buy illegal torture equipment could get a roof over their heads while someone who just wanted to watch Bromley was struggling?

Then I stumbled across the Elstree Inn, a place that sounded perfect. Not only was it within easy walking distance of the ground and station, it was only £40 for the night.

I sat back in relief, proud of myself for having found such a brilliant deal when rooms in and around London were at a premium. I looked it up on TripAdvisor to confirm how lucky I'd been.

'This place should be closed down,' said the first review.

'The bed springs were that bad I had to sleep on the stained floor,' said another.

'There were pubic hairs in the bathroom, stains on the

bedding, an iron burn on the floor and chewing gum stuck to the television stand,' added a third.

Maybe this wasn't such a good idea.

Lines from other reviews leapt out at me: 'shower head was covered in black mould'; 'the carpets were filthy, mattresses were horrendous and one of the beds had stained sheets'.

I was definitely wavering.

'Dust, dirt and hairs everywhere', 'disgusting bathroom with urine stains on the wall and down the radiator', 'water only came out of three holes in the shower head'.

That settled it. I'd give it a miss. I like a fully powered shower in the mornings.

Maybe it was unrealistic to expect accommodation booked late near non-league football grounds to match our experience in the Cotswolds. Since everywhere apart from the Elstree Inn was full, Liz suggested airbnb. This, I discovered, is basically a website where people rent out their spare rooms, and I found one in the perfect location – ten minutes from the station and fifteen minutes to the ground. For less than the price of a room with dust, dirt and hairs everywhere.

I booked and paid for it on the spot, not wanting to risk missing out. The only slight alarm bell rang when the host asked that I bring two forms of ID, including proof of address. Apart from that, it seemed just like a normal B&B.

I'd chosen the train to London on price (£9.50), not practicality. Which meant arriving in Borehamwood at four o'clock with nearly four hours to waste. At least this gave me enough time to bump into an *EastEnders* actor filming at nearby Elstree Studios. Or distraught minor celebs still wandering the streets after being evicted from the *Big Brother* house, which was also in the area.

I was starting to find train journeys increasingly boring, but passed some of the time by picking the Bromley team on the way down. Based on two minutes of highlights, Twitter and the match report in *The Non-League Paper*, I'd picked the following line-up to play Boreham Wood: Julian (he could have the job for life as far as I was concerned); Anderson, Swaine, Chorley, Holland; Cook, Dennis, Fuseini, Prestedge; Wall, Emmanuel. Ben May could consider himself unlucky. On another day he might have got the nod alongside Moses.

The team looked a strong one on paper, and this filled me with excitement – a feeling that only began to fade as we approached the rather dismal-looking Elstree and Borehamwood station. The first thing I noticed as we came to a halt was a Samaritans poster.

I dropped my bag off at the B&B, a pleasant bungalow next door to a house that someone from *EastEnders* had just bought (the landlady swore me to secrecy as to Stacey's identity), and after an enjoyable hour talking to her and her taxi driver husband, it was time to go.

As I walked to the ground, I saw the heavily fenced entrance to the BBC studios, lit up by floodlights. There was a security guard there and I asked him if there was any chance of my getting my photo taken on the *EastEnders* set.

'No' was the curt response.

I was starting to hate the BBC. They seemed to be going out of their way to deprive me of my most basic needs.

Ten minutes later I was at the ground. It was straight out of the old Isthmian League days – small, tucked away in a maze of back streets, dark, bleak and unwelcoming. There was a tiny crowd, a touch over 300 – and half of those must have come from Bromley – and yet there was strict segregation. The away fans were herded into a small pen behind one goal, an uncovered terrace with a terrible view of the pitch.

Most could take that. But they then found out they wouldn't be admitted to the bar. If you want to upset Bromley fans, there is no more effective way to do it.

As the Boreham Wood players came on to the field, one stood out as far as the people around me were concerned. Their goal-keeper and YouTube sensation Preston Edwards (a clip of him being sent off after ten seconds had got over ten million hits) had a short fuse and had reacted to Bromley fans when he was at Ebbsfleet. And football fans, eager to give their team the tiniest advantage, don't forget this kind of thing. The abuse started immediately, but Edwards managed to ignore it.

I was far more concerned with the view we had of the far end. The floodlights were poor and it was hard to make out what was happening. Some of the Bromley contingent even moved to the impressive new stand, which had been opened by Arsène Wenger the previous year, to get a better view. I stayed put, enjoying the atmosphere and singing, and relying on Colin Head (or just Col, editor of the Bromley fanzine *Two Footed Tackle*) to tell me what was going on.

Maybe I should have popped along to the Arms Fair for some thermal imaging night vision goggles. At least then I might have seen what happened after twenty minutes.

That was when Bromley took the lead. I only knew this because I could see a distant player in red with his arms raised in celebration.

'Who scored that?' I asked Col, jumping around in excitement.

'Ben May, with his right foot.'

I was impressed. 'How can you see that far?'

'Contact lenses.'

At half-time, with their team a goal up, the Bromley fans, denied access to the bar, entertained themselves with a series of songs and chants.

'Give me a B,' shouted someone behind the goal.

'B,' I joined in half-heartedly. There were six letters to come in 'Bromley' and I already knew in which order they'd arrive.

'Give me an E.'

'E,' I shouted, confused. Surely R came next?

'Give me another E,' he demanded.

By now I had no idea what was going on, so just gave him another E.

'Give me an R.'

'R.'

'What haven't we got?' he shouted at the top of his voice.

'BEER!' screamed just about everyone in the away section.

Not long after the restart, Bromley got a free kick on the edge of the area. The defensive wall was nearer seven yards away than ten, but since Vanarama National League budgets apparently didn't stretch to providing referees with spray, Boreham Wood got away with it.

But that was soon forgotten. Rob Swaine climbed high, headed the ball past Preston Edwards, and Moses Emmanuel was perfectly placed to nod the ball into an empty net. There was real excitement among the Bromley fans – a first away win of the season looked on.

Minutes later, somewhere in the distance, someone in a white shirt pulled it back to 2-1 and the mood of optimism vanished, to be replaced in my case by the return of jinx thoughts. I was thinking that a draw would still be a really good result.

After a nailbiting spell during which I was convinced Boreham Wood were going to score, Emmanuel played a fantastic defence-splitting ball through to Bradley Goldberg thirty yards out.

Underneath the excitement of potentially regaining our two-goal lead, I sensed that this was make or break for him. He'd been playing low on confidence, reluctant to take defenders on. If this had been a 1970s comic strip, there probably would have been a thought bubble coming from him reading: 'Oh no! I'm through on goal and yet I've only scored once in six games, and that was a rebound from a rubbish penalty. Help!' If it had been me, that's what would have been going through my mind.

Behind the goal, we collectively held our breath as Goldberg advanced on goal, seemingly in control. The keeper came out to narrow the angle, and then . . .

. . . and then Bradley calmly curled a perfectly placed shot over Edwards and the glistening white ball flew into the top corner.

There was an explosion of emotion behind the goal, a genuine outpouring of affection. The thing is, although there was always grumbling about whether or not Goldberg currently deserved his place, the Bromley fans adored him. Bradley was one of them. He'd grown up with them and stood alongside them on the terraces, dreaming of playing for Bromley one day. Much as I had, come to think of it.

It was impossible not to feel happy for him as he stood facing the fans, arms outstretched, relief and joy all over his face. This was more than just a celebration of Bromley going 3-1 up. This was redemption for a favourite (manager's) son.

In a season already full of great moments, this was up there with beating Wrexham, outplaying the League leaders in the Cotswolds and scoring three goals in ten minutes against Gateshead.

I felt for the fans who hadn't been able to make the trip. A couple of volunteers from the club were going to provide their own radio commentary via laptop (since there was obviously no chance of the BBC covering a Bromley game), but Boreham Wood had wanted a £50 fee. Instead, they would have been following the updates on Twitter. And they would have seen the bare fact that Bradley Goldberg had given Bromley a 3-1 lead. As far as I was concerned, that third goal had provided a piece of trivia which will never be bettered, when the scorer, whose sister (Lauren Rose) had sung on *The X Factor* beat the goalkeeper whose sister (Steph Edwards) had sung on *Britain's Got Talent*.

This is the sort of fact that makes me very, very happy.

A two-goal lead deep into injury time would be enough for fans of most teams. But when someone suggested the points were in the bag, Mash wasn't having it.

'I've seen us lose from here,' he said, putting into words what I, and most likely plenty of others, was thinking.

Seconds later, Boreham Wood scored and it was 2-3.

But when the whistle went for the restart, it was followed almost immediately by the whistle to end the game. Our first away win of the season. And it had been done without several key players, including Holland, Minshull, Dubois and Cook (who had come on as a late sub).

The feeling of happiness that washed over me contrasted with the miserable surroundings. There was just the tiniest hint that this team could be on the verge of something special. Our defence – or what I had seen of it – had impressed, with Swaine and Chorley forming a great centre-back partnership. Paul Rodgers, filling in for Jack Holland, had been solid and committed. Ben May and Bradley Goldberg, two of the scorers, hadn't been in the team I'd picked – one reason why Mark Goldberg was manager and not me. I now felt confident that Bromley belonged at this level, and was full of pride that we were unbeaten in six games (with the usual disclaimer about that Forest Green Rovers result).

One of the good things about being an in-form team is that this increases the chances of being featured in a live TV game, and those for November and December were due to be announced soon. It was BT's opportunity to demonstrate that they were a fair and impartial broadcaster.

As I lay in bed a few hours later, I reflected on how things were getting better on and off the field.

Off the field, I was starting to get to know some of my fellow fans and enjoying their company, feeling less of an outsider. Two had even offered me a place to stay next time I was down for a game and couldn't get back.

On the field, Bromley were now in the top half of the table, just below Grimsby in eleventh place. We'd played four of the five teams in the play-off places and done well against them. These were exciting, heady days.

Sleep was hard to come by that night. But that was mainly because I was in a taxi driver's spare bedroom in Borehamwood, missing my wife and wondering if I'd ever grow out of making these trips. At my age, this sort of travelling starts to take its toll.

But if this journey to Borehamwood had been hard, it was merely the hors d'oeuvre. A few days later I'd be eating the main course – the most stupid, ill-considered and senseless Bromley trip I'd ever undertaken.

I couldn't wait.

Gilbert the Gull

#SAVETUFC

HOME
AND
AWAY

Seven

The day started at 5.30 a.m. with some very good news from the Bromley forum. I learned that Torquay manager Paul Cox had walked out, as had four of the club's directors. At 5.35, I learned some very bad news: Alan Julian, arguably Bromley's most important player, had an unspecified injury and was out for an unspecified amount of time.

A replacement, Chris Kettings, had been rushed in. He was billed as Crystal Palace's third-choice keeper, but I wasn't convinced this was strictly true. Alex McCarthy was in my *Telegraph* Fantasy League team (cleverly called CF Yelmorb), so I knew he was the current first-choice goalkeeper at Selhurst Park, while the better-known Wayne Hennessey and Julian Speroni were more likely to be next in line. I just hoped Kettings hadn't exaggerated his CV. As I could have told him from experience, you always get found out in the end.

So there was plenty to think about as I made my way to the station. And as I passed several heavily gelled men in tight T-shirts clutching bottles, and orange women wearing pink sashes along the way, an important question popped into my mind. When does Friday night in Leeds end and Saturday morning begin?

And why had nobody told me it was so cold at this time of day in mid-September?

As I stood shivering on the platform, I remembered my first day back in England, shivering on another platform, at Gatwick. That was over four months ago now. Since then, Liz and I had settled in well. We'd been to Halifax, Bromley and the Cotswolds, started to get used to the cultural differences, and my kids had become a part of everyday life again.

There weren't a lot of people waiting for the 06.10 to Plymouth. Just me and several dozen Irish rugby fans on their way to Cardiff for the World Cup game against Canada. I couldn't help but question their sanity – getting up at a stupidly early hour to trek hundreds of miles across the country for a meaningless fixture. The irony of this somehow evaded me.

The train was on time, and as we began the long journey to the south-west coast I discovered what Irish rugby fans like for breakfast. Carlsberg Export. I opted for the more conventional M&S melon-free fruit salad.

As the sun rose over the South Yorkshire countryside, I sat back and took in the sights. There were cows grazing, painted stations whistling by, and fishermen on riverbanks.

It was idyllic.

By the time we got to Sheffield I was completely bored with idyllic scenery and there were still four hours and twelve minutes to go. I'd already picked the team (Goldberg in for May, new goalkeeper, otherwise unchanged), had breakfast, read the paper, read the paper again, and texted Liz to tell her how bored I was.

The view from the window didn't help. Instead of natural beauty I'd begun to notice some of the less visually appealing aspects of British rural life: towering electricity pylons and unsightly satellite dishes.

I closed my eyes and tried to sleep, but gave up after what seemed like an hour but was, in fact, less than ten minutes.

It was around this point that the idiocy of my day trip finally started to register. In terms of travelling time, it was the equivalent of flying from London to New York, watching a game of football (sorry, soccer) and flying straight back afterwards.

And in terms of likely outcome, the picture wasn't much brighter. Bromley had played at Torquay in January, an FA Trophy tie that did not end well (a 4-0 defeat); although, perhaps a symptom of Torquay's downturn in fortunes since then, their keeper had left to become a car salesman at Dorset's premier Audi centre, Poole Audi. There was more money in it, apparently.

So given the result last time out, I was more than likely making a long trip to watch my team get comprehensively beaten. And the journey was beginning to feel as though it would never end. If I'd been in a car, I would have been pestering the driver by constantly asking, 'Are we there yet?'

As we sat at Birmingham New Street, with three and a half hours still to go, I almost got off and went back to Leeds. Only the thought of Bromley FC kept me going. That and the fact that the platform was absolutely packed with Irish rugby fans.

At least the trip got a bit more enjoyable once we reached Devon, with the track running along the coastline, just yards from the sea. This compared favourably to the football journey between Victoria and Bromley South.

After changing at Newton Abbot, I got talking to a man in his sixties wearing a Torquay shirt. He was a typically pessimistic non-league fan whose ultimate hope was that his team would scrape home. They'd drawn at Kidderminster in midweek, doing a Bromley by conceding a penalty in the last minute of injury time.

His shaven head was covered in a film of sweat. I wanted to think it was brought upon by gut-churning terror at the prospect of his team facing Bromley and the likes of Moses Emmanuel, but conceded it was probably the unseasonal temperature.

It really was a perfect day to be beside the seaside, as I was about to discover. Because minutes later came the moment I'd spent the past six hours dreaming about: we finally arrived in Torquay. Torquay, another in a long list of must-see British places I'd never been to.

As I stepped off the train and took the short walk to the seafront, I was pleasantly surprised. For a start, I was probably the youngest person in town. But what struck me most was how civilized it seemed. Elegant Victorian architecture nestled alongside picturesque gardens, and everyone was polite and welcoming. Even the seagulls were well behaved, keeping squawking to a minimum and sticking to a respectful, unthreatening altitude.

Perhaps this was because I didn't see a single person carrying chips – a first for me in a British town centre.

After a pleasant stroll through the streets, I began the ascent up a very steep hill (this was beginning to seem to come as standard with clubs in the Vanarama National League) towards Plainmoor. For the second time in three weeks it felt like climbing Everest, but without Sherpas to carry my backpack.

When I finally got there, Plainmoor struck me as being the direct opposite to Boreham Wood: it was a lovely, well-maintained stadium that didn't reflect the club's fall from glory over the last eighteen months from Football League towards football obscurity. The fact-packed programme, too, deserved to be a source of pride. It was called *Simon Says*, which was a bit puzzling, but most Vanarama National League programmes had distinctive titles. Halifax's was called *Shaymen Shout*, Grimsby's was *The Mariner*, Forest Green's was *We Are FGR*, and Woking's simply carried the title *Cards*. All further evidence, as far as I was concerned, of programmes' gradual metamorphosis into magazines.

The home support was impressive, and as usual an equally impressive number of Bromley fans had turned out, but the team news contained a huge shock. Bradley Goldberg's mum was getting married again, and he was at the wedding, which was typical: I finally pick him in my starting line-up and he can't play. In his absence, his dad had named Moses Emmanuel and Ben May up front, mainly because they were the only strikers available. If either got injured, we were in trouble.

I was happy to see Bromley in their all-red strip, which had become a bit of a good luck charm. They hadn't been beaten in it all season and most of the hundred or so fans who had made the journey were quietly hoping for a good away draw.

Torquay had replaced their goalkeeping car salesman with Daniel Lavercombe (kit sponsor: Paul Bastard), and picked a strong side packed with names familiar to those of us who obsessively study *The Non-League Paper* every week.

Predictably, Bromley went behind early on, and it was all too easy. A free kick into the box, the right-back James Hurst leapt high above the defence, beating Palace's third-/fourth-choice keeper with a firm header, and that old, familiar feeling came over me.

This was Torquay United away. What was I expecting? A 5-0 win or something?

But you can't get too pessimistic when you've got Moses Emmanuel out on the pitch, and minutes after going behind, we were level. Moses got the ball on the right and, with the defender backing off, struck the ball sweetly past Lavercombe to make it 1-1.

And he hadn't finished. From a corner five minutes later, Torquay failed to clear and Moses was perfectly positioned to poke the ball home from a yard out.

Torquay 1 Bromley 2.

His third goal, on the half-hour mark, was the culmination of a brilliant move involving Anthony Cook, Louis Dennis and Ali Fuseini. Fuseini's shot was half cleared to Moses, who struck the ball cleanly into the roof of the net, giving him a first-half hat trick.

Torquay 1 Moses Emmanuel 3.

The Bromley fans were in football heaven. Apart from Pete, a fellow Leeds resident who told me before the game that we'd win, no one had seen this coming. The singing was louder than ever and the celebrations more exuberant.

But beneath the joy was a tinge of sadness. Moses was now the League's top scorer and bigger clubs would soon be chasing him. The January transfer window was going to be a very nervy time for Bromley fans.

Another nervy time was injury time, which always carried a great deal of stress for the seasoned Bromley follower. Our defence always seems to switch off, and today was no different. Deep into first-half injury time, Tyrone Marsh walked through and scored from close range.

Torquay 2 Bromley 3.

As the teams ran out for the second half, groans could be heard from several Bromley fans. Ben May, one of our two fit strikers, had been taken off injured and replaced up front by centre-back Jack Holland.

But as play got under way, it was soon apparent that the game had entered a parallel universe. Bromley suddenly clicked, and started playing out of their skins. It was all triangles and one-touch football. The movement was so fast at times that Torquay – that's Torquay United, who were in the Football League until recently – couldn't keep up.

This was as good as it got. Here I was, on a beautiful day on the English Riviera, watching the English Barcelona.

An inch-perfect Cook cross from the right was met by striker/centre-back/occasional midfielder Holland, who calmly side-footed home before uncalmly heading towards the delirious Bromley fans. They responded the only way they knew how, with a B-R-O, B-R-O, B-R-O-M-L-E-Y, which had somehow gone from being an ironic piss-take to a heartfelt goal celebration.

Torquay 2 Bromley 4.

From then on, Emmanuel, Cook and Dennis were at the centre of everything. Finding space, toying with the opposition defenders, and playing some lovely passing football. It was dizzying to watch.

After an hour there was yet another crude tackle on Cook outside the area, and another free kick. The keeper organized his defence, but Louis Dennis ran up and Messi'd the ball over the wall and into the top corner. It was now, unbelievably . . .

Torquay 2 Bromley 5.

Minutes later, before the 'Bromley Geezers' song had had a chance to die down, Jack Holland, who was having a great time playing up front, fed Cook who was chopped down in the box. The winger picked himself up and smashed the penalty powerfully past Lavercombe.

Torquay 2 Bromley 6.

The overwhelming feeling was one of pride. You can spend a lifetime following a team, sitting through hundreds if not thousands of Saturdays, and not see anything like this. And to think I nearly hadn't come. I felt the tension drain as I had the novel experience of knowing that Bromley were going to win, despite having twenty minutes left on the clock.

Then, after another fluid move, came the best goal of the lot. Holland once again got involved, setting up Fuseini who curled the ball from outside the box past the flailing keeper.

Torquay 2 Bromley 7.

I was feeling a bit emotional. This was a Bromley I'd dreamed about as a young boy. I took a picture of the scoreboard. It shows the Torquay United security guard staring at it, bemused. The keeper looks shellshocked. He was probably wondering if there were any vacancies at Poole Audi.

I was irrationally upset when Torquay got a consolation just before the end to make it 3-7. I suspect this was because I'd just that minute posted my picture of the scoreboard on Facebook. Out of date after seconds. No wonder it got only a couple of likes.

When the referee blew the whistle on this near-perfect display from Bromley, I immediately regretted not having time to stay around and celebrate. Sadly I was on a tight schedule: my train left Torquay at 17.14, and if I missed it, the next one didn't get into Leeds until 02.20.

Luckily, I got a lift to the station from Rich – another kind gesture from someone I barely knew. I was starting to get the feeling I'd had nearly fifty years earlier, when Roy (who was there today), Derek and Peter, the self-styled Bromley Boys, were like a second family. This was a feeling I'd first noticed in the close confines of the terraces at Boreham Wood.

As I sat on the train, watching the sun set and the tide go out along the south coast, I thought about the day. I'd just read a report on a Torquay newspaper website quoting the assistant manager as saying it was the worst defensive effort he'd seen in fifty-odd years. Maybe it was, but there was another way of looking at it. From my point of view, it was the best attacking effort I'd seen in fifty-odd years. Most of the goals were so good they would have even beaten Alan Julian.

Thrillingly, the table now showed Bromley in ninth place, closing in on the play-off places. I was trying not to get carried away, but some of the football I'd just seen had been a lot better than you'd get from a middle-of-the-table team. Even in the Vanarama National League.

Much of the journey home was spent staring at the picture I'd taken of the scoreboard, which read Torquay 2 Bromley 7. This was conclusive proof that I wasn't a jinx; in fact I must be a good luck charm. The only downside to winning so convincingly – not that I'd had much experience – was the hope it gave you. Because as every football fan knows, hope is what comes immediately before crushing disappointment.

Plus, winning streaks – and we'd now won four in a row – tend to come to a crashing halt, as Forest Green Rovers were finding out. After winning their first seven (again, if you count that 'goal' against Bromley), they had lost midweek and today.

But for now, I was happy. The journey home was rushing by and not even an unexplained thirty-minute delay at Birmingham New Street could dampen my mood. Suddenly the long trips to watch Bromley seemed more sensible than stupid. The only problem, as always, was the dwindling funds which meant I'd be looking at Megabus timetables instead of train ones by Christmas.

To help pass the time, I imagined I had the power to stop the season whenever I wanted to. If I decided to take advantage of this now, we'd finish sandwiched between Grimsby and Tranmere as the League's top scorers, and Moses Emmanuel, with his eight goals from nine games (many from the wing), would win the Golden Boot. Would I take it? Was this as good as it was going to get?

I thought about it carefully, not wanting to make a rash decision; with great power comes great responsibility. In the end, I surprised myself by deciding to keep going with the season, as I was enjoying the adventure so much. The way we'd played today we might well shock one or two other sides during the campaign, I reasoned.

Realistically, though, the first task remained to finish outside the relegation zone. Someone on the forum had come up with a total of fifty-one points being enough to ensure another season in the Vanarama National League. We were already a third of the way there.

When the train pulled into Leeds, it was after midnight. Despite getting tangled up with a giant inflatable penis attached to a piece of ribbon which was being pulled along by a woman wearing a pink sash, I couldn't have been happier on the walk home. This had been the best football day of my life, at the end of the best football week of my life. And, almost unbelievably, things were about to get even better.

We had two home games and, frustratingly, I wouldn't be going to either. But an email from the BBC brought good news. They were responding to my complaint of anti-Bromley bias (to be honest, now, in the cold light of day, it sounded to me more like an unhinged rant than an evidenced-based argument) by pointing out that they were covering both the Kidderminster *and* Chester home games in the next week, and that they'd had Mark Goldberg on after that 'amazing win' at Torquay. Flattering my team paid off. They were immediately forgiven.

The BBC site had everything I needed for the Kidderminster game on one page – the commentary, all the latest scores and, crucially, live tables. They were thus restored to the position of a totally impartial national institution to be proud of.

I made a cup of tea, put a couple of ginger biscuits on a plate, and sat down at the kitchen table to follow events at Hayes Lane.

I was hoping for a repeat of Saturday's heroics at Torquay, and the day had started exactly the same way: Kidderminster's manager had walked out just before the Bromley game. Who'd want to be a Vanarama National League manager? Well, as far as Torquay United were concerned, 129 people. That's how many applied for the job at Plainmoor in the days following Paul Cox's walk-out.

In another repeat of Saturday, Bromley soon went behind. And this was after Joe Anderson had cleared a header off the line. It was all Kidderminster, and Bromley had slipped to eleventh in the live table. The commentator, who was from BBC Radio Worcestershire, described the goal, but had difficulty identifying the scorer. 'The floodlights aren't great,' he said. 'I can't really see.' That was it. He'd already stuck the knife in by sounding happy about Kidderminster scoring, and now he was twisting it.

If he thinks Bromley's floodlights are bad, I mumbled to myself, I'd like to see him commentating at Boreham Wood. I made a note in my notebook. 'Commentator is a twat' it read.

The stress got too much for me and I went to the cupboard for a couple more biscuits, one of which was gone before I sat back down.

Just before the break, Bromley got a free kick on the edge of the box. In yet another repeat of Saturday, Louis Dennis curled the ball over the wall and into the right-hand corner. Obviously Kidderminster hadn't watched the highlights of the Torquay game on BT.

This was understandable. They'd probably set the recorder for it like I had, only to find themselves watching the second half of Marseille v. Saint Etienne when they played it back, like I had.

This would never happen with the BBC.

Recent history continued to repeat itself in the second half. Just like at Torquay, Moses Emmanuel scored from a poor clearance and Anthony Cook won, then scored, a penalty. To complete the parallel, we gave away a soft goal half an hour from the end.

But Bromley held out. It was now five straight wins in the Vanarama National League.

The sixth came the following Saturday, at home to former winners of the Debenhams Cup (an admittedly short-lived trophy in the 1970s) Chester. If the BBC commentary was anything to go by, it was one of the performances of the season. The game was over by half-time, with three outstanding goals – two from Moses Emmanuel and one from Louis Dennis. I saw the goals on YouTube, and each one was stunning. It was impossible to pick the best of the three – they were equally brilliant.

The confidence among the players seemed to be stratospheric. Rob Swaine tweeted that 'If Moses Emmanuel doesn't get Player of the Month, I will cartwheel through Bromley High Street in a g-string.' I suspected that he wouldn't mind too much if Moses missed out, as he didn't seem the shy retiring type. Another tweet reflecting the mood of the camp came from Anthony Cook. 'When Moses gets the ball anywhere near the box, don't think I'm making runs to receive the ball,' he wrote, 'I'm running to celebrate his goal.'

Bromley were fourth in the Vanarama National League – so much higher than and so far removed from anything that had ever gone before, it was laughable. We were becoming known as the most entertaining team in the League, and when Moses picked up the Player of the Month award (possibly to Rob Swaine's relief) and Goldberg was made Manager of the Month, there was an air of inevitability about it.

It couldn't get any better than this, could it? I was pretty sure the answer was no. Blind optimism is not part of a Bromley fan's make-up. Especially when the next game is against the biggest club you've ever played.

HOME
AND
AWAY

Eight

The Merseyside derby, taking place at Goodison, completely overshadowed the next biggest game on Merseyside that early October weekend. The one I was on my way to see.

Tranmere Rovers v. Bromley. It was being advertised as fifth in the table v. fourth, but that gave no indication of the true gap between the clubs. Tranmere Rovers were playing in the League Cup Final at Wembley in 2000, at a time when Bromley were third from bottom in the Ryman League Division One. Between 1993 and 1995, under John King, they'd reached three successive play-offs for promotion to the Premier League.

Tranmere Rovers v. Bromley. It just didn't look right, as though the fixture computer had had a meltdown and was churning out random, nonsensical pairings for its own amusement. This was going to be our biggest test of the season and all I wanted was to avoid total humiliation. I wanted to be proud of the team, and just hoped they wouldn't freeze.

Talking of which, with autumn setting in, I'd bought myself a new football-watching jumper. It had a fashionable Nordic-style grey and black pattern and represented a significant upgrade on my usual Jeremy Corbyn look. It would be making its debut at Prenton Park for a game I'd written a big fat zero next to on the fixture list, when I'd gone through the season's games allocating predicted points.

To make Bromley's task even harder, the Tranmere manager didn't walk out the night before the game; but the sense of feeling cheated by this was partially offset by the fact that both their captain and number one striker were suspended.

As Liz and I stood on Platform 12B at Leeds station, we noticed a young woman with thin-framed glasses and long blonde hair who was wearing a Bromley scarf. This was totally unexpected. A female Bromley fan in Leeds? Who was she? I was too bashful to go up to her and ask, thus ensuring that she would remain a mystery. At least for the time being.

Besides, we would shortly be meeting up with another woman I'd never seen before, because one of the bonuses of playing Tranmere was that I finally got to meet Caroline, who lived nearby. We'd had our first books published by the same publisher at the same time, nine years before. We'd kept in touch and become good friends without actually meeting. This was the perfect chance finally to get together: her husband and son were Tranmere season ticket holders.

The three of them met us at Liverpool Lime Street station, and it was brilliant to see them. Inevitably, after catching up with Caroline, talk turned to the game. Her husband Gary, a big, friendly, outgoing Scouser, seemed supremely confident – something you rarely see in a non-league fan – and was anticipating a comfortable win. He didn't even pretend to take Bromley seriously. This was clearly a game Tranmere expected to win, and the bookies agreed.

I'd even had a bet on them myself, but this was designed to jinx Tranmere. Sports betting as it is today didn't exist when I'd last lived in the UK, when horses were the only thing you could gamble on. Since my return I'd discovered gambling was not my strong point as I lost £20 on Australia not winning the Ashes, £20 on Andy Murray not winning Wimbledon and £40 on the Open golf, when my anticipated Tiger Woods comeback failed to materialize. It was now time to capitalize on my terrible record by putting a fiver on Tranmere to beat Bromley.

After not long enough with Caroline (although we agreed to meet up again in a couple of weeks), it was time for football. Gary gave us a lift to the ground, where we went to our separate ends, arranging to meet up afterwards. I was looking forward to that, as there was every chance he'd have undergone a change of heart about Bromley, and there are few things more satisfying than praise for your team from a supporter of one of your rivals.

Going into Prenton Park was a thrilling experience. It was a huge, well-maintained ground designed for bigger games than this. The crowd was equally impressive, with around 5,000 expected.

And if the intimidation factor was a worry, so was the team news. We needed our strongest side out there, and this wasn't our strongest side. Jack Holland was still filling in up front, although Alex Wall was on the bench. There was still no sign of Alan Julian, Reece Prestedge had come in for the injured Max Porter, and Ugo Udoji was starting at right-back. I was looking forward to seeing Lee Minshull, who had been named as sub. A friend who is a fan of his former club AFC Wimbledon rated him highly, saying he 'gets stuck in, is good in the air and scores a few goals. Expect red cards though.' Exactly the sort you need in a game like this.

The usual songs and chants started up. The only one that didn't quite work was the 'Goldberg, Goldberg, give us a wave' one. Unusually there was no response from the dugout and the plea for a wave got louder and more indignant. It was all a bit puzzling – the manager normally responded straight away. Why was he ignoring us today?

It was only when someone pointed out that he was ill and hadn't made the trip that the chant came to a sudden and embarrassed halt. This was one of the problems playing in a big stadium: we were miles away from the dugout and couldn't see who was there.

A couple of the Bromley fans noticed my jumper. Instead of the expected compliments, all I got was 'Bit early for Christmas, isn't it, Dave?'

The game started well for Bromley and I thought we just about had the better of the opening. But then, after half an hour, Tranmere took the lead when Andy Mangan beat Chris Kettings from the narrowest of angles.

Not long after, Bromley opened up the defence when a ball was played through to Moses Emmanuel and the Tranmere keeper, Scott Davies, slid out to meet him. The Player of the Month saw what was happening and took an early shot, which Davies, a yard outside the area, dived towards and tipped away. My heart leapt. This was a free kick in Louis Dennis territory – almost as good as a penalty given the form he was in. Plus, Tranmere would be down to ten men without a keeper on the bench.

The only problem was, referee Jason Whitely had somehow missed it. His linesman (programmes no longer identify them by the colour of their flag, so I don't know if it was Mark Powell or Oliver Bickle, though I suspect the latter: he looked like an Oliver) was shaking his head vigorously. It had been absolutely blatant. Anthony Cook later tweeted a still of the incident, and it was even further out than I'd thought.

The frustration in the Bromley end, already brewing after giving away a soft goal, was growing. It got even worse just after half-time when the normally reliable Rob Swaine failed to clear the ball and instead passed to the Tranmere winger, who found Jonny Margetts lurking just inside the box. 2-0.

The home fans burst into song and Liz looked at me, bemused.

'What's that they're singing?'

'We're Tranmere Rovers FC, the finest football team the world has ever seen.'

'That's what I thought. Isn't that a bit of an exaggeration?'

I nodded. But while they weren't the best team on the planet, they were definitely one of the best teams in the Vanarama National League. And if the score stayed at 2-0, it wouldn't be a disaster. In fact it would be quite respectable.

With ten minutes left, Margetts made a good run which took him past Swaine and into the area, but his feet got tangled and he fell over, slid along the ground, and his momentum made him punch the ball into the advertising hoardings. When the whistle went I laughed. It was one of the funnier handballs I'd seen. Only the whistle hadn't gone for the handball. Whitely was pointing at the spot after the linesman – the one who was probably Oliver Bickle – had indicated a penalty.

The atmosphere behind the goal was now one of disbelief and anger. No defender had been anywhere near him when he went down. As Mangan converted the penalty, quite a few fans turned their attention to the linesman.

And the frustration wasn't only apparent on the terraces. On the field, Alex Wall and Anthony Cook were booked in quick succession, both for dissent, before injury time became insult-to-injury time when Lee Minshull was shown the predicted red card. Oliver-the-linesman was indicating he'd used an elbow. It hadn't looked worse than any of the other pushing and shoving that had been going on all day, but it was hardly a shock given how things had been going.

No sooner had the attendance of 4,817 been announced than it was reduced to 4,816. Just before the final whistle, to the surprise of absolutely nobody, Naughty Nigel was ejected from the ground. More of a surprise was the fact that Mikey, one of the club's more amiable supporters, followed shortly afterwards. From what I could see they'd both been having a go at the linesman.

I'd never seen a Bromley fan thrown out before. Leaving voluntarily ages before the end, yes. Countless times. But physically chucked out by a steward? This was a first.

While I was watching this unfold, Tranmere added a fourth. I didn't see it, but it was probably offside. The 4-0 loss had taken us from the play-off places to mid-table. It had been a miserable afternoon.

After the game we met up with the considerably less miserable Gary and his son Ben. I desperately wanted them to tell me how unlucky Bromley were, and that they were surprised by how well we played, but the hideous truth is that the game had finished exactly as Gary had predicted – a comfortable win for Tranmere.

In a last-ditch effort to salvage something from the day, I went fishing for compliments.

'So, what did you think of Bromley, then?'

'You won't be going down, there are plenty worse than you,' Gary replied, writing off our promotion chances. 'But you need a new striker.'

That felt like a punch in the stomach. I wanted to point out that Moses Emmanuel was not only the best striker Bromley had ever had, he was also the League's top scorer and Player of the Month, but instead I just sat there. The fight had gone out of me.

All I'd wanted was for Bromley to show that they belonged at this level. And they hadn't done that. Was it the Manager of the Month/Player of the Month curse? Poor refereeing and linesmaning? Or intimidation – playing a big team in a big stadium? Whatever the reason, Bromley were a much better side than the Bromley we'd just seen. Tranmere still had to come to Hayes Lane, in January. I decided I'd definitely be going to that, hopefully to witness redemption.

I also hoped that today's game had been a blip, and I managed to convince myself that with a different linesman it could have been a different result. Some of the decisions were awful. I wondered what Caroline's brother, the 2015 FA Cup Final referee Jonathan Moss, would have made of them.

The next morning I woke up in our cabin (the hotel had a nautical theme) to a new day in Liverpool. Going through my usual social media outlets, it was apparent what a close-knit club Bromley was. On Twitter, Rob Swaine apologized for his performance, taking responsibility for three of the goals (including the penalty that wasn't), and on Facebook, Mikey said how sorry he was for losing it with the linesman.

After passing the Castaway Bar, we found the breakfast room, where Liz and I sat next to a couple of women around my age. One proudly wore a Cliff Richard 75th birthday tour T-shirt, from his concert the previous night, while her friend carried a bag with a huge picture of a cat on it. They were excitedly arguing about which one of them he had been looking at directly as he sang 'Living Doll'.

I drifted out of their conversation. I was thinking about Bromley's season. How it had been sailing along nicely with everything going smoothly, then disaster had suddenly struck, threatening to sink our play-off hopes.

'So, what shall we do today?' asked Liz, interrupting my thoughts.

'Let's go to the *Titanic* exhibition,' I said, wondering why the thought had popped into my head.

'Good idea.'

The walk down to the Maritime Museum on the Albert Dock was glorious. The sun was out and the sky clear blue. Liverpool and Everton fans wandered around, mixing freely. The dock was unexpectedly beautiful and vibrant, a mix of old and new. It was far from the post-industrial dump I'd been expecting.

The *Titanic* exhibition was chilling. Literally: the air conditioning was on far too high for an early autumn morning. But that was soon forgotten as we came face to face with items like the flimsy lifejacket worn by one of the survivors, and letters from passengers who didn't make it back. It was a reminder that the *Titanic* story happened to real people, not actors.

Afterwards, we walked along the dock. We took selfies standing in front of the Liver Birds building. We took selfies with a ferry crossing the Mersey in the background. Then we took selfies posing with a John Lennon statue.

Basically, we did what everyone else was doing.

Once we'd run out of photo opportunities, we continued our stroll around the dock. And it was then that we came across a ship, the *Zebu*, that appeared to be sinking, with just its masts poking out from the murky waters outside the Tate Gallery. Because of its location, I assumed it was an installation, but when I saw half a dozen men in high-vis jackets standing around shrugging and looking helpless (which immediately identified them as British workmen), I realized it was a real-life shipwreck.

When we asked someone what was happening, we were told that the *Zebu* had sunk a few weeks ago, but no one had managed to salvage it yet. This was fairly typical of Liverpudlians; everyone we met seemed happy to act as our personal tourist guide.

We had completely fallen in love with the city. I decided that if a major British TV broadcaster with a keen sense of what the public wants ever offered me a series where I wandered round British cities offering semi-amusing observations, I'd start right here. Liz wanted to come back in the spring. Even though Bromley wouldn't be playing nearby, I found myself agreeing. Liverpool really was that good.

On the train home, I found myself sitting next to the world's most annoying man. He was in his early twenties and started loudly shovelling chips into his mouth as soon as he sat down. When he'd finished, he sat back, spread his legs into my space, scrunched up the bag and threw it on the table. It came to rest alongside my elbow.

He and his girlfriend were going to Leeds to celebrate their friend Sally's twenty-first. I know this because (a) the whole carriage could hear their conversation, and (b) he'd put a cake in a white cardboard box directly in front of me, and I could see 'Happy 21st Sally' through the cellophane window.

What they'd failed to notice, since they were so busy discussing how much they'd be drinking later, was that the strong early afternoon sun was shining directly through the window and on to the cake. As I gleefully watched over the next hour, the wording started to melt into a giant multicoloured unreadable blob, while the rest of the icing began to drip down the side.

I suppose I should have told them. But the feeling of pleasure I got from this tiny triumph, combined with the morning's walk around the Albert Dock and winning a couple of quid from the bookies, was therapeutic, helping to mask the pain of Tranmere.

A chance for instant redemption came three days later. A local derby of our own, although with a lower profile than the Merseyside one. Welling v. Bromley. It was a must-win game, even though I don't think there's ever been a Bromley game I haven't considered as must-win. But this really was, since it would put us back on track and prevent a nasty little not-winning streak from developing.

I listened to it on BBC Radio Kent, expecting the worst after the bubble-bursting experience at Prenton Park. When we conceded the traditional early goal, I felt as though I had been plunged into a world void of hope.

But then Ali Fuseini struck from outside the box in front of a vocal group of ecstatic Bromley supporters to level the score. I felt a touch of envy mixed in with the joy. I wished I was there, on a freezing, wet and unpleasant night in Welling, instead of following the game from the comfort of a warm home. It sounded like a special goal, which got better and better every time I replayed my version of it in my mind.

Just as I was wondering whether I should be happy with a point, given that Welling were on a four-game winning streak, Bromley took the lead with another high-quality finish. This time it was Jack Holland, put through by Moses Emmanuel, who chested the ball down, controlled it and finished in untypical centre-back fashion with a subtle touch past the diving keeper.

The fans celebrated his versatility by breaking into the longest song in their repertoire, sung to the tune of 'Yellow Submarine' – 'Number 1 is Jack Holland, Number 2 is Jack Holland, Number 3 is Jack Holland' and so on, eventually arriving at 'and the subs are Jack Holland', before going on to the memorable chorus 'We all dream of a team of Jack Hollands, a team of Jack Hollands, a team of Jack Hollands'. I don't know who came up with it – it certainly wasn't speediej's mate as it was far too good – but it made for a pleasant backdrop to the commentary. Plus, it passed the time. And when your team is 2-1 up, time is everything. It slows to a crawl.

A sign that Bromley were staying on top of things came when the commentator compared Mark Goldberg to legendary Dutch coach Rinus Michels, and Bromley's style to the total football played by Holland (the country, not Jack) in the 1970s, where positions were interchangeable and the game was played at a dazzling pace. Despite the slight difference in personnel, I could see what he was getting at. Because what was becoming undeniable, even to the most cautious and pessimistic Bromley fan like me, was that this team was capable of breathtaking football. Last Saturday had just been an off day.

Despite this realization, I couldn't listen to the commentary as the game went into injury time with Bromley still only a goal ahead. This was a period that had provided so much angst and heartbreak during the season that it was simply too stressful. I walked away from the computer and turned the sound off, returning half an hour later, long after the game (and injury time) was over. I sat down and forced myself to look at the screen.

It said Welling 1 Bromley 2.

Bromley had overcome the injury-time jinx. Mark Goldberg's black and white army had held on for their seventh win in eight games, and one of the most important. Unbelievably, we were now back up to fourth in the Vanarama National League. Was promotion a possibility? I decided to turn to the people who knew about such things. The bookies.

And this was the exact moment when I came crashing back down to earth. William Hill had Bromley eleventh favourite, only a few places higher than at the start of the season. Everyone else I looked at agreed that we'd finish outside the top ten. Even after the outstanding performances of the last month, and with the best attack in the League, Bromley were no more than an afterthought in the betting market.

I felt deflated. Just like at Tranmere, it seemed my team wasn't being taken seriously by the big boys. And if there was one thing I'd been craving more than anything else in recent weeks (apart from Marmite crisps), it was recognition for Bromley FC.

Still, there was a small run of games coming up that could change all that. These included a home game against Barrow on Non-League Day followed by a visit from high-flyers Cheltenham, who were among the title favourites. Cruelly, I wouldn't be going to either of these – Barrow for the most embarrassing reason ever to miss a football match, and Cheltenham because I couldn't afford it.

But after these matches my mini Bromley drought would be over in one of the best ways possible. I'd be going back to Aldershot, scene of one of my favourite football memories.

HOME
AND
AWAY

Nine

A week before the almost Torquay-length journey to Aldershot, there was Non-League Day. This is a joyous celebration of the game outside the Football League, a party atmosphere with bumper crowds thanks to the international break and slashed admission prices. For the true football fan, it's unmissable.

If your team happens to have a good chance to climb from fourth place to even more rarefied heights, it's even better. So what was I doing on 10 October 2015 that was so important it stopped me going to see Bromley play Barrow on my first ever Non-League Day?

I was getting ready to watch Jenny Eclair's *How to Be a Middle-aged Woman (Without Going Insane)* with Liz at the Carriageway Theatre in Leeds. Months earlier I'd promised to go along and see it with her and had made the schoolboy error of not checking the fixture list beforehand. Like most lessons learned, it was a painful one.

To make it even worse, I'd miss the chance to see Bromley in a match refereed by a Mr Bromley. That's Adam Bromley. From Devon. I'd found this out from the Football League website which has a list of all National League officials and, crucially, their home towns (or sometimes only their counties). A vital resource for all but the most casual football fan.

With the twin temptations of Non-League Day and the appearance of Mr Bromley at Hayes Lane, I briefly thought about getting the train down, watching the first half and then dashing back to King's Cross to catch the 17.03. But for the first time in months, common sense won out. I decided that made little sense financially – or in any other way. Besides, there would be other Non-League Days for Bromley. Unless we got promoted, in which case I wouldn't care what the smaller clubs got up to.

At least I'd be able to listen to the game on the radio. Or so I thought.

Doubts about the BBC's impartiality resurfaced after discovering there would be no live commentary on BBC Radio Kent. It would have to be back to the old-school way – relying on Twitter. Jenny Eclair had robbed me of seeing the game; the BBC had deprived me of listening to it. Resentment against both was growing.

It was a particularly important game because it was the first of three in quick succession against teams that had been in the Football League. What happened in these three matches would be an excellent indication of how far Bromley had come.

And Barrow were first up.

This is how the afternoon unfolded for people who were unable to go to the match because they'd committed themselves to watching a woman talking about coping with the menopause and were having to follow it on Twitter instead:

> 18 minutes GOOOOOOAAAAALLLLLL!!! 1-0
> BROMLEY! Corner swung in, Swaine heads back
> across goal to the goal machine Jack
> HOLLLLLLANNND!!!

25 minutes GOOOOOOOAAAAALLLLL!! 2-0 BROMLEY!
What a goal from Cook! Great turn just inside half,
beats three defenders, smashes a great strike home!

49 minutes GOOOOALLLL!!! Prestedge lobs the
keeper from edge of box! 3-0 BROMLEY!

64 minutes GOOOOOOOAAAAALLLLL!! 4-0 BROMLEY!
Emmanuel with the goal! Unbelievable scenes at
Hayes Lane!

88 minutes GOOOOOOOAAAAALLLLL!!! IT'S FIVE!!!!!!
5-0 BROMLEY! Louis Dennis with an unbelievable
curling effort into the top corner!

It seemed that I had missed another Torquay-like performance, perhaps the best of the season so far, but that didn't stop me feeling totally elated. I was especially impressed with Jack Holland who had been outstanding at centre-back, right-back and striker.

I was still full of Bromley-related excitement when we arrived at the Carriageway Theatre. The audience was made up of around 99 per cent women, but when I complained about being outnumbered, all Liz said was, 'Now you know how I feel when you drag me along to football.'

I thought this was a bit unfair. I'm convinced Bromley have the highest percentage of female fans in the Vanarama National League – in spectacular contrast to the 1970s, when a woman at Hayes Lane was as rare as a Bromley win.

Despite not being in Jenny Eclair's demographic, I actually quite enjoyed the show (apart from the unwarranted mockery of Marks & Spencer's Blue Harbour Collection jumpers, which are no laughing matter). Still, I'd never be able to forgive her. I hold grudges longer than anyone.

The next morning, I rushed out early to get *The Non-League Paper*, which is usually on Sainsbury's shelves by eight a.m. When I got home and read phrases like 'Brilliant Bromley batter Barrow in five-star show', 'a stunning finish that couldn't have been placed any better' and 'an exquisite strike from Anthony Cook', all the pain of missing out came back. It was almost impossible to suppress the seething mass of bitterness towards Jenny Eclair bubbling up inside me.

And the next night, when I watched the goals on BT's high-lights show, that feeling grew even stronger. They were, without exception, brilliant. Cook's and Dennis's were a toss-up for goal of the season. I went for the latter. Just.

When I saw that Bromley had climbed to third – only below Cheltenham on goal difference, so effectively joint second – I suddenly appreciated the enormity of what my club was doing. It crossed my mind that I might have lost touch with reality a couple of months ago and was in the middle of some weird, long-term, dreamlike hallucination. I'd seen a film a bit like that once.

Cheltenham, the second of the three former Football League teams we were playing in a week, were the next visitors to Hayes Lane, which really was turning into a fortress. Maybe that name had been ahead of its time. I then found out that the official name for the ground was now the Bromley Arena. I wasn't convinced that would last too long either.

I did a feasibility study on going to the game (it was a bit late to get a good train price, but National Express could get me there and back for £14 plus £1 booking fee, arriving home at 2.20 in the morning), but decided against it. BBC Radio Gloucestershire were providing commentary, and I was travelling to Hampshire on Saturday.

Cheltenham were coming off a draw with Gateshead on Non-League Day, a game notable for Gateshead striker James Marwood playing without a number on his shirt, as a team-mate had accidentally spilt chocolate milk on the shirt he was meant to be wearing. Other than that excitement, it was a fairly uneventful draw.

Implausible as it sounded, Bromley could climb to second in the table with a win. I was feeling nervously hopeful, and saw on Twitter that Alan Alger, a highly respected tipster from Betway, was going. I tweeted him to get his prediction. 'Cheltenham 2-1' was his reply.

The game could have started better, but only just. Bromley were completely on top – Moses Emmanuel was put straight through and the keeper made a great save, and minutes later Anthony Cook hit the post. Moses then volleyed wide with just the keeper to beat. 'You can see why they score a lot of goals,' said the Radio Gloucestershire commentator, making me feel ten feet tall. Next Jack Holland, who really is about ten feet tall, came close with a header. We'd had four good chances in the first seventeen minutes.

But, gradually, Cheltenham got back into the game, and with just twelve minutes left the inevitable happened and Billy Waters scored for the visitors.

Bromley weren't finished yet. Two minutes from time, Cook won yet another penalty, and once again tucked it away. 'That's it, Bromley have salvaged a draw,' said the commentator, showing extraordinary naivety. This was Bromley, and there was still injury time to go. Something disastrous is usually guaranteed.

I repeated my trick from the Welling game, and walked away from the computer. It was apparent that I could no longer handle the stress of injury time. Too much damage had been done too many times in those few minutes.

I watched an episode of *Lewis* with Liz, then after it had finished I sat back down at the computer, looked at the screen – and was vaguely aware of a bloodcurdling cry erupting from the very depths of my being.

'Arrrghhh, nooooooo. No. No. No.'

Liz glanced over, giving me her irritating 'It's only football' look, then went back to reading.

I continued to stare at the screen. All I could see were words and numbers swimming around in front of me: Bromley 1 Cheltenham 2. They had scored a winner in the very last minute.

I slept badly that night, but by Saturday I had come to terms with the result. It was pretty good, I'd decided, being just seconds away from getting a point against one of the promotion favourites. I did such a good job of convincing myself it was a sign that Bromley remained on track for the play-offs that I almost ran to the station.

I was ready for our third game in eight days against a former Football League club.

Even though it would take nearly four hours to get to Aldershot, it felt great to be back on a train, heading for a Bromley match. It had been two weeks since Tranmere and I'd missed three games. Twitter and radio were simply no substitute for being there.

A couple of minutes from King's Cross came a reminder that the big time Bromley were enjoying wasn't quite as big as I'd built it up to be in my mind. We went past the Emirates Stadium, a spectacular sight – an enormous space-age dome, all curved glass and concrete, surrounded by its own plaza. Suddenly Prenton Park in Tranmere seemed a little less awe-inspiring than it had a fortnight ago.

Half an hour later, as a further reminder that I wasn't quite sitting at football's top table just yet, I was on the train to Aldershot. When we stopped at Woking, it was the first time this season that I'd stopped at the nearest station to a Vanarama National League club while on the way to another Vanarama National League ground. A fact so devoid of interest that I almost didn't put it in my notebook. Almost.

When I got to Aldershot, I was pleasantly surprised. It was much nicer than I'd expected, and after a quick but fruitless wander round looking for a cash machine, I arrived at the Electrical Services Stadium. It was brilliant to get to a Vanarama National League ground without having to climb a seemingly endless steep hill.

Then I noticed a sign outside that read:

AWAY SUPPORTERS
UNDER RAILWAY BRIDGE.
LEFT UP REDAN ROAD.
BACK DOWN THROUGH PARK TO TURNSTILES.

At least this detour gave me another chance to find a cash machine, which seemed to be non-existent in Aldershot. I even asked in Aldershot Kitchen Designs ('Why not let us create the perfect kitchen for you?'). They thought the one at the station was the nearest. I'd left it too late to go back there.

The problem was that I only had £18 in my pocket. If admittance and a programme – just one programme, mind – came to more than that I was in serious trouble. I could either go to the game and not get a programme, or get a programme and not go to the game. Neither option was satisfactory.

This dilemma gave me plenty to think about as I went in search of the away end. After going under the bridge, I turned on to Redan Road. Unsurprisingly, this was a really steep hill which took around five minutes to climb, and I had to stop to catch my breath a couple of times. I then turned into the park and on to another hill, this time more slippery as it was covered in wet autumn leaves. This eventually led to some steep wooden steps which I almost fell down, regaining my balance just in time.

And there, at the bottom, was a small dark green shed, its roof covered in twigs and barbed wire, incorporating a turnstile. A faded notice outside read:

Visiting Supporters Terrace
Adults £17
Concession £13
Juniors (11– U16) £5

This was potentially a huge break. There are very few advantages to being sixty, but this could well be one.

'How old do you have to be to get the concession?' I asked.

'Sixty-five, mate. Are you sixty-five or over?'

I paused, feeling like a deer caught in the headlights. If I could just hold my nerve and not panic, I might just get away with it.

I found myself putting on a deeper voice, a tactic dredged from my subconscious – it was something I used to do to try to sound older and get served in pubs. But then, just like with my pub attempts, I lost my nerve.

'Yes. I mean no. I'm only sixty.'

I handed over the full £17. He took it, but didn't seem entirely convinced.

Once inside, I was left with two stark choices. Do I do the unthinkable and go without a programme, or do I do the unthinkable and ask someone I barely know to lend me two pounds?

I spotted Mickey, one of the fans who had admired my jumper at Tranmere.

'This is a bit embarrassing,' I began, anxious to act before the programmes sold out, 'but you couldn't lend me a couple of quid for a programme, could you?'

He dug into his pocket.

'Sorry, only got this,' he said, holding out a handful of small change. 'I couldn't find a cash machine.'

Luckily, his mate overheard and handed over a £2 coin with a look of disbelief and a slight shake of the head. My gratitude was immense and heartfelt. I thanked him and swore I'd pay him back next week. Even though I'd normally buy two programmes, there are times when you're happy just to have one.

The Aldershot programme (or *Shots* as they call it) was one of the better ones, but there was still a depressing uniformity about modern-day Vanarama National League publications. But would that stop me buying them even if I had to borrow the money from complete strangers? Of course not.

Team news brought very little in the way of good news. Still no Alan Julian, Max Porter, Pierre Joseph-Dubois, Alex Wall or Ben May. Jack Holland would be continuing in an unfamiliar striker role. Bradley Goldberg was still on the bench.

The away end was small and cramped, which helped the atmosphere. I did miss the days of changing ends at half-time, but this was the big time. And I was enjoying life at this level, despite all my worries at the start of the season about not feeling part of the club.

The only thing was, in the euphoria of being at such a high level, being in the play-off places and playing total football, I'd forgotten one important truth. Sometimes, a game of football can be really, really boring.

Different people found different ways of coping with the boredom. Mash advised the locals on integration with the area's recently arrived Nepalese immigrants by shouting 'Embrace your Gurkha community, you bastards' in their general direction.

Stokesy was gazing into the floodlights. 'I really like these old-school lights,' he said to no one in particular. 'If you stare into them you don't get a migraine.'

Mickey sang 'Goldberg, Goldberg, give us a wave', and the manager waved from the dugout. 'Not you,' Mickey shouted back at him, 'Brad!'

After half an hour during which the most exciting moment was when I realized I was standing underneath a tree – surely a rarity at a Vanarama National League ground? – Aldershot took an undeserved lead. A long-range shot which, like the game itself, was going nowhere took a huge deflection, sending Chris Kettings the wrong way. I'd have to look at it again on the highlights, but it looked lucky.

Minutes later, right in front of the Bromley contingent, Joe Anderson delivered a teasing, outswinging cross. In that moment I found myself desperately wishing we had a proper old-fashioned centre-forward instead of a makeshift one. But then Jack Holland, timing his run perfectly, muscled his way past a couple of massive centre-backs, soared and met the cross perfectly, Alan Shearer style, rocketing the ball past the static keeper. Honestly, it was brilliant.

Holland was now our second top scorer since converting to striker. I'd been waiting for several weeks for a newspaper or website to use the 'Jack of All Trades' headline, but thus far they had stubbornly resisted. I didn't mind. I could wait.

The game had briefly flickered into life, but then went back to sleep until an abysmal tackle by Jake Gallagher left Plymouth-based referee Adam Hopkins little choice but to get out his red (actually, it was more of a fluorescent pink) card. I knew I would never be able to forgive him for allowing that Forest Green goal earlier in the season, but this was a small step in the right direction.

Lee Minshull (formerly of Tonbridge Angles, according to the programme) then attempted the most ambitious thing I'd ever seen on a football pitch. The tough-tackling, ball-winning mid-fielder found himself one-on-one with the lightning-quick Aldershot right-back just over the halfway line. Minshull played the ball twenty yards past him into space and set off in pursuit, forgetting that he wasn't blessed with any speed whatsoever. The right-back turned, strolled after the ball, and it was back with the keeper before Minshull had even arrived.

That was the last action of the game. Injury time failed to deliver an Aldershot winner, and both sides had to settle for a draw. The fact that I felt a bit disappointed with just a point showed how far expectations had shifted since the start of the season.

As I set off on the long walk through the park and back to the station, I thought about the last time I'd been to the ground, in 1971. It had been another disappointing game, but memorable for other reasons: the match programme was one of the thirty-two I'd taken with me when moving to the US from New Zealand seven years earlier. My best friend Dave and his friend Keith had driven back from that game singing 'Back Home', the huge football song at the time, and we decided to write our own, in tribute to Keith's beloved York City. It wasn't very good but that didn't stop us recording it and sending it to the York manager.

Thinking about that episode, and how proud we were of the song, gave me a greater understanding of speediej. It was easy to laugh at his work, but at least he was trying. I had once been speediej. We have all once been speediej.

The next morning, I opened *The Non-League Paper* (disturbingly, I had started collecting them) and felt much happier. The report not only mentioned the huge deflection, which to my mind effectively confirmed that we would have won but for a lucky goal, but also carried the headline 'It's Jack of All Trades!'

That evening I watched the Vanarama National League highlights show. I didn't even bother watching from the beginning. The Bromley game would be last; it was inconceivable that there could have been a worse game. Sure enough, just before the end, it finally arrived. All they showed were the two goals. Or rather, they didn't. The camerawork was so shockingly awful that everything was a few seconds behind the play, so you didn't see the deflection for Aldershot's goal, just the ball going into the net, and you didn't see Holland's run, just the ball going past Phil Smith, the Shots' keeper.

The last three games we'd played against former Football League clubs had provided a win, a loss and a draw. As a measure of Bromley's progress, this couldn't have been more inconclusive. But I'd already forgotten about that crucial run of games which turned out to be not quite so crucial. I was thinking back to the magnificent sight that was the Emirates Stadium, and imagining Bromley playing there in January. Admittedly it was a distant possibility, but possible none the less.

We were, after all, just three games away from a first ever appearance in the third round of the FA Cup.

In order to stay on track for that, we had to overcome money-bags Eastleigh at Hayes Lane in the fourth qualifying round.

HOME
AND
AWAY

Ten

As I sat in a quiet carriage on my way to Hayes Lane via King's Cross, I realized I had now moved into full trainspotter mode. This had become apparent when I'd reached into my backpack and taken out the one essential component that had previously been missing: my brand-new Hercules thermos flask, chosen for its durability and exceptional heat retention. I put it on the table and poured myself a piping-hot cup of tea.

My notepad and pen remained packed away. I didn't need them just yet, since I'd given up on picking the team. I'd missed three games in a row in October so didn't feel able to judge who was in form and deserving of a place. Plus, there were too many injuries, with Alan Julian, Alex Wall, Ben May, Pierre Joseph-Dubois, Max Porter and Rob Swaine missing last time out, and the club being rubbish at giving any updates. It all seemed a bit pointless anyway since Bromley tended to go with Mark Goldberg's selection, not mine.

This meant I had more time to dwell on Eastleigh, today's opponents. They were our jinx team – games between us tended to be close before they snatched a late winner. Injury time today was going to be unbearable, unless we were at least four up.

And it wasn't just Eastleigh who were causing me anxiety. The train had been crawling along at Lee Minshull pace ever since leaving the station, and I was starting to worry about missing the game – especially when there was an announcement saying that we were running late due to trespassers on the track between Leeds and Wakefield.

To distract myself from thinking unthinkable thoughts, I decided to read some match previews, starting with the *Bromley Times*. But when I saw the headline 'FA Cup Chance to Stop the Rot', I almost spat out my tea.

The rot? What rot was this? Losing to the two teams that were playing in the Football League earlier this year? Unbeaten in the last ten games against everyone else? There was no rot to stop. If it had been a proper old-fashioned paper I would have screwed it up and thrown it in the bin between the seats. But it was on the iPad, so I couldn't.

Instead, I went to the Eastleigh supporters forum in search of some praise for Bromley, but soon found myself drawn into a heated discussion between what appeared to be fellow thermos flask owners that completely overshadowed football matters.

The great Eastleigh parking controversy.

This raged on over six online pages and had begun when someone had arrived for a home game only to find a car parked in his space. The steward told him to park in the bay next to it. The writer admonished the steward, telling him that this would merely compound the problem. His solution was A4 parking permits. 'I would gladly volunteer to help produce these,' he added.

It was a post that opened the floodgates.

Someone else suggested that since the stewards were under the control of the safety officer they couldn't be expected to control parking arrangements, while suggestions of a pay-and-display scheme were shot down with comments about 'machines that would cost money to install and could break'.

After several more pages of this, with the adult tone of the debate broken only by their local speediej equivalent ('We park where we want, we park where we want, we are the Eastleigh, we park where we want'), I had to concede defeat.

Not because I wasn't finding it interesting – I was – but because my own crisis was deepening. The train was now running eleven minutes late. That was OK, but if the delay crept past half an hour there were potentially catastrophic consequences, ranging from missing at least part of the game right through to the risk of programmes being sold out.

By the time we got to Doncaster we were fifteen minutes behind schedule, and when we finally pulled into King's Cross, the deficit had reached twenty-one minutes. There was still time. Just.

I jumped out of the train as soon as it came to a halt, rushed down the platform and ran to the underground station, FA Cup-inspired adrenalin pumping through me. It was a competition I loved and the thought of missing even a minute was terrifying. It was one of the most exciting things about coming back to England.

I managed to make up most of the lost time, but when I reached Victoria there was more bad news: there were no direct trains to Bromley South because of engineering works at St Mary's Cray. A real trainspotter would have known that.

And so, following a heroic effort involving more running, I arrived at Hayes Lane just four minutes late.

I hadn't managed to persuade Liz to come with me. The romance of the FA Cup had somehow eluded her. Back in May, she had insisted on watching *EastEnders* half an hour into the Cup Final as I'd already 'been watching football all day' and could record the rest and watch it later. When I protested that it was the most important game of the season, she pointed out that according to me *every* game was the most important of the season.

She had a point. But that day's game really was one of the most important games of the season. I had a feeling she'd regret not coming today.

As soon as I got into the ground, I saw something that made me realize Liz had made the right decision. The referee was Nigel Lugg, which meant Bromley were up against twelve men.

Feeling deflated, I made my way to my usual spot behind the goal where I saw Roy, his plastic Tesco bag by his side. He'd been the official seller of golden goal tickets for something like fifty years. I stopped to talk to him. His original cry, which you could hear from halfway down Hayes Lane, was 'Get your golden goal ticket here – every one a winner!', although he had since had to modify this on the grounds that it wasn't actually true. Every game I went to he managed to persuade me to buy a ticket. In all that time I had never come close to winning.

On the train back from Aldershot, he'd begun to tell me about the tens of thousands of programmes he had at home. One of these in particular made me embarrassed to call myself a programme collector and produced a feeling of envy that shocked me with its intensity. It was the programme for the Bromley match that never was, a proposed 1955/56 away game with Cray Wanderers, a friendly to test out Cray's new floodlights. But a few days before it was due to take place, Cray decided that their floodlights were rubbish and the match was abandoned.

And programmes weren't the only things Roy collected. There were also Bromley-related bus timetables, posters and newspaper cuttings. There were badges, pens and match tickets. And scarves, shirts and golden goal tickets. It was a glimpse into what my life would have been like if my mum hadn't thrown everything out the minute I left home.

Some would call it hoarding. I prefer to think of it as extreme collecting.

Roy lived in St Mary's Cray, where engineering works were currently taking place, and his neighbour had told me that a few years ago Roy could be seen on Google Earth standing outside his house, having a fag. People have become famous for less.

After discussing his fine collection, I left him and went in search of Mickey Crouch's mate who'd lent me the £2 at Aldershot. I found him standing just behind Mickey and handed over the money. It was a weight off my mind. I don't like being in debt.

Just after this, Anthony Cook dribbled the ball into the box and was too quick for the defender, whose boot stamped down hard on Cook's left foot, sending the winger tumbling. It was impossible to miss, given the defender was wearing fluorescent orange boots *and* had a handful of Cook's shirt *and* that the referee was about five yards away, but Lugg waved play on. There was no conceivable way it could not have been a penalty.

It was that 2008 FA Cup game against Hornchurch all over again, except then Lugg had given a penalty to our opponents when it clearly wasn't one. How much pain and misery can one man inflict upon another in a lifetime? At that moment I just wanted him to fuck off back to Chipstead and never to see him again.

Cook couldn't quite believe it either. 'Are you serious?' he asked the official, genuinely perplexed.

It had been the pattern of the season. The big decisions were going the way of the big (relatively speaking) clubs. Forest Green's offside 'goal', Tranmere's keeper handling outside the area and their penalty that wasn't, and now this. The conspiracy theories running around my head were reaching Mourinho proportions.

Still, at least it remained goalless. Or so I thought. Because it was then that I discovered we were in fact 1-0 down. Eastleigh had apparently scored in the first minute, just before I'd arrived. According to Mickey, it was a soft goal, a close-range header by a completely unmarked striker.

This was heartbreaking news. To suddenly go from the optimism of being level to the misery of being a goal down was hard to take, especially since we didn't look like scoring.

But after the break something clicked and Bromley looked much sharper, especially Cook and Louis Dennis. Even Mr Lugg couldn't find a reason to disallow Dennis's superb strike midway through the second half. He cut in from the right, beat a couple of defenders and smashed the ball into the roof of the net. As Lugg did the right thing for once and pointed towards the centre circle, the FA Cup dream was back on. I was just glad Mickey had told me about the early goal, otherwise I might already have been celebrating a win.

Which would have been a little embarrassing, but not half as embarrassing as what happened next. Because from the touchline thirty yards out, Jai Reason floated a hopeful cross towards the Bromley goal and Rob Swaine and Eastleigh's Ross Lafayette both missed it, which seemed to put Chris Kettings off. He stood and watched as the ball sailed over his head and into the corner of the net. It was the sort of goal only Bromley can concede.

This made it even more painful when we spotted Alan Julian, who would have saved it, as well as the first goal (even though I didn't see it), wandering around the ground with his little boy.

Bromley pushed hard for an equalizer but luck continued to be on Eastleigh's side. They somehow managed to hold on, and we were out of the Cup.

But as I walked towards the station with the rain pelting down on me, I realized things weren't as bad as they felt. Since all the other Vanarama National League teams had also been involved in the competition today, it meant that we were still in joint third place (although technically sixth on goal difference), only five points off top spot. And Moses Emmanuel was still two goals clear as the League's top scorer, despite having a quiet month. Not only that, but we were still officially among the top hundred clubs in England. Considering, too, that we were heading out of a very tough October into a relatively easy November when Bromley would be free to concentrate on the League, and Moses Emmanuel would be free of the Player of the Month curse, there was plenty to fuel feelings of both pride and optimism.

The importance of the FA Cup faded dramatically somewhere between Hayes Lane and Bromley South station.

On the train back to St Pancras, I got talking to Mash. He'd been a fan for around twenty years and had had similar early experiences to me. His first couple of Bromley games were misleading: Bromley won both and he was hooked. Then reality set in, and in his first three seasons he saw Bromley finishing eighteenth, eighteenth and nineteenth in the Ryman League.

For most people, that probably would have been enough. For most people, a move to one of the more successful clubs would have made perfect sense. Instead, Mash's love for Bromley grew and he followed his team around, watching them lose at places like Moseley (I didn't even know where that was until I Googled it), Ford United (the Ford factory works team in Romford) and Hayes Lane (a 5-2 defeat to Cray Wanderers, Bromley's tenants, in what was technically an away game).

But all this suffering did not go unrewarded. When you've lived through such misery, you can really appreciate it when you get to the dizzying heights Bromley had now reached. And the brilliant thing about supporting a small club is that even when they do unexpectedly well there are none of the big-team problems like, say, riots.

Which is why I was surprised to come across one as I got off the train and walked towards the exit of St Pancras. A line of police blocked my way and a deafening sound of screaming and shouting was coming from outside. I was advised to leave by the entrance at the back of the station and walk round to King's Cross. When I did, I could see what was going on. A hundred or so protesters, scarves covering their faces, were throwing flares and smoke bombs at the police, who had their batons drawn and looked as though they were itching to use them. The atmosphere was loud and threatening, with the acrid smell of smoke in the air; but I only saw one injury, which came when a particularly rubbish anarchist (he had the anarchy symbol on his jeans) tripped when running: the scarf covering his mouth and nose was also covering his eyes, which meant that he couldn't see where he was going, and he promptly fell flat on his face.

But it wasn't just anarchists (who, I soon discovered, were demanding an end to all borders) and police who were gathered in large numbers. There was a third group, bigger than those two put together. It was the bank of bystanders holding their phones up, taking pictures and putting them straight up on social media. I was part of this group. A post on Instagram broke my record amount of likes.

Of all the travel delays today, this was the most novel.

The police soon took control and, entertainment over, I walked across the concourse and into King's Cross. As I went past Platform 9¾, a tourist attraction (it's where Harry Potter and his wizard friends caught the Hogwarts Express), I noticed that the police had shut it down. Take that, anarchists.

The platform for the Leeds train was thankfully open, and as I made my way back up north I had time to think. Specifically about my dad. I'd been to see him, and one of the first things he'd asked about was how Bromley were doing, even though he had little interest in football. When I told him about the season, and the recent successful trips to Boreham Wood, Torquay and Aldershot, I noticed he had the same indulgent expression he'd had when I first hit my teens and could talk about nothing but Bromley FC. It was as though he loved my passion, but just didn't quite understand it.

He no longer lived in Bromley. Having lost his sight and mobility, he'd decided to move into Nightingale House, a delightful care home overlooking Wandsworth Common. He seemed happy there and well looked after.

Being able to see him regularly was one of the best things about moving back to England. As usual, I'd taken him several bars of ginger chocolate, as I could never think of anything else. It was what I'd bought him every birthday and every Christmas for as long as I could remember. He must either really enjoy eating them or have quite a collection somewhere.

He'd seemed in good spirits when I left, and I was already looking forward to a return. But before that could happen, on the last day of October there was the small matter of a trip to the home of Lincoln City, another former Football League club, who were unbeaten at home all season.

And Bromley badly needed a good performance. Not just because a draw could put us back in the play-off places, but also because Liz would be coming with me. And I was sensing I was running out of chances to persuade her to become a full-time Bromley supporter.

HOME
AND
AWAY

Eleven

When Liz was growing up in Connecticut, she probably never dreamed of a future where her birthday was celebrated with a 120-mile trip to watch a game of English non-league football.

But our visit to Lincoln wasn't just about football. I'm not that much of a rubbish husband. I'd also booked us into a very flash restaurant that evening and planned a romantic tour of the city's main attractions on the Sunday morning. When I say planned, I mean hurriedly Googled 'things to do in Lincoln' just before we left.

When we arrived, the walk to the ground took us through, down and past some of the grimmest back alleys, narrow streets and terraced houses I'd ever seen. I don't think either of us had ever walked so fast, and as a result we got there so early that we had time to check in to the hotel, which was a couple of minutes away, before the game.

We were greeted by the owner, a stern, no-nonsense Eastern European woman who immediately gave us a run-down of breakfast times and assorted house rules, and reminded us of the need to lock our door at all times. When I asked if she could give us a number for a taxi into town later, she looked horrified by the interruption. 'I will get to that, you will let me finish first,' she said, before giving us detailed instructions on using the TV and heater in the room. Only after that did she hand me a card with phone numbers for eight taxi companies.

'Which do you recommend?' I asked.

'Discount Cabs,' she snapped, and abruptly walked away.

I decided to go with them.

As we walked to the ground, I thought about the game. It was going to be one of the toughest so far, especially considering Lincoln's impressive home form. They were unbeaten at Sincil Bank all season, including a midweek FA Cup replay win against Tranmere. The most pleasing part of that was when the Tranmere goalkeeper was sent off for handling outside the area. Like any repeat offender, he probably thought if he could get away with it once, he'd get away with it again and again. But this time, unlike four weeks ago, justice was done.

According to the bookies, Lincoln were hot favourites, and it was relatively easy to avoid the mild temptation of backing Bromley at 6-1. Even I could see that wasn't a good idea.

Outside the stadium we met a small group of fellow Bromley exiles – Stu from Cardiff, Will from Manchester and Pete from Leeds. They were drinking, for reasons that weren't entirely clear, beer from Lithuania. It was good finally to see some friendly (if slightly glazed) faces.

Just before we went through the turnstiles, a security woman asked me to remove the top from my water bottle.

'Where should I put it?' I asked, looking around for a bin.

'Wherever you like.'

'In my pocket?'

'Yeah, that's fine.'

'But what if I put it back on as soon as I get in?'

She shrugged. Her job was done.

I noticed that Lincoln also had concession prices, and excitingly these were for spectators aged sixty or over. This was the first time I'd ever qualified, but it was a bittersweet moment. The man behind the grille didn't question me, or say, 'Well, you don't look sixty to me.' He just took my £13. Liz, of course, paid the full whack. The blow to my ego was balanced by the thought that I'd saved a fiver. In effect, I got my two matchday programmes that day for a pound.

It was another big stadium, capable of taking 10,000 – not quite as big as Tranmere's, but not far off. It was impossible not to be impressed. The main stand was the best I'd seen all season and looked as though it had been built quite recently. This was my idea of a glamour club, even if it wasn't the *Guardian*'s. That morning they'd named Lincoln City as one of the six most unglamorous clubs in the entire country. Lincoln unglamorous? Had they never visited Boreham Wood FC?

As we sat down – it was an all-seater stadium – the teams were announced. Still no Alan Julian and still no recognized striker to partner Moses Emmanuel; Jack Holland continued to fill the gap. It wasn't easy to hear the loudspeaker as we had been put right next to the stand occupied by Lincoln's 647 Squadron, a group of fans who showed their support by relentlessly banging the loudest drum on the planet.

As if that wasn't depressing enough, Bromley were playing in yellow, which rarely ended well.

After the first few minutes it had become obvious why Lincoln were unbeaten at home. The pressure on the Bromley defence was intense and all the action was taking place at the other end, where their wingers were putting in a succession of dangerous crosses. As the half went on, a Lincoln goal looked inevitable. The game was following the Tranmere pattern. Bromley just weren't clicking – passes either weren't finding their target or were over-hit, and players were arguing among themselves. They just seemed overwhelmed by the occasion.

Not much was happening on the terraces either. There seemed

to be no inspiration, just a few half-hearted renditions of some of the standards, including 'Shall We Sing a Song for You?', which I think was meant to be ironic as the home fans hadn't stopped singing since we arrived.

On and off the pitch, it was all a bit demoralizing.

Standing there in the deepening gloom reminded me of the last – and only – time I'd been to Lincoln. In 1971, at the peak of prog rock, my best friend Dave and I had hitched to the Great Western Music Festival. The weather was terrible, and I remember feeling miserable, shivering with cold and having to listen to never-ending drum solos. So nothing had changed.

But though things weren't going Bromley's way, at least we were still level. And as half-time arrived there were the first stirrings of excitement among the Bromley fans. If we could hold out for another forty-five minutes we'd snatch a draw. That was the optimistic view. A more realistic one was that Bromley's luck couldn't possibly hold out and that Lincoln had plenty of time for plenty of goals.

As soon as the second half started it was clear that something had changed. Whatever Mark Goldberg had said at the break was having an effect. Within a minute or two Anthony Cook had hit the bar and Bromley were playing with a confidence that had been missing in the first half.

Being stuck behind the Bromley goal – which is usually painful since you get a close-up of the opposition scoring – suddenly opened my eyes to something I'd never really appreciated before. Our defence. You could see how well organized it was, and that bringing in Ben Chorley had been a Goldberg masterstroke. Big and strong, he had formed a powerful partnership with Rob Swaine. There was plenty of talking between them, and no signs of panic. Lincoln's Matt Rhead, the League's second top scorer, wasn't getting a look-in.

I'd never noticed how hard Louis Dennis and Anthony Cook

worked either – they chased every ball and continually tracked back. It was also apparent that Lee Minshull made an effective extra centre-back at set pieces.

Finally, Chris Kettings wasn't just a polite goalkeeper (he and Alan Julian were the only ones I'd seen all season thanking the ball boy when he returned the ball), he'd also grown in confidence since I'd first seen him and as a result was a lot more decisive.

All this seemed to me like good foundations for a huge improvement. And suddenly the one-touch stuff was working again and passes were going to feet, bringing glimpses of the Barcelona-esque form shown in Torquay, but this time against a much better side. We were outplaying Lincoln City. At Sincil Bank. And the way the defence was playing, coming away with a draw wasn't out of the question.

When the clock opposite showed just ten minutes left, and with the League's second top scorer having a quiet time, an Ali Fuseini cross found Moses Emmanuel, the League's top scorer, on the edge of the six-yard box. The Bromley fans were out of their seats. Moses Emmanuel doesn't miss from here. His prod beat the diving Paul Farman and set off mass hysteria behind the Bromley goal. There are few things more exciting in life than Bromley taking the lead against a strongly fancied team.

Soon after that it could have been two but for the best save I'd seen all season. From a Dennis cross, Jack Holland drove the ball powerfully from a yard out. It was a goal all the way until the keeper dived and somehow pushed it away.

The clock on the opposite stand ticked by slowly, and as the game moved into injury time I tried to prepare myself for a Lincoln equalizer. With seconds left, a shot by Farman, who had come up for a corner, was cleared off the line by Swaine a few yards in front of me, and hoofed upfield. And then the final whistle went.

The reaction was the sort of pure, undiluted joy that can only come from beating a very good big team at their ground. At that moment it seemed like our best win of the season so far, even better than the 7-3 at Torquay and the 5-0 thumping dished out to Barrow. Today we had shown a combination of fight and flair and gone toe-to-toe with one of the best teams in the Vanarama National League – and won.

My only regret was not backing Bromley at 6-1.

It was brilliant that Liz was there to see it, as she'd watched my team at their best. I asked her what she thought of the game.

'It was OK,' she told me. 'First half was a bit boring.'

She did, however, enjoy the sight of Lloyd, a Bromley fan built like a WWE wrestler, bending over and kissing the top of Moses Emmanuel's head. By the time I was ready to follow suit, Moses had made a rapid retreat.

But that didn't matter. All that mattered was that Bromley had beaten mighty Lincoln City and were now fourth in the Vanarama National League. Back at the hotel, I lay on the bed thinking of the scoreline and wondering, not for the first time this season, whether I had just witnessed Bromley's greatest ever performance.

Liz seemed more concerned about dinner plans, so while she got ready, I got on to the phone to arrange a taxi. The restaurant I'd booked was on the other side of town, in the cobbled streets by the cathedral, and the table was booked for seven. We'd been told to allow fifteen minutes to get there.

Discount Cabs, recommended by our host, took nearly a minute to answer, and when I tried to book a car for 6.45 I was told that they had nothing until nine. Oh well, their loss, I thought as I moved on to County Cars, where a flustered-sounding man said that I should try again later but he couldn't promise anything.

I felt the first stirrings of panic. What if they were all busy?

I looked over at Liz, who was blissfully unaware of my futile attempts to arrange transport as the sound of the hairdryer was drowning it all out. She was wearing her favourite dress and looked stunning. I was really looking forward to our night out at the Grille at the White Hart. As long as we could get there.

With a renewed sense of purpose, I rang Lincoln Taxis. They answered straight away, which was a good sign. They were booked until ten.

Next was A15 Taxis. They didn't answer.

By now, full-blown anxiety had taken over. It worsened when I tried Handsome Cabs and got a message saying 'The number you are calling is no longer available'. Greenlight Taxis didn't answer, and Direct Cars were booked solid.

There was only one more name on my list. Lincoln Cabs. When I asked for a taxi at 6.45, the man actually laughed. 'No chance, mate,' he said.

After admitting to Liz what had just happened, we went downstairs to see if the owner had any ideas.

'Are there any buses to the cathedral?' I asked.

'No.'

'Well, how long will it take to walk?'

'I think it will be less than an hour.'

I looked over at Liz, taking in her heels, her dress, her perfectly styled hair and her forced smile.

'Let's go,' was all she said.

It was a dark autumnal night, with a cold wind blowing directly into our faces. The road was badly lit and went on and on, taking us over a huge, scarily high flyover bridge. The cathedral was clearly visible in the distance, lit up with yellow floodlights, yet in a cruel visual trick never seemed to get any closer.

After half an hour of brisk walking we arrived at the bottom of a hill which was called, for obvious reasons, Steep Hill. According to my pre-trip research, it had been voted the best street in Britain, while at the top was Lincoln Cathedral, which had once been the tallest building in the world. I would be lost without Google.

It was the steepest hill I had ever climbed. Steeper than the one at Forest Green. Steeper than Torquay. Steeper than Aldershot. It was so steep that not only was it called Steep Hill, it was known as 'heart attack alley' by pretty much everyone apart from the local tourist board.

Thankfully, it was also a part of Lincoln that was the opposite of the football ground Lincoln. This was a Lincoln of beautiful cobbled streets, dusty antique shops, quirky boutiques and quaint tea rooms. If we'd earlier seen a game of two halves, we were now witnessing a city of two halves.

We were both completely out of breath when we arrived at the restaurant, but the meal that followed was worth it. During dessert, when we noticed Count Dracula and Scary Spice climbing out of a taxi, the penny dropped as to why they had been booked solid. It was Halloween.

Halloween didn't exist in England thirty-five years ago. It's another relatively recent American import, alongside waiters calling everyone 'guys' and calling chips 'fries'. The worst thing for me is Alan Sugar saying 'You're fired' on *The Apprentice* when he should be saying 'You're sacked'. Liz, being American, isn't quite as offended by all this as I am.

But although Halloween here was by now similar to the States, with people wandering the streets in horror-based costumes, we were soon wondering if it had been given a uniquely British twist – dressing up then getting drunk and trying to start fights with strangers. I feared the worst when two groups, one containing Batman, the other the Joker, came face to face outside the restaurant as we were leaving . . . but in the end the two comic-book sworn enemies just high-fived each other and staggered along on their separate ways.

The evening, despite a poor start, had ended up being brilliant, much like the game earlier. The only slight downer was that we were a week too early for the switching on of the Christmas lights by a local Gary Barlow lookalike. We later learned that the Gary Barlow lookalike had pulled out, but had been replaced by another local Gary Barlow lookalike.

There was obviously no shortage of Gary Barlow lookalikes in Lincoln.

The next morning I checked the Bromley forum and felt a warm glow when I saw a post from a Lincoln fan saying we were 'the best side to visit all season'. Considering they'd just played Tranmere, this was a perfect start to my day.

Over breakfast, the middle-aged couple at the table next to us were having a difference of opinion over songs. At first I thought they'd been to a concert last night, but it soon became apparent they'd stayed in their room to watch *The X Factor*. When he said 'Well, there's a reason he's always been a backing singer', she got up and walked out without another word.

I was just happy that Liz was a little more forgiving.

The rest of the morning was as enjoyable as the post-walk segment of the previous night. We took a taxi to the cathedral and admired the beautiful stained-glass windows and intricately carved dragons. We stood outside the castle taking selfies, and then moved on to a mid-morning snack of chips in a local pub.

All too soon it was time to go, which meant a stroll down Steep Hill – a lot easier than walking up it – towards the station. It had turned out to be an outstanding weekend.

We took the train to Newark Northgate, where there was an hour to spare before our connecting train to Leeds. Aware that I still had a bit of ground to make up, I asked Liz if she fancied a coffee and something to eat instead of hanging around on the platform. I'd looked at my Google Maps app when we arrived and saw there was a Costa Coffee nearby. She perked up at this news.

We came out of the station and walked into Newark, following the signs to the town centre. My backpack was heavy, and I was still a bit sore from the trek into Lincoln the previous night, but I didn't dare complain. I just hoped we came across the Costa Coffee outlet soon.

The scenery on the outskirts of town was less than inspiring; it was an industrial area and the only shops we saw were closed. Still, there were definite signs of activity in the distance, and ten minutes later we arrived in what seemed to be the high street, packed with familiar names like Argos, Cash Converters and Sports Direct. The only name missing was Costa Coffee. Or any other coffee shop.

'Why don't you ask someone?' said Liz.

'No need. I'll find it. Can't be that far.'

She stopped and looked at me. 'Let's just go back.'

Twenty minutes later, having added another mile to the total distance walked that weekend, we were back at Newark Northgate station.

As we made our way along the platform, Liz suddenly grabbed me by the coat and pointed at something. Judging by her expression, she was deeply unhappy with what she'd seen.

'Look.'

'Look at what?'

And then I saw it. There, on the platform, just towards the end, was a small queue standing waiting to be served at Costa Coffee. There was no mistaking it – the distinctive maroon logo with three coffee beans was impossible to miss.

We travelled home in silence, Liz nursing a hard-earned coffee and me pretending to be deeply engrossed in the *Newark Advertiser*. I felt that it wasn't the time to ask if she wanted to come with me to the next game I was going to, a seemingly routine match at home to Altrincham in a fortnight's time. But I decided to wait for the right moment as I desperately wanted her to be there with me. I wanted her to witness a historic occasion that could never be repeated.

It would be the first Bromley game to be shown live on national TV.

Twelve

It wasn't until Tuesday, 10 November – the day of Bromley's home game against Boreham Wood, and over a week after getting back from Lincoln – that I finally felt the time was right to ask Liz if she wanted to come to Hayes Lane on Saturday.

'If it's live on TV, why would I want to go?' she asked, genuinely puzzled.

I couldn't think of an answer, so got on with throwing some books into a box. We were moving flat (or rather, apartment) over the next few days, so I was combining packing with following the Bromley game on Twitter. This was the first of four winnable games in November, the second being that weekend's historic Altrincham game in front of the cameras, before away trips to struggling Macclesfield and Guiseley.

If we won these and other results went our way, Bromley Football Club could well be top of the Vanarama National League by the end of the month.

I couldn't help sneaking a quick glance at the League Two table, just to see the calibre of teams we'd be playing *if* the season happened to end in promotion. Was it possible I'd spend 2016/17 watching Bromley at places like Crewe, Carlisle and Colchester?

Not to mention easier-to-reach places like York, Accrington and Mansfield?

I was trying hard not to get carried away and had continued to toe the official line that I was happy just to avoid relegation. But this was a lie. I craved more. The tiny taste of success had gone to my head.

The heart wants what it wants.

Boreham Wood were one of the weakest teams we'd played and were deep in the relegation zone. I was having to follow the game on Twitter since the BBC were once again ignoring the in-form Ravens and BT had resisted the temptation to go to Hayes Lane twice in five days.

The first tweet brought some unwelcome team news: three more regulars were out. Ben Chorley was injured, Anthony Cook suspended, and Louis Dennis only fit enough to be on the bench. The midfield was the weakest I'd seen in ages – the kind you end up with in your Fantasy League team when you've spent all your money on expensive strikers and defenders. At least Bradley Goldberg was given a rare start, which, given his brilliant goal against the same opponents earlier in the season, could well be the silver lining in the injury cloud. Maybe it was fate. Considering he had a point to prove and this was an easy game, his inclusion was a rare piece of good news.

As I piled our side plates and dinner plates into a box with a new sense of positivity, a 'ping' from my phone alerted me to a new tweet:

> Late change to Bromley line-up. Bradley Goldberg
> picks up an injury in the warm-up. Paul Rodgers now
> starts. Conal O'Leary added to bench.

It was lucky we were playing Boreham Wood and not someone like Cheltenham or Forest Green.

As I finished stuffing books carelessly into a Heinz baked beans box and sellotaping it shut, there was another ping. I snatched up the phone in eager anticipation.

Currently Bromley 0-1 Boreham Wood after 4 minutes.

Why did Bromley do this to me? Conceding an early goal was almost as predictable as conceding a late goal. Or a goal either side of half-time. Still, I wasn't particularly worried. We'd gone one down to other struggling teams, like Torquay and Kidderminster, and come back.

The next ping had me staring at the 1080×1920 pixel screen in disbelief. I could see the words, but I could make no sense of them.

12 mins: Bromley 0-2 Boreham Wood.

What was going on? I sent a panicky tweet to Mash, who was at the game, for an explanation. 'No real attacking cohesion' was his verdict. 'Just kinda waiting for Moses to do something on his own.'

As I watched Liz carefully repack the plates using bubble wrap and old newspapers (including *The Non-League Paper* containing the Lincoln match report, which I rescued just in time), I could feel the hope draining from me. Not just for the evening, but for the season. It looked like the ten-day lay-off between games had done Bromley no good whatsoever – but still, how can a team go from brilliant to rubbish in such a short space of time?

Five minutes later, another ping. I warily picked up the phone and peeked at the screen through my fingers, expecting the worst. But the news was good, and Mash's wait was over.

39 mins: GOALLLLLLLLLLLL! Bromley back in this
and it's who else but Moses Emmanuel! Right-footed
strike into the bottom right corner.

While packing programmes into a shoebox (I'd previously used a Tupperware container but my collection had now outgrown it), I was interrupted by another ping. I grabbed my phone this time, hoping for news of the equalizer. But it wasn't. Not yet, anyway.

HT: Bromley 1-2 Boreham Wood. A slow start saw the
visitors take an early two-goal lead but Bromley are
not out of it yet!

I couldn't keep on checking the tweets. It was too hard on my nerves. Instead, I decided to focus on the packing and just look at the final score. Liz had split the duties between us and I couldn't help noticing that I'd been allocated all the non-breakable things, like pans and cutlery.

There were seven pings before they finally came to a halt fifty minutes later. Best possible scenario was that Bromley had staged a huge comeback and won 8-2. Worst possible scenario was that Boreham Wood had ripped us apart and won by a similar margin. I would be happy with a draw, with most of the tweets about near misses and substitutions. I could barely bring myself to look. When I did, I felt the will to live drain out of me. The final tweet read:

FT: Bromley 1-2 Boreham Wood.

In a panic, I went straight to the BBC site to check the Vanarama National League table, any thoughts of boycotting the BBC quickly forgotten. The news was bad, but not critical: we had dropped to sixth, level on points with fifth-placed Grimsby.

Three points against Altrincham on Saturday could repair a lot of the damage.

I managed to get over the loss surprisingly fast. Just three days later I was carrying on as though nothing disastrous had happened. I was impressed with my mental strength.

Perhaps the reason for this rapid recovery time was the anticipation of the TV game. My plan to go and watch it at Hayes Lane had been destroyed by Liz's argument that if it was Bromley's first ever live game on TV, then history could only be witnessed by watching it live on TV, not at the ground.

This meant taking a big financial hit as I'd already bought three different non-refundable train tickets for the occasion. The first I'd bought back in September as it had seemed a really good deal, until I realized that it wouldn't quite get me there on time. The second was for my usual train for home games, getting into London at 12.29. The third had come after the announcement that because the game was being shown live, kick-off had been brought forward to 12.30.

Total spent on train tickets to a game I'd now decided I shouldn't go to? £94.

We were due to move into the new flat (it would always be a flat to me, not an apartment) on the morning of the match, but that carried unacceptable risks. The TV needed to be set up at least twenty-four hours beforehand, in case there were unforeseen technical issues. As it turned out, the worrying was unnecessary. BT reception was perfect. I'd brought a spare aerial cable, but the one that came with the flat was fine. The picture was clear, the definition perfect. The equipment was ready for Bromley v. Altrincham.

The next priority was to experiment with viewing angles from the couch. We eventually settled on the classic directly-in-front-of-the-TV-facing-straight-ahead-with-feet-on-coffee-table-and-remote-in-front-of-us position.

It was done. I sat back, relieved. All that remained of the moving in was to unpack the other thirty or so boxes, assemble the IKEA furniture and get rid of all the rubbish the previous tenant had left.

Only it wasn't rubbish. We found out later that the stained mattress, the worn saucepans coated in black grime and the mould-covered bedroom storage system (circa 1985) were all in the landlord's inventory, allowing him to rent the flat as fully furnished.

There were a few other things that hadn't been apparent when we were being hurriedly shown around, and not everything was in working order. Like the fridge, which was again the size of a hotel-room minibar. The door to the mini-freezer was broken, which meant cold air circulated throughout the fridge, freezing every-thing in its path. This resulted in my having to microwave a salad, which was another first in a season of firsts.

But the biggest first for me was this live TV appearance. As I sat waiting for coverage to start, I felt overwhelmed with pride that I was sitting in my living room in Leeds and Bromley were on the telly. The same telly I had watched Real Madrid, Barcelona and Bayern Munich on.

Then it got even better. Liz came and sat down beside me. She had got the Bromley bug. She just didn't know it yet.

The opening shot showed Hayes Lane looking at its best, a proper non-league ground. With Norman Park's naked trees as backdrop, the camera panned around and there, in front of the John Fiorini Stand, was Mark 'Clem' Clemmit, the BT Sports front man.

As he gave a bit of background on Bromley, footage of my home town came up on the screen. They showed Primark and the Christmas trees just put up in the high street. There were pictures of the town's most famous sons – Charles Darwin, H. G. Wells and David Bowie. And then another familiar sight:

one of the horses in the field outside the ground. It couldn't get any better than this, could it?

Actually, it could. 'Bromley,' said Clem, who had seen a lot of Vanarama National League action during the season, 'have proved themselves to be genuine promotion candidates.' To illustrate this, BT then showed the Moses goal against Boreham Wood just four days earlier. It was spectacular and took my breath away. A brief description on Twitter can never do justice to a goal like that.

Clem was now in Hayes Lane's inner sanctum, under the stand. I had once trod the same corridors, as a fourteen-year-old when I sneaked in to look around. I'd sat in the changing room, pretending to be Alan Stonebridge, my Bromley hero. I don't think I've ever felt more excited, before or since.

But this came close.

It was a huge thrill seeing Clem talking to Mark Goldberg, who must love being reminded every time he's interviewed by someone new that he once lost forty million quid. But Goldberg came across very well, as someone who simply loved football. He was articulate and thoughtful.

I felt proud of the manager. I felt proud of the ground. I felt proud of the floodlights. I felt proud of the horses in the field.

Most of all, I felt proud of Bromley for climbing the lower leagues and being on TV.

Just the fact that I was watching it meant that the BT Sports coverage already had more viewers than BT's flagship drama channel, AMC, which had recently registered zero viewers for several consecutive nights, according to the official audience survey. ('We're pleased with the start it has made,' said a BT spokesman.)

As the players came on to the pitch and warmed up, I felt that the signs were good for three points. Altrincham had gone six games without a win and were near the bottom of the table, while Bromley had in-form Ben Chorley, Anthony Cook and Louis

Dennis back. With Bromley expected to have an easy afternoon, I decided to have a just-in-case bet on Altrincham. At least I'd be able to recoup my train ticket losses if the unthinkable happened. I ended up backing the Robins to win 2-1, based on recent history showing that we seemed to lose all our home games 2-1, and the winnings would be more than enough to cover the cost of all those unused tickets.

Clem and his co-commentators Kevin Davies and Peter Taylor were backing Bromley. They all thought we'd win comfortably, and considering both Davies and Taylor had played for England, I found this tremendously reassuring.

As the camera panned across the crowd, it was exciting to see so many familiar faces – I spotted Mash, Jim who ran the club shop, and fanzine editor Col.

Altrincham had most of the early chances, but it still came as a huge surprise when they took the lead. Full-back Adam Griffin, standing wide on the left, controlled the ball with his arm, but referee David Rock of Hertford allowed the game to go on. Griffin put in a perfect cross, which dropped between the centre-backs, and Damian Reeves headed the ball past Chris Kettings.

It was a gut-wrenching moment which would have been hard to take at the best of times but was made far worse by knowing that the world was watching. Or at least a minuscule, insignificant fraction of it.

But was it handball? Both Davies and Taylor thought so. More predictably, so did I. The goal stood, though, and the sixty or so Altrincham fans huddled in the corner near the toilets went berserk.

We were a goal down. This wasn't supposed to happen, and Bromley looked shaken. The match then hit such a dull patch that at one stage the BT director decided it would be more interesting to focus on a brown horse in the field outside. 'A lonely old nag,' observed commentator Steve Bower, scrabbling around for words to go with the unexpected images.

But then the onfield action picked up. Moses Emmanuel twice missed chances he would have buried a month ago. A penalty shout was denied when the ball struck the arm of an Altrincham defender, and Bower endeared himself to Bromley fans by saying, 'For me, that looks a penalty.' The slow motion replay backed him up.

Penalty or not, Bromley were off the pace. Was it the pressure of playing in front of the TV cameras? I always like to find an excuse for the Ravens playing badly and that seemed a good one.

Only Jack Holland looked in decent touch, and I'm not saying that just because he was the only Bromley player to follow me back on Twitter, or because we have the same birthday, or even because we went to the same school. It was because he was perfectly suited to the one-touch game Goldberg liked to play.

In the space of fifteen minutes there was a delicate chip between Altrincham defenders on to Moses' right foot, a couple of headers into Moses' path, and some lovely first-time flicks. And when Moses scored from one of these, with a high, looping deflection off a defender – his scrappiest goal of the season – I ran around the living room in delight, almost tripping over some boxes.

But one of the most heartbreaking things about supporting a non-league team is that sooner or later your favourite player will get poached by a bigger club. And with that goal in front of the TV cameras, Moses Emmanuel had almost certainly made sure he'd be on his way in January.

There was still time left in the first half for Holland to be denied by a point-blank miracle save. I thought he must be getting sick of point-blank miracle saves, especially after Lincoln. This one was particularly galling as Tim Deasy was, like so many goalkeepers, angry and bald. In fact he was the second angry bald goalkeeper

Bromley had faced in a week, following Boreham Wood's extremely grumpy Preston Edwards.

At half-time, Clem, Taylor and Davies stood out in the middle, analysing the first half. The general consensus was that Bromley had all the momentum. Taylor, all five foot nine of him, was holding an umbrella for the much taller Clem, which meant it rested on the top of Clem's head – an area unprotected by hair.

'Can we get someone bigger?' said Clem, indicating Taylor. 'I've got a twelve-inch advantage on him.'

As Clem realized what he'd just said, the camera cut away quickly. The commentators suddenly went quiet, although if you listened carefully you could hear snorting and uncontrollable giggling in the background.

It was time for a hastily scheduled ad break.

A few minutes into the second half came another moment for the history books: the first ever rendition of the 'Bromley Geezers' song on national TV. Speediej, whose rise this season had been as meteoric as Bromley's, must have been a proud man. Surely this would inspire the team to greater heights?

Well, no. It seemed to have the opposite effect. A terrible mistake from the Bromley defence, who were trying to play themselves out of trouble instead of hoofing the ball upfield, let in Josh O'Keefe, who finished well.

I hit the arm of the couch in frustration. It was 2-1 to Altrincham. If the score stayed that way, at least I'd get my train money back. But that was no consolation. I'd rather get a point, preferably three.

'You'd rather your football team get a meaningless point than win a hundred pounds?' was how Liz saw it, disbelief all over her face.

Eighty-three seconds later, I had neither. That was how long it took for Altrincham to add a third, from yet another defensive mistake. They took the chance well; their finishing, unlike ours, had been excellent all day. They'd had three chances and scored three times. That's the sort of thing Bromley were doing not so long ago. Now we were getting loads of chances and scoring very few.

The game deteriorated after that. Even though Moses came close a couple of times and Jack Holland had one cleared off the line, we lost for the second time in a week.

I imagined thousands of families across the country looking at their TVs and saying to each other, 'Bromley are a bit rubbish, aren't they?'

'No they're not!' I wanted to shout back to all these people I'd just made up. 'They're much better than this!'

If only BT had chosen to show our 5-0 game against Barrow instead. Or the 7-3 win at Torquay. But they hadn't. They'd shown our 3-1 defeat to Altrincham.

It didn't help that the Altrincham manager was so nice after the game. There was no gloating, no exaggerating how good his side was. His summing up of the game was both fair and accurate. This was not what I had come to expect from a football manager.

I'd vowed to sit through all two hours and forty-five minutes of the coverage, whatever the result, determined to savour every moment. The worst part was knowing that during the summer, when I'd be deprived of watching Bromley, there would be a choice of watching this recorded game (fast-forwarding through the rubbish bits) or watching nothing. I just knew I would have to relive our humiliation at the hands of Altrincham at least a dozen times before the new season started.

The last, painful, shot of the coverage of Bromley's first ever TV appearance was of several visiting fans holding a PRIDE OF CHESHIRE banner.

We had slipped into ninth place after losing two in a row at Hayes Lane. 'Well, if we can't win easy games at home,' I thought, 'perhaps we can win easy games away.' And we had two of those coming up, at contrasting northern grounds: the big stadium of former League Two side Macclesfield Town and the much smaller venue belonging to former Conference North side Guiseley.

But before these matches there was a Kent Senior Cup game at Whitstable, which was brilliant news, in that it would give a few of our important players coming back from injury, like Alex Wall, some much-needed game time.

It would have been even more useful had the game lasted longer than sixteen minutes.

HOME
AND
AWAY

Thirteen

Yes, sixteen minutes. That was how long the Whitstable v. Bromley Kent Senior Cup tie lasted before the lights went out and everyone, after the inevitable singing of 'pay the bill, pay the bill, pay the bill', went home for an early night.

I was telling Liz about this as the train meandered through the snow-coated Pennines the following Saturday – the first leg of our journey to Macclesfield.

'Does that happen a lot?' she asked, an unmissable glint of hope in her eye.

'Not really,' I said, 'but, interestingly, it's happened to Truro City twice in the last—'

'And do they ever call games off because it's too cold?' she interrupted.

'Not that I know of.'

My hopes of Liz's love affair with Bromley continuing to bloom following encouraging signs during the televised game (she'd only wandered off twice, and had celebrated Moses' goal) were now on the verge of crashing. She was discovering something I'd seen a lot of since my return – that it's easier to support a team in front of a hot fire on TV than from freezing-cold terraces.

And Liz wasn't the only one affected by the conditions. We'd seen the mysterious blonde Bromley fan at Leeds station again, and she'd looked as though she was prepared for an Arctic expedition. When we arrived at the Moss Rose Stadium, we discovered that Mash had given his mittens their first outing of the season, and Iona, a Bromley fan I followed on Twitter, was wrapped in so many layers she could barely move.

The lightest of snowflakes were swirling around. It was late November, and it was bitterly, bitterly cold. The traditional football fan warming-up technique of stamping your feet alternately on the concrete while blowing hot breath into open hands and rubbing them together was as ineffective as always.

When the teams were announced, the Bromley line-up contained a big surprise. Jack Holland had been moved to right-back, with Lee Minshull taking the makeshift striker position.

Our position in the stand was equally alarming. We were standing right in front of Naughty Nigel, and witnessed his attempt to launch a new song. 'All in all it's just another Macc in the wall,' he sang. It didn't catch on.

As the players came out, they were greeted by another adaptation of a well-known song, this time a Monkees classic from the PA system. 'Hey hey we're the Silk Men', it started, and went on, 'and we're the pride of Cheshire.' So, like Altrincham the previous week, Macclesfield were claiming to be the pride of Cheshire. This struck me as being fairly unambitious, especially when Tranmere fans insisted that their team was 'the finest football team the world had ever seen'. I'd only once heard Bromley fans make the same claim, but since they were losing heavily at the time I'm pretty sure they were being ironic.

As the game started, the seventy-odd who had made the journey north burst into the old favourite 'You Are My Bromley'. The fact that it went on for just over twelve minutes raised the strong possibility that some pre-match alcohol had been consumed. No one seemed to be minding the cold. Or even to be aware that it was cold.

Bromley seemed to be enjoying themselves too. They were comfortably on top, and looked certain to score when Moses Emmanuel was put through, but his shot was a weak one. Once again, it was the sort of chance he would have buried earlier in the season. Minshull then had a good chance but he skied the ball over the bar.

At the break it was somehow still goalless but there was every reason to believe that the points drought would be coming to an end. A feeling of confidence I hadn't experienced for a while resurfaced. We were playing well, and the tide appeared to be turning.

As I stood in the queue at the bar under the stand at half-time, a couple of the home fans in front of me seemed equally confident, feeling that their team was comfortably on top. Were we watching the same game?

Macclesfield scored soon after the restart. It was a simple tap-in from a couple of yards out by Paul Lewis (kit sponsor: Clamor Fashion, 'for women with an independent mind'). We were losing a game we should have been winning. It was the story of the past couple of weeks.

To make matters worse, one of the linesmen seemed to have developed an irrational hatred for Bromley. He was flagging furiously for fouls that hadn't actually happened and giving every throw-in to Macclesfield, regardless of who had touched the ball last. When he got bored with this, a minute or so after the goal, he decided to signal for a penalty when the ball hit Ben Chorley's arm at point-blank range.

Referee Ryan Johnson from Bolton (which, suspiciously, is just thirty miles from Macclesfield) agreed, and pointed to the spot – even though exactly the same thing, ball hitting arm, had led to (a) Bromley being denied a penalty the previous week against

Altrincham, and (b) a goal being allowed in the same game when their winger clearly handled in the build-up. It was as though a new sub-law had been introduced stating 'The ball hitting a player's hand from close range shall not be deemed to be handball unless the player in question plays for Bromley FC, in which case a free kick or penalty shall automatically be awarded.'

A thought briefly flickered across my mind that perhaps I wasn't seeing things in a totally impartial light.

I couldn't bear to watch the penalty. I looked away, up into the hills beyond the stadium, and watched the snow gently fall. Seconds later, I wished I hadn't. Chris Kettings' save to keep us in the game was, by all accounts, brilliant.

Then, right in front of us, Moses Emmanuel got the ball on the touchline, cut inside and curled a beautiful shot past Shwan Jalal. It thudded against the far post.

And that was as good as it got for Bromley.

Macclesfield were suddenly playing the kind of football we were playing before we became rubbish, and when Kristian Dennis scored from the edge of the box to make it 2-0 just before the end, the misery was complete.

I'm not sure how much of the match Liz had managed to witness, since her scarf seemed to be wrapped tightly around her face and her bobble hat was pulled right down. I think it may have been some kind of protest.

This was the third of three winnable games, all lost. Bromley had gone from promotion candidates in fourth spot to mid-table (or worse) candidates in eleventh. It had been a depressing three weeks, with things going wrong on and off the field ever since the final whistle at Lincoln.

Further confirmation of this came when the people we were staying with had a power cut just before dinner, and the next morning I broke an irreplaceable bowl in the bathroom when I caught it with my towel, sending it crashing to the floor. Even getting home was a disaster, with all trains from Manchester to Leeds cancelled for most of the afternoon. We ended up going home via Sheffield.

Worst of all was an email I got from Mickey, a man who seemed remarkably well informed about what went on at the club. 'Whisper is Cookie is off back to Ebbsfleet shortly,' he wrote. 'Julian has sciatica [possibly the worst thing a keeper could ever have]. Moses and Dennis even money to be on their bikes in January window. It seems it's going to be business as usual at Hayes Lane again soon.'

So, just three weeks after the most impressive win in Bromley's 123-year history, the season was threatening to fall apart in spectacular fashion. And it couldn't have come at a worse time. Because accompanying me to the next game, at Guiseley, was my friend Giles. And Giles was bringing a friend of his, Duncan Hamilton.

The same Duncan Hamilton who had won the William Hill Sports Book of the Year twice. A man who had written definitive books on Brian Clough (*Provided You Don't Kiss Me*, which is my joint favourite football book of all time) and George Best. A man who had covered some of the biggest games on the planet for national newspapers.

And here I was, hoping for him to be impressed by non-league middle-of-the-table Bromley.

The anxiety I was feeling turned to jealousy when I got a text from Giles on the morning of the match: 'Just had a chat with Lee Minshull at King's Cross. Your boys are on the train.' If only it was me on the 9.03 to Leeds instead of him, although I probably wouldn't have known what to do. Ask Minshull to sign my senior railcard? I wondered how Giles had recognized him, then I remembered that Minshull had once played for AFC Wimbledon, whom Giles supported.

When the train carrying Giles and Bromley FC pulled into

Leeds, I was there to meet it, which came as a surprise to Giles. I assured him it had everything to do with welcoming him to Leeds and nothing to do with hoping to catch a glimpse of the players.

Apparently they hadn't left the train, and I couldn't really hang around until they did, so Giles and I made our way to Guiseley, where we met Duncan and his wife Mandy for lunch. Once I'd got over the realization that I was sitting across the table from one of my favourite football writers, I relaxed enough to enjoy the meal.

It was only a ten-minute walk to Nethermoor Park, and as we went through the ancient turnstiles and into the ground, I experienced a burst of nostalgia. Not that I'd ever been here before, but I'd been to loads of grounds just like it in the distant past. Small, intimate and friendly, with ageing stands and rusty floodlight pylons, where you are free to wander anywhere. There were even large nets strung up behind one of the goals to catch wayward Lee Minshull-esque shots that at bigger grounds like Tranmere's or Lincoln's would end up in Row Z.

Just inside, an old couple were selling programmes. I imagined they were a permanent fixture at the ground, having occupied the same spot for the past thirty or forty years. The man handed me a separate sheet, with the teams neatly typed out on it. There was no Joe Anderson. No Anthony Cook. No Louis Dennis. No Alan Julian. No Max Porter. No Bradley Goldberg. No Ben May. No Sean Francis.

'Oh no,' I said, feeling my shoulders sag.

The programme sellers started laughing.

'We've heard that a lot today,' said the woman.

As I flicked through the programme, my heart rate doubled when I saw that the player profile for right-back James Hurst included the fact that his worst day in football had been playing Bromley when he was with Torquay earlier in the season. I imagine not many footballers would say that their worst day in football was when they'd faced Bromley. It made me feel warm inside.

Which was just as well, since outside it was freezing cold.

Despite the weather, I'd taken an instant liking to Guiseley. There were no police, no stewards. The only people in uniforms were the Salvation Army band, which was playing 'Once in Royal David's City' as the rain from the grey skies pounded the corrugated tin roof covering a ramshackle stand on the side of the pitch. It was the most northern thing I'd ever seen.

As I was running Giles and Duncan through my list of excuses why Bromley might well lose (terrible conditions, fill-in goalkeeper, injuries, makeshift striker policy), the game got under way. Not a lot happened in the first twenty minutes, which in my mind was a bonus. Surely Duncan would be impressed?

'What do you think?' I asked him.

He just looked at me. I sensed the game was not reaching the heights of the last game he'd been to: the Champions League Final between Barcelona and Manchester United.

After half an hour, Rob Swaine got the ball just inside the box, with just the keeper to beat. He hit a rising shot first time, and found the net with ease. Unfortunately it was the one strung up behind the goal: he'd missed the target by a good ten yards.

The rain turned to sleet and fans of both sides huddled together, shivering. Everyone in the ground was either under the same roof or in the stand opposite. Then I heard a couple of home fans muttering in bewilderment and pointing.

Through the darkening gloom I could just make out a small but determined procession of Bromley fans – a couple of dozen at most – leaving the comfort of the covered terraces and walking directly into the storm. Unbelievably, they were making their way over to the Guiseley goal, hunched over in single file like Arctic explorers bravely battling the elements.

I couldn't make out who they were, but I had a pretty good idea. Even though I wasn't particularly proud of the team at the time, I'd never felt more proud of the fans. Some of them – I'd managed to identify Ian and Mash – had travelled to Whitstable on Tuesday night for that meaningless game that lasted only sixteen minutes. Now here they were, standing behind the sticks in the worst conditions imaginable, supporting Bromley. These were genuine fans. They'd travelled a few hundred miles just to be here.

I continued to watch from the comfort of the terraced stand but could clearly hear the 'Bromley Geezers' song being sung in the far distance.

It was during this that Duncan turned to me.

'That winger looks all right,' he said, approvingly.

It was a heartwarming moment that meant a lot to me since no one else had impressed him.

The feeling of pride faded when I realized he was talking about the Guiseley winger.

I felt even more demoralized soon after, when the curse of injury time struck once more. Oliver Norburn, a player best known for having had a celebrity girlfriend, Chelsee Healey, when he was with Bristol Rovers (they split after disagreeing over her boozy lifestyle, according to the *Daily Mail*), hit an unstoppable swerving rocket from forty yards out. It was so good that it later made the *Guardian*'s Goal of the Week round-up, alongside efforts by Luis Suárez and Lionel Messi, and it reminded me of Halifax's injury-time goal from a similar distance. Yorkshire has not been kind to Bromley, and the pain of conceding such a goal – especially in front of Duncan Hamilton – was unimaginable.

By the start of the second half the Bromley fans had moved behind the goal at the other end, and Giles, Duncan and I joined them. The rain had eased to a drizzle. As we arrived, Ian was shouting something to the Guiseley goalkeeper about sheep drench. The keeper looked bemused. As was I. Why was Ian talking to him in an Eastern European accent about sheep drench?

Was he from that part of the world? He didn't look or sound it.

It took me a few seconds to register that Ian had adopted the most terrible Yorkshire accent imaginable; he sounded more like a Hungarian with a cold. It took a few more seconds to work out that what he was saying was 'Ee by gum, where's t'sheep drench?' But it was only when I discovered that the goalkeeper's name was Steve Drench and that Ian was actually asking 'Where's the sheep, Drench?' that it finally made sense. To me, if not the Guiseley stopper.

Still, he had plenty of time to think about it in the second half: Bromley were so ineffective up front that he barely had to touch the ball.

Guiseley were simply too good for us.

If true football happiness is watching your team tear apart a big-name team like Torquay in the blazing hot sun, then true football misery is watching your team capitulate to a solid, no-name mid-table team on a cold, wet afternoon, without a single shot on goal.

Bromley were awful. The supply line to Moses Emmanuel had completely dried up and the only threat on goal came from a decent Reece Prestedge header that clipped the bar. Only one player shone, and that was the man I'd warned Duncan was hopeless. Chris Kettings.

Crystal Palace's third-/fourth-choice keeper had an absolute blinder, following on from his penalty save from Kristian Dennis at Macclesfield. He was keeping Bromley in the game with some astonishing saves. The cruelty of football was illustrated when the best of the lot was deflected into the path of Anthony Dudley, who made the score 2-0.

The final insult came when news filtered through that Dennis had scored twice for Macclesfield at Wrexham to move ahead of Moses as top scorer. Actually, that wasn't quite the final insult. That came when the BBC called the previous top scorer Ade

Moses – a bizarre sort-of reversal of Moses Ademola, the name he'd played under before taking his mother's surname.

As we walked back to the station, I avoided asking Duncan what he thought of my team. I already knew. At least Giles had seen similar performances in the past and had pretty much known what to expect.

Bromley were having a terrible run. In the space of a month we had plummeted from fourth to twelfth. Instead of dreaming of spending next season watching Bromley at places like Portsmouth, Plymouth and Port Vale, my thoughts were now turning to a more realistic return to the Conference South, where teams like St Albans, Wealdstone and Sutton awaited.

After the game, to take my mind off the misery I was feeling, I took Liz to see a punk band called Bear Trade. Their bass player was Bromley fan Lloyd (the man who had kissed Moses Emmanuel's head), who had persuaded me to watch one of their videos – not by threatening to kiss my head if I didn't, but by pointing out that he was wearing a Bromley scarf in it. In all likelihood, this was a first for a punk video.

The song, 'Son of the Manse', was unexpectedly brilliant (have a look on YouTube if you don't believe me), and Liz showed a lot more enthusiasm for going to see them live than I'd ever seen from her while watching Bromley.

Bear Trade was my first punk gig since seeing The Adverts at the Greyhound in Croydon ('Surrey's Premier New Wave Venue') in 1978. They'd opened, with thrilling audacity, with their irresistible debut single 'One Chord Wonders'. The energy was incredible; everyone was pogoing and singing along. By the third song, however, the entire crowd were sitting on the floor, talking among themselves, completely ignoring what was happening onstage.

Bear Trade were a lot more entertaining, and it was good to see several Bromley fans like Stu, Pete and Rob there. The gig made me forget I was sixty. The reminder came later, when I slept for twelve hours and then started complaining about my ears ringing.

Still, there was plenty of time to recover. My next game wasn't for a fortnight – the FA Trophy first round. This was a superb chance to reset the season, get it back on track. A good cup run – and this was a big trophy – could bring (a) money into the club, (b) more trips for me and Liz, and (c) a visit to Wembley, which would be the perfect way to finish the season. I'd only been to see Bromley play at the spiritual home of English football once before, albeit not Wembley itself but Wembley Arena. This was where I enjoyed one of the most magical nights of my football life as Bromley lifted the Prince Philip Five-a-Side Cup, having seen off star-studded opponents like Wycombe Wanderers and Enfield in the process.

So at lunchtime on Monday, with 'Son of the Manse' still running through my head, I sat down to follow the FA Trophy draw, wondering which glamorous team we'd be thrown up against. Would it be Bromley's near neighbours and hipster darlings Dulwich Hamlet? A trip to the seaside at either Eastbourne or Truro? A nice day out in Buxton?

I didn't really care, to be honest – as long as it wasn't someone like Cheltenham, or Forest Green, or . . .

HOME AND AWAY

Fourteen

Braintree away.

It was a nightmare of a draw.

An eight-hour round trip to a nondescript Essex town famous for having more outlet stores than pretty much anywhere else on the planet, just so I could witness almost certain defeat to one of the Vanarama National League's strongest teams. In a relatively meaningless trophy. On a cold and wet Saturday in December.

This was one game I would be almost happy to miss.

But it's one thing deciding not to go, and another waking up on a Saturday morning when the cold, hard truth hits you that Bromley are playing later and you won't be there to see them.

Just as an exercise, I checked train times and fares. If I left within an hour, it was doable, although tickets were so expensive that I'd have to conceal the exact price from Liz. Luckily, I was saved from having to make a questionable decision when news came through that the game had been postponed.

And when I saw that another FA Trophy game – Southport v. Worcester City – had also been postponed because of a water-logged ground, I was suddenly filled with heart-pounding terror. Bromley were due to play there in the League in a week's time. I'd already prepaid for travel and accommodation, as well as booked the hotel restaurant. If the game was called off and the weather remained wet and miserable, we would be stuck for three days in a seaside hotel described as 'a disgrace' and 'thoroughly dreadful' in reviews *on its own website*, one which boasted the Lawnmower Museum as its nearest attraction.

That could make for a very long weekend.

On the plus side, it could be a chance to take a closer look at the kind of solar-powered lawnmower used by Forest Green Rovers, although there probably wouldn't be much sun around to power it.

But there was another, bigger reason I was desperate for the game to go ahead. By 19 December, the date of the fixture, I'd have had no football for three long weeks since Guiseley. That was a taste of what the proposed mid-season break would be like. And so far it wasn't a happy prospect.

The fall from eleventh place in the Vanarama National League pre-Guiseley to twelfth place post-Guiseley, without playing a game, had caused me immense psychological damage and I was still struggling to come to terms with it.

And that wasn't the only major catastrophe. As Mickey had predicted, Anthony Cook, one of our best players until the recent slump, had moved; although what motivated him to drop down a division to sign for extremely wealthy Ebbsfleet was a mystery.

This heartbreak was slightly offset when I discovered that several Bromley fans, who were a lot more knowledgeable than me about Kentish non-league football, seemed very happy that we'd got striker Adam Cunnington as part of the deal.

There was also a rumour that an ex-AS Monaco first-team player had joined. If this was true, I knew, on a rational level, that it would be someone who had once come on as sub for the last ten minutes in the French equivalent of the Kent Senior Cup. But that didn't stop me daydreaming about the possibilities. You never know, it might be George Weah. Or Youri Djorkaeff. Or, best of all, Dimitar Berbatov, the only former Monaco player I could think of who would still be under forty.

I allowed my thoughts to run riot. Weeks without a game can do that to you. I imagined the languid Bulgarian running, or rather ambling, around the edges of the Hayes Lane penalty areas, with 'INTU Bromley' emblazoned on the front of his untucked white shirt and 'Dean Wilson Funeral Directors' on the back of his black shorts, scoring goals whenever he could be bothered.

These are the sorts of fantasies a sixty-year-old man has.

The reality was, of course, very different. The ex-AS Monaco player turned out to be Steve Pinau, whose last club was the Rochester Raging Rhinos. I'd never heard of him or the team he'd come from, but he couldn't be *that* rubbish if he'd played at the highest level in France.

I was cautiously optimistic about both new signings and excited about the possibility of seeing them at Southport – if the match was on. In the week building up to the game, I nervously checked the weather forecast every day.

On Tuesday, rain was predicted, and plenty of it. I got a sinking feeling and, resigned to yet another football-free weekend, visited the Lawnmower Museum website. It was open on Saturday afternoons. I then noticed a link to Car Key World, its sister site. What fresh hell was this? A museum of car keys? Surely we'd be able to find more interesting ways to pass the time in Southport?

By Wednesday the forecast for rain was still there, but it would be less heavy. The temperatures were also looking better, reaching a high of twelve degrees.

By Thursday my confidence that the game would go ahead was growing, albeit on a damp afternoon with light rain falling.

On Friday we were on our way to Southport where a relatively scorching fifteen degrees awaited us. This could turn out far better than expected, I thought; we might even be able to have a paddle in the sea before the game, so that Liz could enjoy the full British seaside experience.

Arriving in Southport was a shock. We'd been told it was tired and run down but it didn't look that way as we walked through town. There were tree-lined boulevards with Victorian canopied shops and the people were friendly, even when they saw my Bromley scarf. Liz and I were already talking about coming back in the summer when it might be even warmer – perhaps up to eighteen or nineteen degrees.

But as we got nearer the seafront, which was where the hotel was situated, an old foe awaited. Swarms of seagulls, flying menacingly low. Southport wasn't considered a seagull danger zone like, say, Dover and I wasn't aware of any history of attacks in the area. But there's always a first time.

It had taken a grandmother from Herne Bay to find the solution. Her name was Dina Wilson, and she had come up with an ingenious way to protect herself from seagull attacks in her garden – by wearing a colander on her head when she was hanging out the washing. The trouble was, while this might work in her back garden, I couldn't imagine walking through Southport with a colander on my head. People might notice. I decided to face my fears.

By the time we'd got to the hotel (which was nowhere near as dreadful as the website had led us to believe), my mind was totally focused on the game which was now only twenty-four hours away. The forecast, once again, was for a lot of rain, with strong, cold winds coming in from the Irish Sea.

I'd warned Liz that there probably wouldn't be much in the way of goalmouth action since Bromley had only scored twice in the last four games and Southport had the worst attack in the Vanarama National League. I then tried to explain why I'd be really happy if neither team scored, since it would put an end to our run of defeats, but I'm not sure a goalless draw on a cold, wet and windy day appealed to her as much as it did to me.

During dinner at the hotel that night we bumped into Jim, who runs the Bromley FC club shop, and his friend John. We decided to meet up in the morning and explore Southport, starting with going down to the sea, since this is one of the main attractions of a seaside resort.

By the time morning arrived, everyone's enthusiasm had dimmed noticeably. The unseasonal weather that had greeted us the previous day had turned into more typical December fare. Even though the wind and rain had already set in, we decided to go ahead with the plan and made our way down to the beach. Since there was nothing but sand and no sign of the sea, we agreed to walk along the pier.

As we strolled, I pumped Jim for club shop gossip. He revealed that new striker Adam Cunnington had already been in with his young son to buy him a full Bromley kit. I took an immediate liking to Adam Cunnington.

I was not so fond of the walk. We were being buffeted by the winds and soaked by the rain, but we carried on. Surely the end of the pier couldn't be far away now? It turned out that it was. We found out afterwards that it was the second longest pier in Britain, after Southend.

There was further disappointment when we reached the end – nothing but sand as far as the eye could see. Southport was a sand lover's paradise, but not so good if you wanted a paddle in the sea. Or even if you wanted to see the sea.

I should have known: the football club's nickname is the Sandgrounders.

We turned around and started to make our way back. After another mile or so of walking, nearly being blown off the pier and a quick lunch, we took a taxi to the Southport ground which was no longer known as Haig Avenue but was now called the Merseyrail Community Stadium. This was up there with similarly evocative and romantic names like the Checkatrade.com Stadium (Crawley), the Abbey Business Stadium (Cheltenham) and the London Borough of Barking and Dagenham Stadium (Dagenham and Redbridge).

As I waited by the turnstiles of the Merseyrail Community Stadium, I suddenly felt myself getting slammed into the wall with tremendous force. This could only mean one thing: Lloyd had arrived – a shoulder charge being his form of greeting. After pretending it didn't hurt (never show pain), I told Lloyd how much I'd enjoyed the Bear Trade gig.

We went into the ground together and there were quite a few Bromley fans in the covered stand which ran along the side of the pitch. Mash had arranged a coach, which had been just about full, and I felt a slight tug of envy that I'd missed out on what sounded like an entertaining trip north. They had left late, which is standard for Bromley supporters' coaches, for the usual reason: Roy had arrived fifteen minutes after departure time as he'd once again overslept.

I had a quick look through the programme and saw that Southport, who were currently twentieth, had come up with an enterprising way of bringing glory to an indifferent season. They had invented the North West Championship, a table made up of meetings between the seven teams in the north-west. Thanks to their recent win against Macclesfield, Southport were in third place in this non-existent competition.

But the more I thought about it, the more I liked it. If there was a Kent Championship, we'd be second, on account of there only being three teams, one of which was Welling, who were rubbish.

While I considered the thrilling possibilities, Liz was looking even less interested than usual. I had to take some of the blame.

Telling her to expect a really boring game in terrible conditions wasn't the best sales pitch I'd ever come up with. And the weather had turned particularly nasty, with rain pelting down and the pitch quickly turning into a mudbath.

But Bromley started quite well. Our ex-AS Monaco winger had already got his own song. To the tune of 'Que Sera, Sera', it went 'Steve Pinau, Pinau, he's better than Cook, you know', which, although factually incorrect on the evidence of the opening twenty minutes, made me laugh.

And then things took a predictable turn for the worse – Southport took the lead. Andy Wright, unmarked at the far post, headed one of the easiest goals he'll ever score and it was 1-0. To the team with the League's worst attack.

It was a lead that lasted only a few minutes. A powerful Lee Minshull shot from just outside the area found its way into the net with the help of some bizarre goalkeeping from Alan Coughlin (it looked as though he was trying to push the ball, which was skidding along the ground, over the bar), and it was 1-1.

Then, on the stroke of half-time, came one of the most glorious moments of the season. Rob Swaine was quickest to react when Coughlin punched the ball out weakly, smashing it home from close range. Suddenly the rain didn't matter. We were potentially on our way to a much-needed win, and the relief was heartfelt. Lloyd was dancing with a Lloyd lookalike. Roy was screaming with delight. People I didn't know were hugging each other. Even Liz was smiling. We just had to survive a minute of injury time and we'd go into the break ahead.

Only one thing had been forgotten in all the excitement: Bromley's complete inability to cope with injury time. From the kick-off, Gary Jones took the ball forward, and the defence kept backing off. When Jones got to twenty-five yards out he took a speculative shot, Chris Kettings made a mess of it, and Southport had equalized.

To make this even harder to take, Jones then came over and celebrated right in front of us, doing that annoying sliding-along-the-grass-on-his-knees-with-arms-outstretched thing.

As I stood there, numbly, during the break, I tried to remember the last time I'd felt so deflated. I settled on the time earlier in the season when I'd started following Rob Swaine on Twitter, and an hour or so later got a private message from him. Bromley's captain sending me a private message! Had he heard of me? Did he want to tell me how much he'd enjoyed *The Bromley Boys*? I opened the message with nervous anticipation.

'Hi,' it read, 'I'm currently recruiting people to join my Herbalife team. We have some amazing opportunities available, let me know . . .'

The theme of crushing disappointment continued two minutes into the second half when the Bromley defence, which was in the process of disintegrating, allowed Mike Phenix to tap the ball past Kettings. An impartial observer might have been impressed with the speed and passing game of Southport's front four, but I'd never seen Bromley's back four play so badly. I felt sorry for Joe Anderson. He was totally isolated, and had no cover whatsoever. Everyone was arguing among themselves or shouting at the manager. Some of the fans had had enough, Lloyd in particular letting the hapless defenders know what he thought.

None of this had any effect, and the inevitable happened shortly afterwards. Southport were given a hugely unfair penalty when Ali Fuseini was adjudged to have brought down Paul Rutherford, even though it was clearly a dive. To me, anyway. Remarkably, none of the Bromley players or fans were protesting. Was it because they were so used to decisions going against us that they now accepted it without question? Or, unthinkably, was my judgement so biased that I was plain wrong? Regardless, Louis Almond made it 4-2.

Then, unexpectedly, came a glimmer of hope. The scoreboard

went out. Hopes leapt that this was a symptom of imminent flood-light failure – which, as I almost told Liz, had happened to Truro City twice in the last two seasons, so maybe it would happen to Bromley twice in a couple of weeks.

'Where's your scoreboard gone?' sang Ian.

'Call it off, call it off, call it off,' came the chant from half a dozen optimists at the back.

But referee Simon Bennett of Kidsgrove in Staffordshire ignored their advice and was soon blowing his whistle for Southport's fifth goal, Jamie Allen outpacing Sean Francis to finish comfortably.

It was getting genuinely painful to watch, and the last hope vanished when the scoreboard came back on just in time to remind us that we were now 5-2 down. Or, as the ground announcer said, 'Southport 5 Bromley Town 2.' I absolutely *hate* it when people call us Bromley Town. Especially when we've conceded five goals.

A couple of fans behind me were no longer talking about the uselessness of the back four. They were now earnestly discussing the risk of corrosion caused by sea air on the iron girders support-ing the roof of the stand. Although this wasn't the sort of conversation you'd hear at Anfield or Old Trafford, it was fairly typical in the world of non-league.

Then, shockingly, Bromley got their third to revive hope among the travelling fans. Francis scoring the goal of the game (as long as you disregarded most of Southport's five) with a strong volley from the edge of the six-yard box.

'We're gonna win 6-5!' sang the Bromley contingent, but we didn't. We lost 5-3. Against a team that had barely scored five goals all season.

After the final whistle I asked Mickey, who had spent the entire game standing behind the goal in his Santa outfit, what he thought of it. 'Two quid for a cup of tea was a bit strong' was his verdict. There was nothing more to say.

When we got back to the hotel, I lay on the bed staring blankly at a piece of peeling plaster on the wall.

'I don't know why you put yourself through this,' said Liz, getting ready for dinner.

I smiled, but the smile masked a near-broken spirit. I was getting used to defeat; it's an unavoidable part of football, and you don't have much choice after five in a row. But this felt worse than usual. It was heartbreaking to see games so carelessly tossed away after battling so hard, body-on-the-line style, for every point earlier in the season. Where was the fight now? Where was the commitment? Where was the English Barcelona?

Over breakfast the next morning I was trying to elaborate on this to my frankly uninterested wife when I was distracted by the sight of a blonde girl pouring herself an apple juice.

It was the girl from Leeds station.

We went over and introduced ourselves, eager to find out her story. It turned out that her name was Georgie and she was a student in Leeds who had grown up in Bromley. Her parents, John and Angie, who soon joined the conversation, were Bromley fans and had taken her along with them when she was younger. Inevitably, she'd fallen in love with the club and now rarely missed a game.

In an era when parenting is often criticized, this was a timely reminder that sometimes they can get it absolutely right.

It was a relief to solve the mystery of the girl on the train and I wondered if she'd be making the long journey to Braintree on Tuesday for the postponed FA Trophy game. I had reluctantly decided, just like ten days earlier, to give it a miss. And it was just as well I did. We lost, obviously. To an injury-time goal, obviously.

Up next for us was moneybags Eastleigh, who could match our five League losses in a row with five League wins in a row. There couldn't possibly be a worse time for me to take my sons Billy and

Frank on the most important rite of passage of their lives: their first ever visit to Hayes Lane.

Yet that was exactly what we'd arranged several months ago. And it was far too late to pull out of it now.

HOME
AND
AWAY

Fifteen

I wondered if John and Angie had been this nervous when they'd taken Georgie along to see Bromley for the first time.

We were driving down the M1 for the home game against Eastleigh after our first family Christmas in ten years. We'd spent the day at my daughter Hazel's house in Burntwood and it had been everything I'd hoped it would be, enjoying simply being together. It had been the perfect Christmas, and was being followed by the perfect Boxing Day – one that was built around a Bromley game.

I kept looking in the rear-view mirror for signs of excited anticipation from Billy and Frank, but just saw two young men with eyes shut, wearing hoodies and headphones. There were two possibilities: either they were internalizing their excitement or they weren't excited.

I felt a twinge of concern that I'd left it too late. They were both in their twenties now and, having grown up in New Zealand, had little interest in football, preferring rugby. But I remained hopeful that once they got to Hayes Lane, set eyes on the ground and experienced the atmosphere, things would change. And then I reminded myself that this was exactly the same thought I'd had about Liz, and that hadn't worked out as I'd hoped.

At least she was now showing a flicker of interest, asking how we could be playing Eastleigh at home in the Vanarama National League when we'd already played them at home in the Emirates FA Cup. Explaining that to an American is harder than you'd think.

It was becoming increasingly clear that almost the only thing Liz found interesting about Hayes Lane was that it was home to Gareth, the Bromley FC office cat, whose progress she followed enthusiastically on Twitter.

I was just glad that she had agreed to come along for this one. It was a long drive, taking just over three hours to reach Bromley. We didn't go straight to the ground, but headed for the Crown and Pepper on Masons Hill instead. We'd all been invited to a pre-match function hosted by a little-known organization with just four members – a number unchanged since its formation in 2011, when they began their annual sponsorship of a Bromley fixture.

We walked through the bar to a room at the back. As soon as we saw these words printed on a piece of A4 paper sellotaped to the door, it was clear that we had reached our destination:

RESERVED
for
The Dave Roberts Fan Club

Bizarrely, my sons burst out laughing when they saw this, which I felt undermined my enviable standing in the literary world. I greeted each member of my fan club by name (there can't be many authors who can say that) as I recognized them from a picture Howard and Robin – who described themselves as 'the committee' – had emailed. The numbers were swelled by twenty or so guests, most of whom clearly had no idea who I was, but had probably been tempted along by the promise of free food, a few drinks, plus admission to the game.

Following an elaborate ceremony, which was rushed through as we were late arriving, I was presented with some programmes from matches previously sponsored by the fan club and a magnificent T-shirt with my name on it.

After that it was time for a quick lunch, a bunch of photos (mainly taken by me to prove that the Dave Roberts Fan Club existed) and the short walk to Hayes Lane.

I was first through the turnstiles, and once inside, stood and waited.

I will never forget watching my sons taking those first steps. Nor will I ever forget watching them take their first steps inside the majesty of what was currently known as the Courage Stadium, after the beer – though still known to everyone outside the marketing world as Hayes Lane.

'Well?' I said, unable to disguise my pride. 'What do you think?'

I saw a look pass between them.

'It's very small, isn't it?' said Billy, looking a bit embarrassed.

'How do you mean?'

'Well, the way you've always gone on about it,' said Frank, 'we were expecting something a bit, you know . . .' He tailed off, not wanting to hurt my feelings.

Why weren't they seeing what I was seeing? A beautiful, awe-inspiring stadium that still had the power to take my breath away nearly fifty years after my first visit. Had I inadvertently given a false impression when they were young in my desperation to get them to like my team?

As we walked around the ground, I tried some emotional blackmail.

'See that bench over there?' I said, trying to make my lip quiver and look as though I was barely able to suppress my emotions. 'That's where your dad used to sit and watch Bromley.' We stopped and looked at it, unsure of what I was expecting us to find.

We took up the optimum position, behind the goal Bromley were attacking, along with the other fans whose hearts ruled their heads. This included half of the members of the Dave Roberts Fan Club, Howard and Robin.

When the team was announced, unsurprisingly it contained a few changes. Aaron Tumwa was in for Joe Anderson, and, most intriguingly, centre-back Ben Chorley had been moved to a make-shift defensive midfield position, covering the back four. Paul Rodgers had moved from full-back to makeshift winger.

After a fairly even start, Moses Emmanuel sprang into action and slotted home an excellent through ball from Lee Minshull right in front of us, only to have a linesman flag for offside against makeshift winger Rodgers. I automatically protested, and had just about managed to convince the boys it couldn't possibly have been offside when I realized, just like at Southport, that nobody else was protesting.

This was forgotten a few minutes later as Tumwa played a long ball over the defence for Moses to run on to. It bounced just as he was closing in on the keeper. An ordinary player would have pan-icked and skied the ball over the bar. Not Moses. He calmly waited for the ball to drop, before lobbing it exquisitely into the back of the net without touching the ground. This was the Moses from earlier in the season. The Moses that made everything look easy.

If this was going to be his last appearance at Hayes Lane, it was the perfect way to bow out.

Billy and Frank were loving it. They both joined in the celebra-tions and even sang the Moses Emmanuel song, which has just two words, 'Moses' and 'Emmanuel'. I looked at them with real pride, remembering how excited I'd been when I first saw Eric Nottage (the Moses of the 1960s) score.

At half-time we were a goal up against one of the best sides in the Vanarama National League, the boys were thoroughly enjoy-ing themselves, and Liz had even stopped asking if we could go and see Gareth the cat – although that was more to do with the bar being open than anything else.

And the bar was where we spent the break.

Just a minute into the second half, Paul Rodgers scored one of the goals of the season to put Bromley 2-0 up. That's what I was told, anyway. I missed it because I was trapped in the corridor at the side of the bar while someone told me exactly where Mark Goldberg was going wrong.

By the time I'd managed to escape, I wasn't so concerned that I'd missed it. What mattered was that Bromley were two up against a play-off contender, and that the boys were really starting to enjoy themselves. It was a brilliant time for Bromley to start turning their season around. The football gods were finally smiling on me.

The only clue that things weren't going quite as well as they seemed was when I noticed that Alan Julian was in a lot of pain. He was only playing because Chris Kettings' loan spell was over and, as far as I could make out, the club had no other goalkeepers. I think Eastleigh sensed he wasn't 100 per cent as they began to pepper his goal. It paid off when the dangerous Ben Strevens headed home.

My heart sank. Billy and Frank didn't know what was coming. They still thought Bromley were on top, just because we were the better team and were winning. But I knew what was about to happen, and the goal took only a minute to arrive – Strevens once again, from close range.

And a few minutes after *that*, Strevens found himself a couple of yards out with an open goal in front of him. It was impossible to miss. My fellow fan Roy, the worst footballer I'd ever played with and who was now closing in on his seventies, would have scored. Yet somehow the Eastleigh striker mishit his shot so badly that the ball sailed, unexpectedly and gloriously, over the bar, over the stand and into the car park.

Unbelievably we were still in the game.

Moses was unlucky not to grab a second when his shot missed by inches, and Eastleigh also came close, but Bromley held out to pick up their first point since so long ago I couldn't actually remember.

We retired to the bar to meet up with the Dave Roberts Fan Club, who had booked a cordoned-off area. Liz was already there. She had been there since half-time and was noticeably enjoying herself more. We stayed for an hour, then it was time to go. It was a long drive back to Staffordshire.

As we were leaving, several people asked when my next game would be. The truth was, I didn't have anything planned until the trip to Cheltenham, a month away; but that didn't make me sound like the committed fan I wanted them to think I was. After all, these were people who went to just about every game (in Sue's case, literally every game).

So when Stu asked the same question, I found myself answering with the word 'Dover' – even though the game was two days away and I hadn't even considered going.

What had I done? I was already exhausted after a busy Christmas. Could I really face travelling almost the length of the country so I could watch Bromley lose?

On the morning of the Dover game, I woke up around 6.30 a.m. Every fibre in my body was screaming, 'No, Dave, go back to sleep. You're tired, and going to Dover would be one of the most stupid things you've ever done.'

I turned to Liz, tapped her on the shoulder and whispered in her ear, 'Fancy coming to Dover?'

'When?'

'Now.'

'Seriously?'

'Yes.'

'No.'

I tried to convince her that it would be spontaneous and exciting, as opposed to rash and disorganized, but she wasn't having it. She went back to sleep. Something I was sorely tempted to do. I really was tired. The last thing I wanted to do was spend something like ten hours on trains.

Besides, if I went, I would have to break one of the immutable rules of the long-distance football fan: never buy train tickets on the day of the game, as that is when they are at their most expensive.

I made up my mind, went online and bought train tickets on the day of the game, getting very little change from £100. But I was already looking forward to the trip, and not just for football reasons. Anticipation among Bromley fans had been building since the Monday after the Guiseley match a month ago, when an ad appeared in the London *Metro* 'Rush Hour Crush' section. It read: 'Pretty Dover FC girl in pink football shirt. I enjoyed our talk on the Leeds train back to London. I regret not asking for your number. Fancy a drink? Bromley Boy.'

A Bromley fan with the ability to chat up girls on trains? It wouldn't have happened in my day.

It took just under a week for the young man to be identified. After all sorts of wild theories on the forums, it turned out to be Tom, a tall, pleasant young man in his early twenties I'd spoken to a few times.

Further information dripped through over the following weeks. She had got in touch, and her name was Camilla. Then word came through that they'd met up for a meal and things had gone well.

Would they meet up at Dover? I would soon – well, in about five hours – find out.

The hugely expensive train journey just went on and on. It felt like an endless tour of every railway station in Kent. Places I never knew existed, despite growing up in the county. Once, when I checked, there were still fifteen stations to go.

I closed my eyes. I'm not sure if I fell asleep, but when I opened them we were pulling into Dover Priory station. I felt a jolt of panic. I was meant to get off at the stop before, Kearsney.

To pass the time before the next train to Kearsney, I walked into town, as I had always wanted to take a look at the famous white cliffs. To be honest, they were a bit disappointing, failing to induce the stirring feeling of majesty and proud Britishness I'd expected. They just looked like white cliffs. There were no blue-birds flying over them, just psychopathic seagulls swooping low and squealing threateningly. This was a town with plenty of form as far as seagulls were concerned, with several reported attacks. Colander sales must be going through the roof, I thought.

A further thought struck me on the way back to the station when I saw a tanning salon that had been closed down and had a 'For Sale' notice on the window. If a place like that couldn't sur-vive in a place like Dover, the next global recession must already be on us.

As I walked through a tunnel, I came across a busker playing a drum loudly, and not very well. It brought back unpleasant mem-ories of Lincoln so I gave him a quid and got out of earshot. As a busker experience, it was the Dover equivalent of the violinist who plays 'My Heart Will Go On' outside Marks & Spencer in Leeds. All day.

I arrived back at the station and took the train to Kearsney. It had already been a long day and I was a bit worried about a scarily steep hill Sue (who had been watching Bromley since she was a few weeks old – her mum worked in the tea hut) had warned me about. But by the time I got within sight of the ground the only hill I'd had to climb had been a bit on the steep side – well, quite a lot on the steep side actually, but no longer than a hundred yards. It had seemed pretty easy anyway. Maybe I was fitter than I thought.

I went through the gate and asked a security man where the

away supporters were meant to go. He pointed to a gate at the far side of the car park. When I got there and turned the corner, I found myself at the bottom of one of the steepest hills I'd ever seen within the confines of a football ground. Looking up, I got a sinking feeling. I really wasn't sure I'd be able to make it.

I asked a passing Dover fan if there was any other way to get there. He said that there wasn't, but you could normally get a ride in a golf cart if you needed it. I looked around. There was no sign of any golf carts.

I set off on the long trek, only the lure of watching Bromley keeping me going. It wasn't long before Ian, who was so fit that he could climb the hill and talk at the same time, caught up with me. He began telling me about an end-of-season game he was arranging, between the fans and the Bromley staff.

A game that would be played at Hayes Lane.

I immediately began lobbying for inclusion, perhaps to come on as sub, with twenty minutes to go. It would be the perfect end to the season – and possibly my and Liz's time back in England – as well as the culmination of a dream I'd first had when I was fourteen years old. In an attempt to prove my fitness, and therefore suitability for selection, I made an extra effort to keep up with Ian, disguising the fact that I was out of breath and desperate for a rest, making sure he did all the talking.

The only slight reservation I had about playing was that in my last competitive game, in the US six years earlier, I'd pulled both thigh muscles and was carried, screaming, from the pitch after less than ten minutes.

At least now I'd have a chance to slowly build my fitness, and the steep climbs at places like Forest Green, Aldershot, Lincoln and now Dover should definitely have helped.

I distracted myself from the discomfort I was experiencing by drifting off into a world where I scored the winning goal at Hayes Lane in the ninetieth minute. I was enjoying it so much that I almost missed an unexpected bonus when I finally reached the top of the hill. As I propped myself up against the wall outside the stand, getting my breath back, I saw they had a concession for the over sixties. It was just a tenner to get in.

I felt a rush of pleasure wash over me, the intensity of which took me by surprise. I had never thought that saving four quid could make me feel so euphoric, but this felt like the most glorious thing that had happened in years. When I told Liz about it later, she said that it was probably the endorphins kicking in after I'd given my body a rare burst of sustained exercise.

She was probably right, because the feeling soon went, not least because when I got inside the ground I was faced with a potentially serious problem. There was nowhere to buy a programme – apparently the seller had already been and gone. I asked a security man if I could go out and get one somewhere else. He shook his head.

This could be Moses Emmanuel's last game for Bromley. And I was faced with the unthinkable possibility of not having a programme to commemorate the occasion with, and to help me look back on it in years to come.

I decided to contact Dover when I got home. I was sure they'd be able to sort one out for me.

The Bromley faithful were in good voice, singing a bunch of songs that seemed to be aimed exclusively at embarrassing Tom. 'Love is in the Air' was followed by 'She loves Tom, yeah, yeah, yeah' and 'Cami-lla, you're breaking Tom's heart, you're shaking his confidence daily'.

And then came 'Camilla, Camilla, give us a wave'.

It was Camilla who would have been happier with the early stages of the game. Dover looked like a team pushing for promotion while we looked like a team without a League win since October.

It wasn't a massive surprise when the home team took the lead.

Rob Swaine was badly caught out, leaving their number 9 (name unknown due to poor eyesight and lack of programme in hand) to slot the ball past Alan Julian.

Ten minutes later, by which time it should have been at least 3-0, history was made when a dubious decision went Bromley's way. The Dover number 23 got in a tangle with Lee Minshull and apparently lashed out (although it didn't look that bad to me). He was shown the red card.

While most of the away fans were cheering, Sue looked alarmed. 'We're rubbish against ten men,' she pointed out, accurately, before pleading with the referee to change his mind.

He wasn't swayed, and the game continued. The next goal, ten minutes before half-time, came from a totally unexpected source. A Bromley player. A superb Moses Emmanuel shot from the edge of the box was pushed out by the goalkeeper and Adam Cunnington was perfectly placed to knock the ball home from close range for his first goal for the club.

We were level. Against one of the best teams in the Vanarama National League and runaway leaders of the unofficial Kent League.

Bromley then got another piece of luck when Dover's appeals for a penalty, after a blatant Jack Holland foul, were waved away and the teams went into the break level.

At half-time, all eyes were on Tom. He was rumoured to be meeting Camilla during the interval, and sure enough, against a background of a drunk and tuneless 'Love is in the Air', he slowly walked across to the fence segregating the two sets of fans. On the other side, heading towards him, we got our first glimpse of Camilla emerging from the crowd.

Tom hadn't been exaggerating when he'd called her pretty. Her long blonde hair caught the late afternoon sun as she hurried towards her man, wearing her pink Dover shirt, a large brown coat and a tartan scarf.

I felt as though I was watching a Cold War romance, with the Crabble Athletic Ground fence standing in for the Berlin Wall and the Dover Athletic stewards taking the roles of the East German border guards. It was the greatest, and possibly only, love story in the history of non-league football.

But then, just as the Bromley fans were singing their encouragement, the stewards took the bizarre decision to try and stop the young couple from talking. First, one of them put an arm out to prevent Tom getting any nearer. Then they were told that they had to stand a couple of feet away from the fence, which one of the stewards was leaning against, watching them. A few minutes later, Dover security decided that enough was enough: Tom and Camilla were told to stop their conversation and move away.

I couldn't help but think back to when Bromley used to play at a lower level and supporters of both sides mixed freely. This was incredibly heavy-handed and I really, really hoped that Bromley could hold on for a draw and put a small dent in Dover's promotion hopes.

This looked unlikely as the second half got under way, with the home team on top. Then, against all expectations, Bromley took the lead – a Joe Anderson corner was met perfectly by former makeshift striker Jack Holland to give us a shock lead.

Predictably, it didn't last long. The Dover number 9 scored his second of the game and the momentum swung the home side's way. Which made it even more shocking when Bromley grabbed a third to go back into the lead, Reece Prestedge nodding home from a corner with his first touch of the game.

Numbers 5, 7 and 10 all came close to equalizing for Dover, but Bromley hung on. Even during injury time.

When the referee – whose name and home town I didn't know because I didn't have a programme – blew the final whistle, I experienced euphoria for the second time that afternoon. But this time it had nothing to do with exercise-induced endorphins and everything to do with getting our first win for two months.

The only disappointment was that once again I couldn't hang around to join in the celebrations as I had just twenty-five minutes to get to Kearsney station. I walked as fast as I could, passing small groups of Dover fans along the way. As I did so, I heard snatches of conversation, all with similar themes – 'the ref must've been blind', 'he'd better not come here again, I can tell you', 'dirtiest side we've played all season'.

They sounded just like me when Bromley lost.

I tried to increase my speed as it was touch and go whether I would make the train, but my body wouldn't respond. This is what I hate most about ageing. I was not only tired from all the travel involved in watching two games in three days, but also physically incapable of running, or even walking fast. My legs were aching and I was out of breath.

How was I going to be fit enough to play football at Hayes Lane if I couldn't even jog more than a hundred yards?

I arrived at the station with four minutes to spare, and promised myself that I would be joining a gym when I got back to Leeds.

The anger from Dover fans continued on the train, with more accusations of cheating, daylight robbery and a naive, incompetent referee. I sat back, basking in the outpouring of bitterness and sense of injustice from people other than Bromley fans. It made the journey a lot more pleasurable and the time pass a lot quicker.

When I got home, I emailed Dover and asked if I could get a programme. No response. The next day, I tried them on Twitter. No response. And when I went to look at the goals on the Bromley site, I discovered that Dover had refused to release footage of the game.

Dover Athletic, it seemed to me, were the most unobliging team in the Vanarama National League. Not only that, they made visiting supporters climb a massively steep hill, so I felt even better about coming away with the three points which kept us in thirteenth place.

Mid-table is a unique experience for football fans like me who tend to overthink things. Depending on your mood, you can either get excited about promotion prospects or feel a sense of impending relegation doom. This is why, despite our seemingly strong position, I was genuinely worried when during the Dover game Manchester Will had mentioned his dream that we'd finished bottom of the table. It was only when he added that in the dream he had provided the assist for Moses Emmanuel to score in the last game of the season that I felt a sense of relief. It destroyed any credibility the dream might have had. It would never happen: Moses was bound to be gone long before the end of the season.

His possible departure was on my mind a few days later as Liz and I stood side by side watching fireworks light up the sky as the bells of Leeds Minster rang out, signalling the start of 2016. For the two of us, the new year represented a time of opportunity, of exciting new beginnings; a time for change.

I couldn't have foreseen just how much change the year was to bring.

Sixteen

When I heard that the Oyster Card system had crashed and people were travelling across London for free, I was sorely tempted to do a U-turn on my decision not to go to moneybags Eastleigh to watch Bromley play them for the millionth time this season. The temptation was magnified by the fact that we had a chance to extend our unbeaten run to three games, which would be the second-longest unbeaten run of the 2015/16 campaign. Plus, it was taking place at the Silverlake (previously Sparshatts) Stadium, where Bolton Wanderers would be the next team to play Eastleigh, after Bromley. This tenuous connection with one of the country's most famous clubs and four-time FA Cup winners might have been enough for a last-minute change of heart, had not word come through that the match had been postponed due to heavy rain.

It was just as well. The reason I was having to sacrifice the trip was purely financial. A combination of living beyond our means and a refusal to check the bank balance had led to the hideous realization that it was touch and go whether our savings would last until May, which would be when our year was up.

Rather than worry about that, I found myself worrying about Moses Emmanuel instead.

The forum and Twitter were an endless source of rumours

about his future. He was going to Portsmouth. He was going to Ebbsfleet. He was going to Barnsley. Someone knew someone at Brentford, and knew for certain that he'd be re-signing with them. Someone else had contacts at Peterborough, who had come in with an offer he couldn't refuse. Blackpool were also interested.

Only one thing seemed certain: by the end of the January transfer window, Moses Emmanuel would no longer be a Bromley player.

But while we had him, there was hope. And what gave me a further boost was seeing his name in the starting eleven against Southport at Hayes Lane for our first game of 2016. Southport were on a six-game winning streak, we were on a one-game winning streak. But even with this clash of two teams on winning streaks, the BBC weren't interested.

Once again I had to rely on Twitter. That was how I learned that, just as it had for the reverse fixture, the rain was pelting down. Unlike the reverse fixture, the game ended scoreless, and I discovered that few things in life are less exciting than following a 0-0 draw on Twitter.

Next up was Grimsby at home. Naturally, there was no coverage on radio, so I had no option but to use Twitter again. But I was fed up with Twitter. It is a truly rubbish way to follow football, because most of the time you have no idea what's going on. So I felt particularly pleased with myself when I had the brilliant idea of trying the Grimsby website. Sure enough, for 'just £4.49' I could have unlimited access to Mariner Player, which would let me listen to commentaries of all games played within the next twenty-four hours. In other words, one.

This was Rip-off Britain at its worst.

Normally I was able to rely on the BBC for biased anti-Bromley commentary. At least that was free. Now I had to pay the best part of a fiver to hear my team insulted? In an attempt to get my money's worth I forced myself to sit through an interview with manager Paul Hurst looking ahead to the game. It wasn't interesting.

After checking the weather forecast (BBC again), I learned that the area would be dry and sunny but very cold despite light winds. Which made me glad I would be listening to the game on Mariner Player and not watching it in person.

Only the game never took place. A frozen pitch was the official reason given for postponing it. Which meant £4.49 down the drain.

Four days later, on 23 January, I was throwing away another £4.49, this time on Tranmere Player. Once again the BBC showed no interest in covering the game, despite the fact, as Col pointed out, that sixteen years ago we were bottom of the Ryman League while Tranmere were at Wembley in the League Cup Final.

I'd been counting down the days to this fixture ever since we were humiliated 4-0 at Prenton Park back at the beginning of October. It promised to be an entertaining game, too. The previous week at Barrow, Tranmere had been 3-1 down after ninety minutes. Then Barrow out-Bromleyed Bromley, conceding three goals in injury time.

Throughout the first half, I had an uneasy feeling. It was hard to concentrate; something felt wrong. I didn't even feel any outrage when Andy Doyle, the co-commentator, chipped in with comments like 'Take Emmanuel away and Bromley have nothing to offer', 'Cunnington's a bit of a journeyman', and 'Chorley in midfield isn't working – he's too old'. It just didn't seem important. And when Bromley went behind, it barely sank in. I felt anxious and unsettled and found myself pacing around the room. At one stage I stared out of the window with an overwhelming feeling of sadness. The commentary had become background noise.

Half an hour after the game finished, my phone rang. As soon as I saw that the caller was Nightingale House, the home my dad was in, I knew what was coming.

I stared at the screen, not wanting to answer. When I did, I heard the words I'd been dreading. He'd passed away suddenly that afternoon, the kindly-sounding nurse told me, about an hour ago. A fortnight short of his ninety-sixth birthday.

On the Monday, I went down to Nightingale House as they wanted me to go through his things. What struck me most was the reaction of everyone I spoke to. From administrators to managers, ward nurses to activities supervisors, tears welled up in their eyes when they talked about him. These were people I'd imagined would be immune from grief, given the nature of their jobs. For me, this was a measure of how much they cared about my dad.

The ward nurse took me to his room, the room I'd visited regularly since moving back to England. She said she'd leave the door open so I wouldn't be disturbed, then left me alone to go through his belongings.

I found letters I'd written, photos and cards I'd sent. I found things I'd made at school and long forgotten about. Everyday objects took on an unexpected poignancy – an uneaten bar of ginger chocolate, a much-used shaving razor, an old jumper. When I'd finished, I didn't feel ready to leave, knowing it would be my last time in this room. I sat on his bed, thinking of all the things we'd done together, like going to football when I was too young to go by myself even though he didn't really enjoy the games, and the lessons he'd taught me. Finally, and reluctantly, I decided it was time to make a move. I put my backpack on, took one last look around and walked towards the door.

And that was when it suddenly slammed shut as though blown by a sudden gust of wind. But that couldn't have been the reason. There was double glazing throughout the building, and no windows were open in January.

As I slowly opened the door, I noticed that the hairs on my arms were standing on end. Had he, like me, tried to delay the moment of parting? Or was there a perfectly rational explanation?

The funeral took place two days later in driving sleet, in a desolate cemetery in north London just a few miles from where he had been born. It was the second time in a month that the family had come together and we held each other as the box was lowered into the ground.

I knew it was going to be hard. I had no idea just how hard it would be.

Four days later I wasn't sure I felt up to going to Cheltenham, but I remembered that I'd promised Liz a return to the Cotswolds and I knew she'd been looking forward to it, even though she insisted it was fine if we didn't go. Besides, it would probably be good to get away.

I'd booked the train tickets a couple of months in advance. As part of my economy drive, I'd chosen them on price, with no consideration given to practicality. This meant that a journey which would normally take just over two and a half hours going direct from Leeds would be taking us just over five hours, which included sitting around at Waterloo station for an hour in the cold and Swindon station for twenty-five minutes. In the event it took a little longer as one of the trains was delayed, but at least it was still daylight when we finally arrived.

After checking into the hotel, we walked around. It was gorgeous, some of the Regency townhouses in particular catching the eye. But it was already becoming apparent that even England's most beautiful towns weren't immune from the decline of the high street. Every other building seemed to be a betting shop, a charity shop or a fast food outlet.

Instinctively I reminded myself to tell Dad about how much the place had changed since we'd visited the town as part of a family holiday at nearby Stow-on-the-Wold, over half a century ago. I was then, almost simultaneously, hit hard by the realization that this was a conversation we'd never be able to have.

The next day, after a pub lunch, we set off for the ground, which, according to the bloke behind the bar who drew a map on a napkin, was extremely easy to find.

After nearly two miles I felt the first stirrings of uncertainty so I stopped walking, stared at the napkin, tried looking at it from different angles, and took a look around for the reassuring sight of floodlights. None of these strategies proved helpful.

'Do you actually know where you're going?' said Liz.

'Yup, pretty sure we're going the right way.'

'Really?'

Given that we'd been walking for nearly half an hour, and given that the ground was only fifteen minutes from the pub, I had to admit that there was a small chance we had missed the turning.

'Why don't you just ask someone?' said Liz, managing to make an order sound like a question.

As she spoke, a shortish, bespectacled, balding man in his early forties clutching a bulging plastic carrier bag came scurrying towards us. I sensed that this was someone who would know the whereabouts of the nearest non-league ground.

Sure enough, he did. In fact he was on his way there himself to watch the game and we were welcome to join him. Which meant that we had to turn round, as it appeared we were heading in the wrong direction.

I couldn't help wondering what was in the carrier bag, though I didn't have to for long.

'I've got nine bacon baps in here,' he volunteered proudly, waving the bag in front of us.

'Really?' I said.

'Yes. Farmfoods have a really good deal on frozen bacon this week – four packs for six pounds.'

'Wow,' said Liz, which is what she says when she can't think of anything else to say.

'That's great,' I added.

'Do you know where Farmfoods is?' he asked.

'No,' I said, 'we've just come down from Leeds for the game.'

'I could show you if you like?'

Despite the fact that neither Liz nor I had any interest in buying frozen bacon (she's a vegetarian for a start), I did what any self-conscious Englishman would have done.

'Yes, please,' I said.

He stopped, and pointed at a tree-lined street across the road. 'You go down there to the lights, turn left, and it's about ten minutes away on the left, just after Greggs. You can't miss it.'

'Thanks – we'll go later.' I felt I had to say that after he'd gone to the trouble of telling us how to get there.

As we arrived at the ground, he obligingly took us past his usual entrance, just so he could show us the way into the Hazlewoods Stand, where the visiting supporters stood. We then shook hands and went our separate ways.

Thirty quid later, Liz and I were inside the World of Smile Stadium. Seriously, who calls their home ground the World of Smile Stadium? It was a terrible name. Even worse than its previous name, the Abbey Business Stadium.

As we walked over to find a place behind the goal, I was touched by the number of people who approached me to say how sorry they were to hear about my dad. I'd only known most of them for a few months so it was further proof that there was a real sense of family among those who followed Bromley around the country.

And the ones who had made the long trip to the World of Smile Stadium had precious little to smile about. Reece Prestedge, scorer of our most recent goal just over a month ago, had been sent out on loan, together with Ugo Udoji. The bench was a mix of kids and reserves. Max Porter, one of our better midfielders, was rumoured to have a career-ending injury. And since this was the last game before the transfer window closed, it was probably going to be Moses Emmanuel's last game in a Bromley shirt too.

Everything seemed to be falling apart.

Our ex-AS Monaco player Steve Pinau had vanished, replaced by an ex-Chelsea player called Adam Coombes who, at twenty-four, had played nine games in his entire senior career – an indication that he might possibly be injury prone. Still, he did once score an equalizer for Notts County against Liverpool at Anfield. I looked it up on YouTube. It really did happen.

Despite this, there was no optimism among the Bromley fans.

Within a few minutes of Mr Wigglesworth (Doncaster) getting the game under way it was apparent that Cheltenham were not only hugely impressive, but also a side that didn't fit the Vanarama National League blueprint. In a league of giants, it seemed that the best team was also one of the smallest. Many of them were average height or below. Dan Holman, a fast and skilful attacker, was causing all sorts of problems for a static Bromley defence. Cheltenham were ruthless at identifying their opponents' weaknesses (to be fair, they had plenty to choose from) and exploiting them. They were a class above most of the other leading teams I'd seen during the season and several classes above Bromley.

The first goal, a superb finish from Holman, came as no surprise. Nor did the second, five minutes later, when Holman scored again. Or the third, a Danny Wright header just after half-time. Or the fourth, an embarrassingly easy tap-in by Wright on the hour mark.

After that they seemed to take pity on us and eased off. Bromley were looking as bad as I'd seen them in years. It was enough to make Mash growl – not in the sense of talking in a growling tone, but quite literally *growl*. The long, drawn-out 'grrrrrrrrrrrrr' that escaped from his lips told anyone within earshot that he was unhappy.

The first bright spot of the game came after eighty-five minutes, when Bradley Goldberg, who had come on as a late sub, hit a shot on target. The Bromley fans behind the goal went wild. 'We're gonna win the League!' rang out amid frenzied celebrations.

It got even better after that. Alex Wall, played in by the ex-Chelsea man Adam Coombes, finished impressively to notch up Bromley's first goal in thirty-one days. We should have had another, too, when Goldberg, clearly onside, finished neatly but the linesman, wrongly, had his flag up.

But when Mr Wigglesworth blew his whistle for the final time, things turned bad again. After most of the players had made their way back to the changing room, Mark Goldberg appeared with his arm around Moses Emmanuel and brought him towards the end where we were standing. He said something into his ear, and Moses shyly joined his manager in waving to the fans. A murmur went round as the implications of this sank in. He was waving goodbye. What was already a depressing day had just turned into one of the most miserable imaginable. Bromley had won just two of their last fifteen games. And soon there'd be a new set of fans singing the Moses Emmanuel song.

Liz and I walked back into Cheltenham (without stopping off at Farmfoods for frozen bacon), once again enjoying the Promenade with its Regency buildings and wide, open spaces. In one of these, Pittville Park, bright yellow crocuses and daffodils were bursting through. At the end of January. Which was just plain wrong.

After stopping to take a selfie in front of the *Minotaur and Hare* sculpture (listed only as a sub-attraction on the Visit Cheltenham website), and checking Waterstones to see if they had any of my books in stock (one copy of *32 Programmes*, which I transferred to a more prominent position), it was time for an early dinner.

In the curry house we went to was proof that we were now in the most civilized town in Britain. The diners were impeccably dressed, with suits, waistcoats and ties everywhere – although we later found out they'd come straight from a day at the races. I started to relax for the first time in a week as Liz and I talked about Dad, sharing memories.

Although our visit hadn't been totally satisfying, given that we'd suffered a humiliating defeat, it was impossible to hate Cheltenham. This was an attractive town with friendly, helpful people and a team that played quality football. The opposite of Dover, basically.

So all too soon it was time to go home. We took a taxi to the station, and when the driver found out that we'd come down for the football, he started complaining that Cheltenham would be top of the table had Forest Green not snatched a winner in injury time in their match.

He wanted to talk to *me* about injury-time injustice? To have enough time to hear about all the injustices Bromley fans had suffered this season, he would have had to drive us all the way home to Leeds.

Of course, he didn't. Instead we climbed aboard a series of trains while following one of the most tortuous routes between Cheltenham and Leeds anyone could ever dream up, arriving five hours later, tired and hungry.

'Another successful trip,' said Liz wearily as we walked out of the station into a dark and rainy Leeds. 'This is what we do. Travel around, watching Bromley lose.'

It was hard to disagree with her.

Further misery came on the Monday, when BT announced which of the Easter games were being televised. Bromley were once again missing from the list.

It was also the day our chances of relegation could potentially be quadrupled. The transfer window was due to close at midnight and the fear that someone could make a last-minute bid for Moses Emmanuel had me glued to the TV and the *Guardian* website all evening, forcing myself to stay awake.

By 11.30 p.m. there was still no news and I went to bed, emotionally exhausted.

'Do you think there's a chance he'll stay?' I whispered to Liz, not knowing whether or not she was already asleep.

'How should I know?' she said, turning her back on me. 'Goodnight.'

I checked my phone again. The transfer deadline had now officially passed and there were no more updates. Miraculously, it seemed as though Moses was still a Bromley player.

But a few days later, some genuinely shocking news filtered through from Hayes Lane. And that was when I realized that when Moses and the manager had come on to the pitch at Cheltenham, it hadn't been Moses waving goodbye.

It had been Mark Goldberg.

HOME
AND
AWAY

Seventeen

My brother-in-law Nick had just come back from Spain after a week away, and Liz was desperate to follow his example and take a break from the English winter.

Her wish was about to come true. We were on our way to Wales for a Valentine's Day weekend in Wrexham – because nothing says romance quite like a weekend in Wrexham, with a Bromley game thrown in.

And for once it was Bromley that Liz wanted to talk about as we trundled through the Cheshire countryside on the TransPennine Express. Like me, she had been shocked by the news that Mark Goldberg, manager on-and-off for ten years, had been dramatically sacked and replaced by Neil 'Smudger' Smith, his assistant and former joint caretaker manager of Woking. Smudger had already had his first game in charge, four days earlier. He'd had to face the twin threats of Grimsby Town and referee Nigel Lugg. Inevitably, Bromley lost 2-1, the winning goal coming late in the game from a free kick given for an imaginary foul seen only by the man from Chipstead.

But while I wanted to discuss the fact that the previous time Lugg had refereed a Grimsby game they'd equalized after being given a late penalty, Liz was more interested in why Goldberg was no longer in charge. I repeated the official line, which was that 'the club has new investors who have higher expectations than current performances on the pitch are showing'. This was typical Bromley, sacking the manager just after the transfer window closes with no one lined up to replace him. Apart from the assistant manager.

After changing trains at Manchester we were joined by Lloyd and Manchester Will. Lloyd placed a plastic Tesco bag on the table, removed a four-pack of Strongbow Dark Fruit cider (which he'd done every time I'd been on a train with him), and got through them all by the time we reached our destination (ditto).

The brilliant thing about Wrexham General station is that you can see the Racecourse Ground floodlights from there. It can't be more than a couple of minutes away. It was just a shame I'd rented a flat for the night on the other side of town, where we had to go to drop off our bags before the game.

Apart from that, the weekend was reasonably well planned. By my standards, anyway. I'd learned from the Lincoln experience that leaving things until the last moment wasn't always a good idea, so I'd booked a table at Black Pepper's restaurant before we left.

The call had been fairly routine until the manager asked my name.

'David Roberts,' I said.

'David Roberts?' he replied, hesitating slightly.

'That's right.'

And that was when I'd realized there could well be at least half a dozen David Robertses dining there that night, given that a significant percentage of Welshmen shared my name.

I just hoped that this wouldn't lead to some kind of mix-up over the booking. This was our Valentine's Day dinner. It needed to go smoothly.

So I also popped into the broom-cupboard-sized taxi office at the station as Lloyd and Will went off in search of the nearest Wetherspoon pub. I wanted to get their card just in case we needed a taxi later, and Station Taxis (as they were unsurprisingly called) had got really good reviews, apart from the one complaining of 'dire service' and calling them 'totally unreliable'.

I picked up a card ('A Local Firm for Local People'), then Liz and I climbed into one of several cabs waiting outside the office and gave the driver the address. On the way there, I noticed a lovely old-fashioned pub called the Cambrian Vaults, which looked like the sort of place you'd find oak beams and a welcoming log fire.

'Let's go there for lunch,' I suggested to Liz, who nodded in agreement.

The taxi driver spoke for the first time: 'That was closed down a few years back. Someone died there.'

'What happened?'

'Stabbed.'

While this was sinking in, he went on to tell us about the Cambrian Vaults football team: they'd played a game which ended in a riot with something like 150 people injured and around a dozen ending up in prison.

We decided to look at alternative lunch options.

When the driver discovered that we were in town for the Bromley game, his voice took on a weary tone. Things were not going well for Wrexham because the players all 'liked a beer, see' and the manager, Gary Mills, 'wasn't 'appy'.

This was brilliant. Not just the discovery that Welsh people really did talk the way they do on telly, but also the glimmer of hope that had been revealed to me where none was previously present. By the time he dropped us off at the flat I was feeling much better about Bromley's prospects, and we decided to take the half-hour walk to the ground and get something to eat along the way.

After finishing a bag of disappointingly undercooked chips and handing over £19 each (the highest admission of the season), we found ourselves inside the world-famous Racecourse Ground. One of the many impressive things about it is that it was one of the first stadiums to go completely smoke-free, a move that would have been welcomed by both the CEO at the time, David Roberts, and the club's highest-profile celebrity supporter, Paralympian David Roberts.

I looked around. This was the ground where Mickey Thomas scored the goal that knocked Arsenal out of the Cup. The ground where more Welsh internationals have been played than at any other venue. A ground which had even seen Champions League action.

Now, Bromley would be playing here. In a League match. If ever there was a two-programme fixture, this was it. I even briefly considered getting three, until I realized that would be totally pointless.

Thankful that the rain had stayed away, I placed one of the programmes carefully in Liz's bag and, leaning against the railing facing the magnificent Mold Road Stand, flicked through the other one.

The first page that caught my eye was the 'Ten to Tackle' segment. This was a trivia quiz with ten questions, some of them so obscure that they would be unanswerable by all but the most obsessive of fans. The one that excited me most read: 'As expected, the burger van at the away end did good business when Wrexham visited Bromley on the opening day of the season, but it was out-sold by another van. What was this second van selling?'

'Ice cream!' I wanted to shout. 'It was ice cream!'

If there had been a bonus point for naming the van's owner, I would have got that as well. That warm day in early August had seen the much-anticipated return of Shirley to Hayes Lane after an unexplained absence of several seasons. Mickey, a huge fan of Shirley's 99s, had spotted her selling her ice creams opposite

Princess Royal University Hospital and immediately started a campaign to bring her back. When her return coincided with the re-release of the Lyons Maid 'Happy Feet' ice cream bar, Mickey's happiness was complete.

The rest of the 'Ten to Tackle' questions weren't quite so easy, but I still managed a respectable three out of ten.

By the time I'd finished, most of the Bromley contingent had arrived and were taking up their places. I found myself standing next to Tom, so asked him about Tom and Camilla – or Tomilla as I had started to call them.

'There is no Tom and Camilla,' he told me. 'We decided it would be better if we were friends.'

The thing is, he really meant it. He clearly liked her so much that he was happy to have her as a friend. This was not what I wanted to hear. I tried to persuade him that an end-of-season wedding between supporters of rival non-league teams would be a perfect and heart-warming climax for my book, but he wasn't having it.

'Sorry,' he said, shrugging.

I'd just have to hope something else came along.

Meanwhile, the Bromley team was being announced. This week's new wingers were Reise Allassani (on loan from Palace) and Rohdell Gordon (on loan from Stevenage). Last week's new winger, Adam Coombes, was on the bench and God knows where the previous month's new winger had gone – although I was pretty confident he hadn't gone back to AS Monaco.

Ironically, this was the most Goldberg-esque team I'd seen in a while and I wondered if it indicated there would be no major changes in the way Bromley played. I'd soon find out.

When the game started and the ball (sponsored by Peter Gwyn's Quality Potatoes) was rolled from Adam Cunnington to Moses Emmanuel, I felt an irrational sense of expectation. We'd already beaten Wrexham earlier in the season for the biggest win in Bromley's history. A win here would be even bigger.

And it could definitely happen, especially given the recently discovered possibility that our opponents had enjoyed a few beers the previous night.

If they had, it was giving them a boost. They were all over us. They had hit the post and had a goal disallowed within the first few minutes. I had never seen a Bromley team look so lethargic and uninterested, and that's saying something.

Was it some kind of protest at the Goldberg sacking? Or struggling to adapt to a new way of doing things even though it looked exactly the same as the old way? Or perhaps – and this was more credible – it was the absence through injury of Rob Swaine? He was very much the team's leader, and earlier in the season we'd seemed incapable of winning when he wasn't on the pitch.

Whatever the reason, Wrexham were completely in charge and thoroughly deserved the lead they took after thirty-one minutes when an unmarked Lee Fowler headed a cross past Alan Julian while the Bromley defenders stood pointing at each other.

It was 1-0, although they really should have been three or four nil up.

From then on a succession of Wrexham shots, headers and crosses rained down on Julian, who, unlike his team-mates, was having an outstanding game. The score stayed at 1-0 until Paul Rodgers helped the Reds out with a daft trip on Connor Jennings, who easily converted the resulting penalty.

It is a very difficult thing for me to admit that Bromley might not be the best team on the pitch. Even if we're losing badly, I can usually be relied on to come up with a reason for it, such as refereeing bias, cheating or unnaturally bad luck – basically, all the excuses I heard from Dover fans after we won there. But this was a day when even the most deluded Bromley fan would have to admit that we were awful. And the fans, most of whom had travelled hundreds of miles, weren't happy.

Sunderland Sean, ranting at no one in particular, was storming off in the direction of Wrexham General station after just forty-five minutes of football.

We were playing so badly that Mickey, who is usually quick to give advice, had nothing left to offer. 'I genuinely don't know what to suggest,' he shouted plaintively.

A few fans had their backs to the pitch, talking. A young couple standing near me had brought their baby boy, and he had to be fetched every couple of minutes as it looked as though he was trying to crawl, in determined fashion, towards the exit.

Manchester Will left to catch an early train and missed both of Bromley's second-half attacks, which at least gave the underemployed Rhys Taylor in the Wrexham goal something to do.

The contrast between this game and the Wrexham game at Hayes Lane earlier in the season was spectacular. Every player wearing a white shirt ran himself into the ground that day. Today was the complete opposite.

If it hadn't been for my lifelong need to witness every minute of every Bromley game I attended, I too would have left long before the end. There was nothing enjoyable about the game and, apart from a quite good Bradley Goldberg shot, no positives to take from the performance.

When referee Joe Johnson (Liverpool) finally put us out of our misery, the new Bromley boss gathered his players in the centre circle and laid into them. Loudly. Or, as a Wrexham fan put it on Twitter, 'lots of F words being dropped in a cockney accent'. Smith then undid the good work by telling the media, presumably with a straight face, that 'the players have given me plenty of effort'.

Over curry that night, I tentatively brought up the disaster that had taken place at the Racecourse Ground earlier, but Liz hadn't registered any difference between Bromley's performance today and all the other times she'd seen them lose.

She was, however, keen to talk about her new love. Strongbow

Dark Fruit cider. It was, she had decided, the best drink ever. And as I watched her get through her third glass, I felt a burst of envy. Why did I ever stop drinking? Being a non-drinker and a Bromley fan simply weren't compatible.

Unfortunately, Liz wasn't too drunk to notice that I hadn't come up with any ideas for what to do after dinner, so in desperation I suggested a romantic night-time stroll through Wrexham. Making sure that we kept well clear of the Cambrian Vaults, we trod the streets and soon came across one of the must-see local sights. The Tesco Extra. This had become famous towards the end of the previous year when it advertised for the UK's first professional Christmas Tree Light Untangler. The job, which ensured plenty of press coverage, was landed by the conveniently photogenic Anya Mugridge and the shop was in the news for about a week.

We went inside to see if there was any sign of her or her famous 'Light Untangling' stand, but both were long gone. Liz bought a four-pack of Dark Fruit instead.

And that, to be honest, was the highlight of our mini tour.

The next morning we realized we had no breakfast, so I suggested a visit to the Farmfoods across the road. I quite fancied bacon and knew for a fact that you could buy a lot of frozen bacon there for very little money. Maybe we could also get some of Peter Gwyn's quality potatoes and fry them up, too.

In the end, much like Bromley yesterday, neither of us could be bothered.

Liz was deeply hung over and absorbed in a cartoon on TV. In it, a giraffe, a dragon and a lion were in a kitchen talking to a character consisting of a photographed baby's head on cartoon legs. In Welsh. She wasn't really up to eating but decided to try to get a coffee at the station. But unlike Newark Northgate, there was no Costa Coffee at Wrexham General.

There was, however, an unexpected alternative.

'Hot + Cold Drinks available in taxi office' said a scrawled note on the wall outside Station Taxis. Considering the place was so tiny and cramped that it looked like something from a documentary on obsessive hoarders, the thought crossed my mind that it might be best for them to focus on their core business. But I had to admire the entrepreneurial spirit.

Liz didn't seem so impressed, saying that she'd wait until we got to Manchester before getting her coffee. She barely said another word on the way home, although that was more to do with her hangover than any crushing disappointment over the way Bromley had played.

But that was the reason *I* could hardly speak. It had been a shockingly bad performance. With one or two exceptions, they hadn't even seemed to be trying. The resignation and lethargy so apparent on the pitch at the Racecourse Ground even seeped into the match report on the Bromley website, which began 'Bromley fell to another away defeat, this time at the hands of Wrexham'.

After a spectacular start to the season, we were now, in the middle of February, in the bottom half of the table, just nine points clear of the relegation zone. Teams below us were winning, we were in freefall. The manager who had led us into the Vanarama National League was gone and it was impossible to see where the next win would come from.

It had all the hallmarks of a typical Bromley season.

Yet by the middle of the week my mind was no longer filled with doom-ridden scenarios that resulted in a humiliating return to the Vanarama National League (South). Instead, it was filled with nervous excitement.

Because on Saturday, Bromley would be playing Woking, and I would be going home.

Literally.

HOME
AND
AWAY

Eighteen

I was in the room I grew up in, getting ready for bed. No, it wasn't a dream – I was back there for the first time since leaving home forty-five years earlier.

I'd had the idea in July, when the fixtures were released. The couple who had bought the house from my parents back in the 1980s had made the mistake of saying that I was welcome to stay at any time. So I decided to take them up on their kind offer for the weekend when Bromley would be playing the only fixture that survived from the 1969/70 season, which was when my childhood fanaticism peaked: Bromley v. Woking.

Part of the reason for wanting to do this was because it would be a journey into the past. The other factor was a belief that if I could relive the build-up to that game, by sleeping in the same room before making my way to Hayes Lane, it might somehow mean that the result would also be the same, a 1-0 win to Bromley.

The room felt much smaller, but everywhere I looked brought back strong memories. I opened the wardrobe, half expecting to see a small pile of carefully stacked shoe boxes containing my chronologically arranged collection of Bromley programmes, with KEEP OUT written on each box. I'm no longer sure who this was aimed at. My sister, probably.

Running along the side of the room, beneath the window, was the space my desk once occupied. The top drawer was home to my collection of enamel badges and pens from every club in the Isthmian League apart from Corinthian Casuals, who frustratingly didn't sell either. As for the desk itself, I would sit there every Thursday evening poring over the *Bromley Advertiser* to find out which players were injured or unavailable before picking the team for the upcoming game. Every week I'd drop the useless Phil Amato, but every week he'd play.

On the wall, placed strategically so that I could stare at it when I was lying in bed, was a framed photo, which I'd cut out of the *Advertiser*. It was taken from behind the goal at Hayes Lane and showed my hero Alan Stonebridge coolly slotting home a penalty against Enfield. My dad had made the frame, and the photo had been signed by Alan Stonebridge himself, using a Bromley pen that I never used again and put on permanent display on my window sill.

And in one corner of the room was the area of floor I set aside for my Subbuteo pitch, which I'd glued down to give me a smoother playing surface, unaware that the glue was permanent. I wondered if it was still there, under the carpet.

It felt good to be home. There was sadness mixed with excitement, with a lot there to remind me of Dad. I remembered him teaching me how to shave in the bathroom, how to cook scrambled eggs in the kitchen, and how to play a forward defensive stroke in the garden.

As I stared out of the window at the road outside I suddenly felt myself turning red as a memory surfaced of the time I tried to steal the family car (a Fiat 124) and drive off to Oxford. I was thirteen. I didn't really know how to drive but had seen Dad jump-start the car by rolling down the hill. I decided to use the same method.

What I'd forgotten in all the excitement of my one-boy crime wave was that he'd had a 'Krooklok' steering lock fitted. As a result, as soon as I took the handbrake off I found myself slowly rolling down the road, across the road, then up the road, in an ever-diminishing U-shape, backwards and forwards while a queue of beeping traffic built up behind me. I finally came to a stop diagonally, in the middle of Grasmere Road. A fellow motorist helped me push it back to where the journey had started, appearing to buy into my story of 'having left the Krooklok key in my other trousers'.

Even the roof directly above me held memories. It was where I had sat, refusing to come down, until my parents changed their minds about sending me to boarding school. They didn't.

As I got into bed, the excited anticipation of the night before a game came rushing back. This was how I used to feel on the eve of every Bromley matchday, even when we were on a losing streak, which was most of the time.

The fact that I couldn't sleep because the next day I'd be watching a mid-table non-league game of football confirmed something I'd suspected for a long time: that I was a fourteen-year-old trapped in an old man's body. I finally dropped off some time after midnight, feeling both disorientated and completely at home.

The next morning, I jumped out of bed the second I woke up and rushed over to the window, urgently opening the curtains. This was a day-of-the-match ritual I'd carried out in this particular bedroom hundreds of times. It was to check that the weather wasn't putting the game in doubt.

I was relieved to see that the sun was shining and the rain had stayed away. Bromley v. Woking would definitely be going ahead.

I spent a pleasant morning talking to my hosts, and after lunch it was time to get going.

As I walked past the huge house which I was convinced when I was ten belonged to an arms dealer, who turned out to own a chain of dry cleaners in Croydon, I thought about the first time I'd seen Bromley play Woking.

It was also one of the first times I'd noticed The Grubby at Hayes Lane. He was easily recognizable, not just because he was the only hippy in the entire school (hence the nickname); he was also the only other pupil who wore an enamel Bromley FC badge. It was inevitable that we would find each other. He had long, flowing ginger hair and, in schoolboy terms, ours was the perfect friendship. This was because he fancied himself as a goal-keeper while I was convinced I was a born striker. This meant our roles were never in question whenever we went down the park and we never had to play out of position.

By the end of that season, we were going to every home game together.

The Grubby, or John as he was now known, would be going with me today, too. As I trod the familiar streets on the way to his flat, I remembered that our pre-match ritual in the old days was to go for a kickabout at the park. But we wouldn't be doing that today.

When I got to his flat, I rang the bell. A couple of minutes later the door opened and there was John. The hair might have gone, but the bright, friendly smile was still the same. The reason he took so long to answer the door was because of a hereditary condition called spastic paraplegia, which meant he could no longer walk and had to drag himself around with crutches.

Not that he let it bother him. His flat was spotless, and the last time Liz and I visited we'd arrived as he was clambering up a ladder to clean the gutters on his roof. At worst, he saw his condition as a minor inconvenience. And since it's hard to feel sorry for someone who doesn't feel sorry for themselves, it was easy to treat him the same way I always had.

John had a history of bravery. We were once on our way to a party in Croydon when five or six skinheads got on the bus, carrying bottles. One of them told him to get his feet out of the way so they could get past. He just looked at them and said, 'No.' This confused them to such an extent that they walked around him.

Recalling this confirmed a realization I'd had the previous night, while standing in my room thinking back to my football-obsessed, programme-collecting schooldays: the boy is a pretty good indication of the man he'll become.

Today, John would be driving us in his specially adapted car, and he was clearly excited about going to see Bromley again. He'd last been to Hayes Lane a few seasons ago, but because of his inability to stand up he hadn't been able to see the game. I'd mentioned the problem to Barrie, another long-term fan, and he'd arranged parking right outside the ground and a seat with one of the best views of the pitch.

As we arrived, and I saw the board with BROMLEY V. WOKING on it, my mind went back to the first time I'd come to this fixture, in 1969. It stood out in my memory because my best friend Dave had ambitiously insisted that I forget about going to Hayes Lane, and instead go with him to a free concert in the Library Gardens. Obviously, I declined. Bromley at home to Woking had far more appeal than sitting cross-legged on wet grass while some earnest long-haired singer/songwriter went on about stars and the cosmos. So Dave went on his own while I went to Hayes Lane. I remember thinking afterwards how glad I was that I hadn't fallen for his sales pitch. Bromley notched up a rare League win, which, even though it was only mid-September, would turn out to be the last of the season.

Dave came round that evening and I wasted no time before gloating about my day, smugly describing the superb displays from greats like Alan Soper, Eric Nottage and Jim Watson that I'd been privileged to witness, while he was having to sit through a free concert by David Bowie, whoever he was.

I'd seen John at the match, although I hadn't had the courage to go up and talk to him, since he was in the fifth form and I was in the fourth. But surely the fact that we were both there back in 1969 would help persuade the football gods to deliver a similar result for us today? Especially considering that I'd spent the previous night in the same house. Not only that, but Bromley had also played their part with a similar record to those far-off days: they'd won just two of the last seventeen games, playing with an almost complete absence of ability, flair and imagination. It was as though nothing had changed.

We took the lift upstairs, operated by a helpful steward, and made our way to the seating area, where John was regularly asked if he needed any help. I felt proud of the club, *our* club, for going out of its way to make him comfortable. As we took our seats it was a powerful feeling sitting alongside John once again at Hayes Lane. I was really glad we were back there together, even though it meant I'd had to cancel my programme-selling duties. There'd always be another time for that.

Once or twice I caught John looking down at benches we used to watch from, behind the goal at the far end. That brought back memories of splinters in the bum, scalding tea in china cups and saucers, and stale crisps. The way football should be watched. These seats were due to be ripped out soon, and apparently they were going to be replaced with corporate boxes as part of a massive redevelopment project earmarked for the summer.

Luckily, there was no further time to dwell on this as the players ran out from the tunnel and it was time to start concentrating on the game.

Obviously, with our record of just two wins in seventeen starts, this was a good time for Woking to be playing Bromley. But it was also, in theory, a good time for Bromley to be playing Woking. Their players had, according to BBC Radio Surrey, been promised a bonus at the end of the season, but in a classic moving-of-goalposts scenario had now been told they'd only get it in the unlikely event of finishing in the top five.

I was hoping that they'd be feeling demoralized and bitter, but if they were, they weren't showing it. Instead, they took just five minutes to cruelly dash my hopes of a repeat of the 1969 scoreline. A cross by the Woking right-back was nodded back across the goal by Joe Quigley, finding an unmarked John Goddard at the far post. It was 1-0 to the visitors.

For the next few minutes I found myself watching John as well as the action on the pitch. He was totally absorbed in the game, rocking backwards and forwards, living every move. It was hard adjusting to seeing him without a fag sticking out of his mouth, but a bout of cancer had put an end to that. He'd had a section of his tongue removed, which initially made it hard to understand him, although you soon got used to it.

Again, he just saw it as something he had to live with. He was that rarest of things – an Englishman who was just happy to be alive.

As I checked the other scores on Twitter, I saw a tweet from Vanarama asking 'Which of these 4 strikers will score most goals this season, Amond, Dennis, Rhead and Wright?' Rhead and Wright. I liked that. But it was a sign of Bromley's decline that Moses Emmanuel's name was missing from the options.

Bizarrely, at that very moment he was about to get a chance to add to his total of seventeen goals. A clearance from Cameron Norman hit the legs of referee Brett Huxtable (who, interestingly, was one of the youngest ever to be promoted to the national list of assistant referees in North Devon). Instead of going out for a corner, the ball rebounded to the feet of Adam Coombes who was then nudged in the back by the unfortunate Norman. Huxtable immediately signalled a penalty.

Moses confidently strode up and sent goalkeeper Jake Coles the wrong way, slotting the ball into the bottom left-hand corner. And with that, he moved into fourth place on the Vanarama National League leading scorers list, level with Cheltenham's Danny Wright.

Only a fool ignores Moses Emmanuel.

Moses (ex-Woking) proved this yet again with half an hour gone, when he won the ball and played it through to Adam Cunnington (ex-Woking), who lashed a first-time shot into the net. He then ran into the arms of manager Neil Smith (ex-Woking) to celebrate.

John was punching the air, and I knew that the tea I'd planned on getting him at half-time with his traditional six sugars would taste even sweeter with a 2-1 lead. Only he turned it down, telling me that he'd had one before he left home, and these days liked to limit himself to a couple a day.

I knew people changed. I just never knew anyone could change this much.

The pace of the game dropped several notches in the second half and midway through John was noticeably tiring. It came as no surprise when he announced that he'd be making a move.

I went with him down to the car park, somehow managing to operate the lift (apart from getting it stuck between floors for an agonizing twenty seconds which felt like an hour). Once we were in the car park, John insisted I went back inside. He knew I didn't like missing any of the action. But rather than rush back to my seat, I stood at a downstairs window, watching him slowly drag himself to his car, grimacing with the effort. He then lifted his head to take one last look at the stadium he'd just been in, unaware that I could see him, and suddenly a broad grin broke out over his face.

As I watched my old friend drive away, a warm feeling came over me, knowing how much it had meant to him being back at Hayes Lane.

I watched the remaining twenty minutes or so with the Dave

Roberts Fan Club, or rather three-quarters of it. The other member had apparently gone off on some sort of religious journey. Had he forsaken the Dave Roberts Fan Club? If so, it was now in disarray; a couple of resignations away from being a one-man fan club. And that wouldn't really be a fan club, just some bloke who likes my books.

When the fourth official held up a board indicating four extra minutes, there was a cry of anguish from the people around me. A minute or two of injury time is usually enough to wipe out any lead Bromley might have. Any more than that virtually guarantees at least one goal to whoever we're playing.

But not today. Perhaps it was down to an improved performance from Bromley, or perhaps it was because I'd relived that day back in 1969 when we beat Woking by the same margin, but we held out to win 2-1.

Apart from my shrinking base of admirers, it had been a great trip home. Staying at the house I grew up in had unleashed all sorts of fond recollections, as had the trip to Hayes Lane with John. The match itself hadn't been bad either, although I was so used to suppressing emotions after the final whistle that it wasn't until I was on the train back to Leeds that it finally sank in. Bromley had actually won for the first time in 2016.

It was a dizzying feeling.

Instead of studying the programme – my usual post-match entertainment – I decided to read *Two Footed Tackle*, the Bromley fanzine. I particularly enjoyed Col's memories of 2000/01 which seemed like a typical Bromley season: a Northwood striker turned up late after taking his exams at college and still scored a hat trick against us; a 6-3 loss at home to Dulwich with no sub available left Col too depressed to speak; two players were picked for the 6-0 loss to Braintree even though the manager had never seen them before; and the team managed eleven defeats in a row yet still, somehow, managed to stay up.

The main theme of the fanzine, however, was the fight against relegation, with the headline 'Still 12 Points to Safety'. After today, we still needed four wins from fourteen games. It was going to be close.

Next Saturday I'd be going to bottom-of-the-table Kidderminster to see them take on in-form Bromley in a crucial relegation battle. And next Sunday I'd be off to Old Trafford, to watch Manchester United against Arsenal.

I wanted to see if there would be any difference between the experiences.

HOME
AND
AWAY

Nineteen

Significantly, I did not make my usual Marmite and chicken sandwiches before setting off to Kidderminster. This was because I wouldn't be needing them. Instead, I would be tucking into one of the Harriers' famous cottage pies.

This was an experience I'd been looking forward to from the time I first surveyed the 2015/16 fixture list. Much had been written about these pies and I was finally getting the chance to try one for myself. According to the BBC, they were the most expensive in the whole of British football – quite an achievement for the team that currently lay at the bottom of the Vanarama National League.

And they sounded good. Very good. The *Birmingham Mail*, in my experience a highly reliable newspaper, described it as 'a cottage pie consisting of almost a pound of beef from local butchers, accompanied by veg and mashed potato cooked to a crisp. It is a tinfoil-based treat to behold.' This was a pie rated so highly among football fans that in a 'best of' list it had even been placed above Kilmarnock's previously untoppable Killie Pie ('Say aye tae a Killie pie').

It was lunchtime when I arrived at Birmingham New Street station, which is much the same as any other station in Britain except that it's inside a massive shopping centre. This meant having to walk past multiple temptations in the form of the Handmade Burger Company, Ed's Diner and Square Pie before I could even get out on the street.

I was starving, but had to be strong. Football's most expensive cottage pie awaited me. I somehow found Snow Hill station, despite being given inaccurate directions by almost everyone I asked which turned a ten-minute walk into a thirty-five-minute walk. This was particularly galling as I'd chosen this trip to break in my new Adidas Samba trainers.

The journey to Kidderminster seemed to drag on for ever. And everyone on the train seemed to be eating. Everyone except me.

I couldn't wait to get to the ground, and it wasn't just the cottage pie, or the football. It was also seeing the familiar faces of the away fans. Someone I was especially pleased to bump into on the way out of the station was Rob. This was because in all my pie-related excitement I'd omitted to find out how to get to the ground, and Rob was one of the best-prepared football fans I'd ever met. He was super organized and was bound to know the shortest route there, having researched it thoroughly.

And he did, leading me through the narrow streets and back alleys of a well-maintained housing estate as though he'd lived there all his life.

We arrived at the equally well-maintained Aggborough ground (complete with sign outside saying NO BALL GAMES ALLOWED) and I bought a programme. Obviously. The first thing I noticed about it was the level of confidence in the lure of their cottage pies, which was so high that they'd audaciously run a full-page ad *in their own publication* for their gourmet takeaway rivals, Foley's award-winning fish and chips.

I made my way straight to the catering outlet under the stand, and as soon as I reached the window I saw it. A mouthwatering row of perfectly formed cottage pies, steam lazily rising from them. I pointed at one, and the woman plucked it from the heated tray. Then, tantalizingly, she held it back, asking if I wanted gravy. After confirming that I did, I was delighted that it wasn't slopped on but lovingly ladled into the middle.

She finally, almost reluctantly, handed it over. Its size reminded me of the pies one of my favourite childhood comic characters, Desperate Dan in the *Dandy*, used to devour. His Cow Pies were so huge they had horns sticking out of the crust. The Kidderminster cottage pies weren't much smaller.

I sat on the step at the bottom of the away stand, used a plastic spoon to shovel the eagerly awaited pie into my mouth, and thought about what lay ahead. Until a month ago, Kidderminster were rubbish, but since then they'd beaten moneybags Eastleigh (which was something we would never be able to do), Macclesfield and Boreham Wood. We were fourteenth going into the game, just nine points clear of relegation. If we lost today and the teams below us won, we could drop to as low as eighteenth in the table (although Guiseley would need to win by at least twelve goals for that to happen).

Once again, this was the most important game of the season.

I was feeling more nervous than I had for weeks. But at least the pie was living up to my hopes. Everything about it felt perfect, from the crisp potato topping to the moist, tender meat. And it was made all the more satisfying because I was ravenously hungry. I am not someone who enjoys going without food for any length of time.

Although I thought it was close to perfection, there were others who weren't so impressed, including Sunderland Sean who called it tasteless and pointless. He felt that the pies at Sunderland's Stadium of Light were a lot better.

It was supporters of another Premier League club who were soon making their presence felt at Kidderminster. Crystal Palace were playing West Brom in a 5.30 kick-off, and about a dozen of their fans had come along, hoping to fit half a game in before travelling the twenty or so miles to see their team in action.

Before the game was fifteen minutes old it was already apparent that they were operating at a different level of anger and frustration at Bromley's inept performance than the regular away contingent, perhaps because they weren't used to it. They were screaming abuse at the players, management officials and Kidderminster fans. Even Bromley fans. I suppose when you're used to the Premier League, the Vanarama National League must come as quite a shock. I'd be seeing if the reverse applied just twenty-four hours later, when I went to Old Trafford. But for now, my full attention was on Bromley's need to get three points.

They came close to opening the scoring a couple of times. First, Moses Emmanuel had a goal disallowed just because he was blatantly offside, and then another effort was shockingly ruled out on account of an obvious double foul by Adam Cunnington. Kidderminster also had their chances, but were denied by the brilliance of Alan Julian, who was back to his best after the injury lay-off.

At half-time, with not much else to reflect on, I looked around the small part of the stand we'd been allocated. The Palace fans had gone, leaving the same seventy or so men, women and children I'd seen at badly named stadiums across Britain over the past seven months. I'd seen them in all weathers – rain, snow, sleet and even sunshine. I'd seen them banging their fists on the ground in frustration and I'd seen them dancing with joy. I'd seen them witness horrific defeats and celebrate unlikely victories. I'd heard them shout things that made absolutely no sense and I'd heard them come out with comments that had me laughing for days afterwards – in one case, both at the same time: that was when Mash shouted, 'Oi, Whitaker, you look just like Garvo' to Macclesfield's Danny Whitaker, who not only didn't resemble

Garvo in the slightest, but also was unlikely to know who Garvo was.

As I scanned the small crowd of Bromley faithful, it occurred to me that there wasn't one of them I disliked, not one I wouldn't mind having an orange juice with. These people, most of whom I'd never met before the season started, were one of the things I would miss most if Liz and I had to go back to the US come May. And that was starting to look like a real possibility. Although Liz had had a couple of interviews and I'd written a few articles, we needed steady work.

I was pleased to see that a lot of the people in the away end were eating cottage pies. They were so popular among the Bromley fans that they'd sold out. I wanted to start singing 'We ate all the pies', but didn't. My fear of no one joining in still haunted me after trying, unsuccessfully, to start a chant over thirty-five years ago. It was a fear that never seemed to worry Naughty Nigel.

When the second half got under way, very little happened. The game only came to life in the last ten minutes. First, Rob Swaine pulled down substitute Evan Garnett (who was so unlucky he hadn't even been able to find a kit sponsor) and even I couldn't argue it was a penalty. In fact, as far as I could make out there was only one person in the entire stadium who wasn't convinced.

That was Alan Young from Cambridgeshire. The referee.

As he waved play on, the stunned silence was broken only by angry cries of 'You're a waste of space, referee!' and 'You dick-head!', both of which were clearly heard on the BT highlights the following day.

Then, a couple of minutes from the end, traditionally a danger time for Bromley, we got a free kick thirty yards out. Joe Anderson floated the ball in, but it was a poor one, going over the heads of Swaine and Cunnington, and into no-man's land behind them. As goalkeeper Dean Snedker watched helplessly, the ball bounced and then slowly drifted inside the far post.

237

The ground fell silent for the second time in a few minutes.

Then the mini-Jumbotron behind the goal flickered into life. KIDDERMINSTER 0 BROMLEY 1, it said. Kidderminster players sank to their haunches. The crowd behind the goal (which consisted of four ball boys) turned away in disbelief.

I found myself doing some weird kind of dance on the terraces and punching the air. I have rarely felt happier. There is huge satisfaction in getting a late winner, because by then you've convinced yourself that your team is never going to score and a draw is the best you can hope for.

It was the sort of goal teams stuck at the bottom tend to concede. And I should know.

Bromley held out for the last few minutes and extended the winning streak to two games. The celebrations were a bit muted because we all knew that a poor decision and a jammy goal were all that had stopped us from sliding further down the table. Still, three points is three points and we'd taken a big step towards safety.

Afterwards, Neil Smith demonstrated that he had taken to convoluted manager-speak like a born natural. 'Joe Anderson put a ball into the right area,' he said, 'and it's one of those that if someone gets on the end of it, it goes in, but nobody did and it goes in at the far post.'

The apprentice had become the master.

I was beginning to feel confident – with one proviso: Alan Julian not getting injured – that we now had a decent chance of avoiding relegation. We were still fourteenth, but five points clear of fifteenth-placed Chester.

In the euphoria of victory I even briefly fantasized about finishing in the top ten of the Vanarama National League. This was world-class denial of reality, considering how bad we'd been recently, including today.

I walked to the station with Pete, who took a detour to the off licence on the other side of the ground where he picked up a four-pack of Dark Fruit cider. As he drank it on the train back to Leeds, we swapped Bromley stories. He reminded me of myself, especially when he revealed that he would be going to Eastleigh in a few weeks for an evening fixture, getting home at six the following morning. For a game we would almost certainly lose. I have rarely felt such admiration for a fellow human being.

Fourteen hours later I was on another train, on my way to my first ever Premier League game, Manchester United against Arsenal. Obviously there would be nothing at Old Trafford to compare with the thrill of that Joe Anderson free kick slowly bouncing inside the far post, but the Sunday papers were giving the game quite a build-up.

I was having to read about it while squashed in a carriage with hundreds of sweary middle-aged men drinking lager. Overcrowding was nothing new on the TransPennine Express, which, as I had soon learned, many regarded as the most inept train operator in Britain. I nearly always ended up standing, even when I had a reserved seat, like I did today. All reservations had been cancelled – not for the first time – because the system had broken down.

When I got on a tram to the stadium, it became clear that this was going to be very, very different to a Bromley matchday experience. Once again I was squashed, this time against a window, which meant I had an enforced view of the streets of Manchester. Like Leeds, it had changed enormously from the time when I lived there. The Arndale Centre, which was an exciting, modern showpiece in the early 1980s, now looked tired and dated.

After a couple of stops, the tram had got so full that any form of movement was impossible. The real shock about this was that there were still two hours before kick-off.

The masses poured out at the Old Trafford Metro stop, and straight into a world of people trying to sell you things. By the time I'd got to the ground I'd been offered T-shirts, chips, match-day scarves, hot dogs, fanzines and tickets.

Getting a ticket for myself hadn't been straightforward. I'd had to pay £20 for official membership of the One United club and then £40 for a seat right at the back behind the goal. I wasn't going to buy a programme, in protest at the fact that they were £3.50 each; but there were so many programme shops strategically placed across the concourse that by the time I reached the ninth one I weakened and bought one. Disappointingly, it was really good.

There were about half a dozen uniformed security guards when I got to the turnstile. One of them patted me down before I reached the turnstile itself, where there was a barcode reader instead of an old bloke with a precariously balanced stack of coins – a common sight at Vanarama National League grounds.

It is rare for me to go to a football match without being subjected to a really tough climb, and this was no exception. Four flights of steep stairs before reaching the top. Once there, I queued for a meat and potato pie, a Twix and a bottle of water (part of the '3 Items for £7' multi-buy deal). The pie was good, but not as good as Kidderminster's.

I then walked up the steps to find my seat.

It was quite a thrill getting my first sight of the inside of the stadium, a vast, glorious expanse that was filling rapidly. As a few of the subs warmed up and I gazed down from over a hundred yards away, I thought about distances between supporters and players.

That was one of the good things about Twitter. It allowed players to communicate directly with fans, something in which Bromley excelled. I loved reading Rob Swaine (who was also busy on Instagram and Facebook), keeping everyone up to date with what was happening and his honest appraisals of matches. Most of the others also joined in, with Moses Emmanuel and Louis Dennis particularly enthusiastic.

Manchester United players were also keen to communicate with their supporters via Twitter. When I'd last looked, a mass outbreak of anticipation for one of the most bum-numbingly dull films of the year had apparently swept the United dressing room.

'Got to say *Revenant* movie looks brilliant,' tweeted an enthusiastic Ashley Young, adding a big thumbs-up emoticon.

Matteo Darmian was also in a hurry to watch it. 'Can't wait to see *Revenant* movie!' he typed. 'Looks amazing!'

Morgan Schneiderlin was relieved that 'at last I can take my girlfriend to a Dicaprio film', pointing out that it had '12 oscarnoms'.

And so it went on. Juan Mata thought *The Revenant* looked great and couldn't wait to watch it. Chris Smalling, displaying an almost telepathic link with the Spanish midfielder, used exactly the same words.

Another who couldn't wait to see it was Bryan Robson. 'How good does *Revenant* movie look?' asked the former Captain Marvel, rhetorically.

Andy (now Andrew) Cole also found himself giddy with anticipation. 'Really looking forward to this movie,' he confided. '12 oscar nominations. Can't wait to see.'

'This *Revenant* movie looks good,' said Memphis Depay, a master of understatement compared to his team-mates.

It looked as though the nearest multiplex to Old Trafford would soon be packed out by Manchester United squad members and ex-players for showings of this apparently unmissable blockbuster. But for now they were running on to the pitch in front of me. Miles in front of me.

I was crammed into a plastic seat a budget airline would have rejected as too much of a tight squeeze. I could just about identify people coming out of the tunnel based on their distinguishing features – Petr Cech with his protective headwear, Arsène Wenger's oversized padded coat, Olivier Giroud's sheer handsomeness.

And just like at the King's Cross riot, all around me smartphones were held high, capturing images of a stadium packed with over 75,000 fans.

The game was played at a furious pace, and mistakes were rare. Whenever United got anywhere near the Arsenal goal in front of me, everyone stood up. If, like me, you weren't used to that, it was impossible to see what was happening. That was how I missed both of United's first-half goals.

Some of the quality on display was way beyond anything I'd ever experienced. I love football, and these were some of the best players in the world. People around me were saying it was the best game of the season. On a technical level I could appreciate what was taking place, but I wasn't enjoying it and didn't really care how it finished.

I thought back to how much I'd enjoyed watching a vastly inferior match twenty-four hours earlier, settled by the kind of goal you'd never see at a place like Old Trafford. But much of that enjoyment was down to the camaraderie. *That* was what made watching Kidderminster against Bromley, a terrible game, such a pleasure. It gave me a sense of belonging. Today, I felt like just another face in a massive crowd.

With five minutes left on the electronic clock it was 3-2 to United and the match was hanging on a knife edge. Looking around the vast, packed stadium, I realized that I wanted to get out early while I still had a chance of getting a tram back to Manchester. So I got out of my seat, climbed down the four sets of stairs and found my way back to the station, along with thousands of others. Perhaps two games in two days had been too much?

The platform was already packed, and I arrived just before they stopped letting people through.

As I stood on the train crossing the Pennines, I couldn't wait to get home. I rang Liz to let her know when I'd be arriving and my feeling of being a little lost was enhanced when I saw that Dad was still in my list of phone contacts. I wondered if I should delete it, but couldn't bring myself to do it. It was too soon.

I couldn't wait to get back to watching Bromley. And for once, I wouldn't be getting a train the next time I saw them; I'd be getting the supporters club coach instead.

The Guiseley Supporters Club coach.

Twenty

The Tuesday after going to Old Trafford, I was celebrating my birthday at a restaurant carefully selected because my son Billy worked there and could get us a 50 per cent discount. The day had already got off to a special start with a personalized email from the Manchester United One Club, hoping that I'd have a great day. Then, just as Billy, Frank, Liz and I were getting stuck into our starters, it got even better. Billy's phone made a buzzing sound, he picked it up, he looked at the screen and said, 'We're one-nil up against Welling.'

This was doubly rewarding. Bromley taking the lead was a thrill. So was Billy referring to Bromley as 'we', thus proving that our children never lose the ability to delight. Perhaps he wasn't quite as unimpressed with his Hayes Lane experience as he'd seemed.

And the same applied to Liz. As soon as Billy announced the news, she picked up her phone and went on to Twitter to find out who'd scored. 'Rohdell Gordon,' she announced, nodding as though that was exactly what she'd suspected. The irony was that I had deliberately left my phone at home as I was determined not to keep checking the score.

During dessert, there was another update. Moses Emmanuel

had added a second, with a penalty. Since Welling hadn't scored for four games, it was unsurprising that we managed to hold out. And for a birthday present, you can't ask for much more than a 2-0 home win against Welling.

On the way home I had a few sneezing fits and wondered if I'd picked up a cold. Things got worse during the week, and by Friday my temperature had crept up and I was coughing violently. I was genuinely concerned. If it didn't get better overnight I was in real danger of missing the trip to Chester on 5 March.

My initial thought was that I'd got the flu, but after consulting Google, I self-diagnosed bronchitis. By Saturday morning I was in no state to do anything but sleep, and had no choice but to miss the game. It was one I'd been looking forward to for two slightly irrational reasons. The first was that it was being played at the Deva Stadium, which is an anagram of the Dave Stadium. Of more interest was that this was probably the first time Bromley had played a fixture where you could park your car in one country (England) and watch the game in another (Wales).

I watched the day unfold on Twitter and it soon became apparent that Dark Fruit's grip on Bromley fans was strengthening (Lloyd, Pete and Manchester Will, the three I would have travelled with had it not been for my bronchitis, had renamed themselves the Dark Fruit Ultras). Bromley were chasing four wins in a row, and I'd discovered a fresh and exciting new way of following the action – a totally biased commentary which, unlike the BBC and Tranmere Player, was biased in favour of Bromley. The commentators, using a laptop app, were Bromley's media manager, Cookie, and the man holding my dream job, James the programme editor. I listened to their live stream on my phone.

Cookie, who reached David Beckham-like levels when it came to overusing the word 'obviously' in his commentary, was, um, obviously a fan. Decisions against us were rubbish, we were unlucky, and the ref was terrible. It was fantastic. When we went a goal down, he sounded like I felt. Distraught. And when Moses or Rob Swaine brought us level (it was unclear whether Moses' effort had crossed the line, although he was later credited with the goal), the relief and excitement were heartfelt.

A draw wasn't a bad result, even though it put an end to the winning run. At least I took a small measure of satisfaction in not losing, as I'd felt a bit hurt when the *Chester Chronicle* had described the fixture as 'the first of two winnable games'. They went on to hit eight past Aldershot in the other one.

My bronchitis, which Liz wrongly insisted was just man flu, was starting to get better by Tuesday, but I wasn't quite up to a trip to Hayes Lane on a freezing wet March night. Luckily, nor were Halifax. Bromley took the three points with a lateish goal from Adam Cunnington, who smashed home Bradley Goldberg's excellent-sounding cross.

It was fitting revenge for those never-to-be-forgotten injury-time goals earlier in the season, as well as for having their ground in a rubbish part of town. Mash's match report was the first time in ages that I'd seen the words 'dominant' and 'swagger' used to describe a Bromley performance.

By the next day, perhaps buoyed by this, I was finally starting to feel better. But even the relief of finding out that I would probably survive couldn't detract from the fact that I'd missed three huge Vanarama National League games which had taken us up to a scarcely believable eleventh place. There was no way I could miss four in a row.

And that was why I found myself heading to Hayes Lane in the Guiseley Supporters Club coach early on the morning of Saturday, 12 March. I'd been getting increasingly bored with getting the train to King's Cross, tube to Victoria and train to Bromley South, so when I saw an opportunity to get from Leeds directly to Hayes Lane, I took it.

I'd contacted Paul, who organized travel to Guiseley's away

games, and he was fine with me coming along. I'd been counting on that: of all the grounds I'd visited watching Bromley, Guiseley had probably given the friendliest welcome. They were like us – a small non-league club that had suddenly found itself dining at the top table and couldn't quite believe what had happened.

Pete, who is exactly the sort of person who would find this kind of thing appealing, joined me. Two Bromley fans in the midst of about forty Yorkshiremen who wanted our afternoon to turn out miserably.

It wasn't long before I felt the first tap on my shoulder.

'Hey Dave, want a beer?'

This was followed by a huge bag of toffee bites being passed around. Not long after that came the wine gums. As everyone got stuck into their sweets, the discussion in the nearby seats was of George, one of their own, who was absent today. It sounded as though they'd banned him, despite his evident popularity. His crime, I soon learned, was bringing a pizza on board their last awayday, to Woking, and eating every one of the ten slices himself.

'He didn't even bloody offer,' said Paul, the man in charge, as though he still couldn't quite believe it.

I was thinking about how brilliant this sharing thing was when I was interrupted by a shout from the back. I looked around and saw a shaven-headed man in his mid-twenties holding up his phone. On its screen was a picture of a young Cilla Black.

'Oi, Dave, who does this remind you of?' he said, grinning.

I soon saw why. Sitting next to him was a red-headed man in his late forties with a haircut that could best be described as a 1960s Cilla Black bob. Apparently it was one of the Braintree coaching staff who had first called him Cilla. If that had been meant as an insult, it certainly hadn't been taken as one. He seemed genuinely proud of the resemblance, and even used a picture of her – with identical hair – on his Twitter profile.

Finding lookalikes for various people on the coach became the new game for the people sitting at the back. Every few minutes the same man would hold up his phone. Unfortunately, when it came to my turn, the picture wasn't of Jeremy Corbyn, as I was expecting. It was Rolf Harris. Eighty-six-year-old Rolf Harris.

The talk soon moved on to football. It seemed that they'd be happy with a draw, although a Bromley win would test the limits of our newfound friendship. If that happened, Pete and I were informed, we would be travelling back in the toilet.

The Guiseley fans were great – just like ours, but with different accents – which made the segregation that had been announced for the game (at the request of the Metropolitan Police, apparently) even more pointless. This had been a theme on the Bromley forum leading up to the game, with Ian, in particular, outraged by it. It was an insult to Guiseley, he wrote. Col agreed. 'Take down the barriers,' he said, channelling his inner revolutionary. Eddie, a fellow old-timer, thought it was 'Unbelievably stupid segregating fans like this that have no history of trouble'.

We stopped off at the Chequers Inn in Bickley for a pre-game drink. This was a pub that had been in the news recently because the landlord claimed it was haunted, citing as evidence the fact that he'd once caught his two-year-old daughter talking to a little boy who didn't exist.

I'm pretty sure that most two-year-olds talk to people who don't exist.

I stood in the bar talking to Cilla, who ran a courier business and possessed the levels of self-assurance you'd expect from someone who was happy to be compared physically to Cilla Black.

Just before we left, I checked the Bromley forum and it seemed that Ian hadn't yet calmed down over the segregation. He was just leaving the Bricklayers Arms, heading for the game, and was still ranting about it, saying that it was a terrible decision. It was hard to disagree. Everyone had got on really well when we visited their ground in November and now they wouldn't even have the chance to renew friendships. The Guiseley fans were puzzled by the whole thing.

We climbed back on to the coach for the short trip to Hayes Lane and it was great being dropped off right outside the ground. Once inside, we had to split up – they went their way, Pete and I went ours.

As this was happening, the teams were being announced on the tannoy. The news that the Bromley fans had been waiting for had finally arrived: Louis Dennis was making his long-awaited return from injury, starting from the bench.

For Guiseley, goalkeeper Steve Drench was absent, possibly traumatized by the prospect of having to put up with Ian's awful northern accent again. I'd been told his replacement was every bit as good, which wasn't what I wanted to hear. The news proved to be accurate as he made a couple of excellent saves early on which were probably the highlights of the opening forty-five minutes. It was a quiet game, with the visitors clearly playing for a draw.

I watched the second half with Col, behind the goal Bromley were attacking. This meant that we were separated from the Guiseley fans – the people I'd travelled down with – by half a dozen security guards and metal barriers.

After Guiseley had hit the bar, which caused much excitement on the other side of the barriers, Bromley made a change that would have had the manager chased off the park six months ago, but now made perfect sense: Moses Emmanuel went off and Bradley Goldberg came on. Both were applauded – something else that would never have happened earlier in the season.

Ten minutes later, it looked like a piece of tactical genius from Smudger. Bradley, all five foot six of him (or five foot seven if you included the man bun), beat a huge defender in the box and glanced one of the best headers I'd seen all season into the top corner.

Few things in life are more pleasurable than standing directly behind the goal when a player you really like scores a classic. In fact, the only thing better is if he does it twice.

And he did. Playing with a freedom he hadn't enjoyed under his dad, Bradley got the ball twenty-five yards out, drifted across the edge of the box and curled an inch-perfect shot right into the same corner. It was 2-0, and even the most pessimistic Bromley supporter could see that the three points were safe.

I wondered how my new mates from Guiseley were feeling about this turn of events, so looked over to where they had been herded. Cilla, Paul and everyone else from the bus were there. But they weren't alone. There were a few familiar faces in their midst. Ian, Pete, Sue, Gary, Garvo and Mash had somehow managed to infiltrate the away end and were standing shoulder to shoulder in solidarity with the Guiseley fans. It was a small but defiant protest against segregation.

It was only later that I found out how they'd managed to get past security. Ian, unbelievably, had managed to fool them by reviving his terrible northern accent, last heard at Guiseley. 'Ahm from t'Leeds,' he had announced – a sentence that has, to the best of my knowledge, never been uttered by any northerner ever. They'd waved him straight through.

Mash had got in when Pete, who was already there due to being able to do a proper Yorkshire accent, had a loud and blatantly staged conversation with him while he was standing by the barrier.

'Oi, Pete,' Mash had shouted, in an indistinguishable accent, trying to catch his attention.

'Come oop 'ere, mate,' said Pete, standing with a group of Guiseley fans, indicating for Mash to join him.

Security let him through.

Garvo, Sue and Gary joined in stealth mode, one at a time. From what I could make out, they hadn't even bothered to put on northern accents. They just said they were from Guiseley.

A sharper security operation would have identified at least Ian and Pete as being impostors since both were wearing Bromley shirts. But they'd somehow got away with it.

Until midway through the second half, that is. Because that was when someone grassed them up. But as three security staff waded into the crowd, the Guiseley fans formed a human barrier, shielding the Bromley Six from view. The men in their orange high-vis jackets scanned the crowd looking for them, then gave up, shrugging helplessly.

It was a stirring act of rebellion. This was the true spirit of non-league. Hayes Lane had become a small pocket of resistance against senseless regulations.

And when some of the younger Bromley fans started chanting anti-Guiseley comments towards the end of the game, they responded by singing 'Your proper fans are over here'.

I looked forward to the trip back to Leeds with these people. As long as they didn't lock me and Pete in the toilet for the next five hours. Luckily, they seemed fine, apart from singing 'It's a long walk home, from Bromley to Guiseley' as we stepped on to the coach.

An hour into the journey, Pete, perhaps spurred on by the Polish lager he'd somehow acquired, decided to treat everyone to a song of his own. 'We hate Gravesend and Northfleet,' he began, referring to a team that went out of existence nearly ten years ago. 'We hate Welling, too. We hate Sutton United, but Guiseley we love you.' Predictably this caused mass confusion, but Pete looked satisfied as he was handed yet another can of the Polish beer. I wasn't sure how the Dark Fruit Ultras would react when they heard about this act of double betrayal.

And with alcohol being passed around freely, conversations began to get increasingly surreal.

'He's going out with some Polish girl,' said someone behind me.

'Where's she from?' asked his mate.

There was a lengthy pause of nearly a minute as he thought about this before finally finding the words he was looking for: 'Poland, I think.'

The rest of the journey passed quickly. Pete and I were presented with enamel Guiseley badges, as well as a couple of supporters club ones. I love badges and was seriously excited by this.

I talked at length to Adam, who was responsible for all the Guiseley social media, and Si, one of their most outgoing and friendly fans. We were all still a bit astonished by the level our teams had found themselves playing at.

As we passed the 'Welcome to Yorkshire' sign, Paul was making his way down the aisle taking bookings for the next away game, at Southport. He was being followed around by Tom, his thirteen-year-old apprentice, an ambitious young man who would be taking over the role one day. For a moment I was almost tempted to sign up for the trip, since Bromley had the day off, but couldn't face another day in Southport. I just hoped Guiseley could stay up so we'd see them again next year.

The day had demonstrated to me why I loved non-league football so much. You probably wouldn't have got many London-based Manchester United fans welcomed aboard the Arsenal coach the other weekend.

When we reached Leeds, Pete and I shook hands with everyone and got off into the cold night air. As the coach pulled away, they were all waving. It had been a memorable day.

I woke up early the next morning, since 6.02 a.m. on a Sunday is apparently the ideal time for the council to start drilling holes in municipal roads. Just under an hour later I was standing outside Sainsbury's waiting for it to open as I couldn't wait to get *The Non-League Paper*.

It was worth the wait. Bromley were named as the form team and Bradley Goldberg had made their team of the week. We'd now gone six games unbeaten. Staring at the table, I couldn't help wondering what would happen if we went through the next six games unbeaten.

The brilliant thing was that leading teams like Cheltenham and Forest Green wouldn't be keeping an eye on middle-of-the-table Bromley. We could sneak into the top five by stealth – the technique used successfully by some of our fans the day before.

It was possible in theory. But to get there, Bromley had a mountain to climb.

And so did me and Liz.

HOME
AND
AWAY

Twenty-one

At the start of the week leading up to the visit to Barrow, I shocked Liz by announcing that I wouldn't be going to Eastleigh on the Tuesday night. The reason being that I couldn't take any more Eastleigh-inflicted pain. Together with Nigel Lugg, they had unfairly knocked us out of the FA Cup, and then clawed back a 2-0 deficit *in front of my children* in the League. Why would I want any more punishment?

Plus, even I could see that it would take a borderline certifiable Bromley fan to make the arduous midweek journey from Yorkshire to Hampshire in the middle of March just to watch a certain defeat.

That didn't stop Pete, though. He left late in the morning and after a nearly four-hour journey wandered aimlessly around Southampton for a few more hours before getting another train to within walking distance of the Silverlake (previously Sparshatts) Stadium.

His efforts were not rewarded. The game was predictably rubbish. I listened to it on BBC Radio Solent, and even their biased commentators admitted that the pitch was just about unplayable: it had so much sand on it that it was like watching beach football.

The opening goal was so ridiculous that one of the commentators was laughing in the background as it went in. Alan Julian's rushed clearance hit Jack Holland, who was standing outside the box, and the ball spun back, in slow motion, past the keeper and over the line.

The second goal was another lucky one for Jai Reason, whose mishit cross had put us out of the Cup. A series of rebounds left the ball bobbling around, and with Rob Swaine getting his boot stuck in the sand (probably a career first), Reason was left with an open goal. He didn't miss.

Eastleigh won 2-0 and our unbeaten streak was over. Of course that hurt. It always does. But this was so expected, so obviously pre-ordained, that the damage to my mental state was minimal.

Pete got a lift back into London, arriving just after midnight, which left him just enough time to get on the one a.m. Megabus which got him back to Leeds around six in the morning.

Around the time Pete was making his way home from the bus station, I was woken by noises coming from the living room. Liz was already up, preparing for the weekend and the non-football highlight of our trip to the Lake District to watch Barrow v. Bromley. We would be mountain climbing. And not just any mountain, either, but the highest one in England, Scafell Pike. All three thousand feet of it.

Unlike me, Liz is not the kind of person to throw a few things together at the last moment. She was stuffing the backpack with everything she felt was necessary for our expedition. Among other things, this included two large bin bags (as makeshift sleeping bags in case one or both of us got injured), three days' worth of food (for the same reason), waterproof clothing, jumpers, protein snacks, water, Panadols, bandages, scissors and an emergency charger. She'd even downloaded a compass app on her phone.

A few days later, as we were about to leave for our football/mountaineering trip, my hopes of a win were raised by a headline on the *North West Evening Mail* website that read 'Virus Strikes Down AFC Barrow Trio Ahead of Bromley Clash'. Disappointingly, it turned out to be some fringe players who wouldn't have been playing anyway. It took me a while to get over this, but once we were on the road in our rented car I started getting excited about the weekend.

Right up until the moment we caught sight of the snow-covered peak of Scafell Pike in the distance. That was when reality set in. It was massive, which shouldn't really have come as a surprise. There was no way I would be able to climb it. My preparation had been limited to climbing a few hills to get into football grounds and going to the gym a couple of times before losing interest. I had to admit that I'd been a bit overambitious in thinking I'd be able to get to the summit of the highest mountain in England, and back.

Liz wasn't overly impressed with me bailing out, so to demonstrate that I really wanted to do some strenuous outdoorsy stuff, I pulled over and began Googling alternative walks. One called The Old Man of Coniston seemed perfect. It would still be a tough way to spend a Sunday as it would mean a four-hour climb, but it promised beautiful views of Lake Coniston and spectacular scenery along the way.

It was a perfect compromise and Liz seemed happy, unlike the residents of Barrow, which was officially the most miserable town in Britain, according to the Office for National Statistics. As we drove down the road into town it didn't seem that grim, apart from the first hill we saw being called Cemetery Hill.

After meeting up with Giles, who had come up from London hoping to see a better game than the last one he attended at Guiseley, we walked to the Furness Building Society Stadium (previously Holker Street Stadium). As we joined the tiny queue to get in, the Vanarama jingle came blasting out of the tannoy – a chirpy singalong number that was irritating but catchy, much like speediej's best-known work.

'Vanarama! Vanarama! Vanarama! They're the ones to call,' it went. 'Vanarama! Vanarama! We're the ones you need to call.'

After it finished, there was a short pause. Then it started up again.

'Vanarama! Vanarama! Vanarama! They're the ones to call. Vanarama! Vanarama! We're the ones you need to call.'

Either the League's sponsors were in attendance or Barrow had limited pre-match entertainment options.

We joined the Bromley contingent behind the goal, most of whom had spent at least six hours getting there. As always, it was brilliant to see so many familiar faces. Only the truly committed travelled to places like this to watch a mid-table non-league match. Some would call them certifiable. I call them soulmates.

Although technically it was the last day of winter, it felt like a gorgeous, sunny spring day, the only dark cloud being the presence of seagulls circling the stadium. To distract myself I looked through the official matchday programme, called *Fly with the Bluebirds*. As usual I went straight to the 'Today's Visitors' page to see what flattering things they had to say about Bromley, and was a bit puzzled to find it written in a strange language – a bit like English but with random words left out. Adam Cunnington 'Has wealth of experience', it said, while Moses Emmanuel signed in 2014 'when did not renew his contract with Dover', and Rob Swaine was 'now in third season with club'. There was a strong suspicion that the editor had run out of space and decided to remove some words to make everything fit.

When the game got under way, I was relatively relaxed. The warm, dry weather had plenty to do with this, as everyone knows that Bromley are useless in cold, wet conditions – winter is traditionally a time for lengthy spells without a win. But when the sun comes out, things usually improve. And a win today would put us in the top ten – and, more importantly, within five points of the play-off spots.

In truth, not much happened in the first half. The highlight came at the break when Rich put up his BROMLEY GEEZERS banner behind the goal Bromley would be attacking. It was great to see it in such an unlikely place – a small unhappy town on the Irish Sea best known for building nuclear submarines.

Seeing it inspired a feeling of nostalgia for the B-R-O song. It hadn't been heard for a month or two and I wondered if it would ever return.

About a quarter of an hour into the second half Bromley's passing game finally paid off, Moses Emmanuel's clever lay-off leaving Adam Cunnington to finish beautifully, before rushing towards the Bromley fans, only to find himself getting his head rubbed by Lloyd.

A few minutes later came what could, potentially, have been the most embarrassing thing I'd ever done at a football match. Moses tried his luck from just inside the box and the ball went a matter of inches wide, making the net ripple. From where I was standing, it looked like a goal. I screamed 'YES!' and charged forward, arms in the air; then I noticed that everyone else was standing around looking bored. I just about managed to put the brakes on and nonchalantly strolled back up the steps, glancing around to see if anyone had noticed. I didn't think they had. Certainly not Liz, who was still in the bar at the far side of the ground – with a Dark Fruit in her hand no doubt.

The action then switched to the other end, Barrow coming close. I felt the anxiety returning. I was quite relaxed when the game had started, but now, with the slenderest of leads and only ten minutes left, I began to fear the worst.

Then Jack Holland got tangled up with substitute Jason Walker, who threw himself dramatically to the floor. Preston's Michael Salisbury (the second referee this season, after Adam Bromley, to share a surname with a former Conference South team) pointed to the spot. The inevitable agony was prolonged when Alan Julian saved Walker's effort, but the Barrow man followed up and headed the ball home to make it 1-1.

And that was how it ended. A bad result, but not a disaster. We were still on track for the play-offs, as long as we won our remaining games and the teams above lost most of theirs.

After the match Liz and I took the short drive to Bowness-on-Windermere, where we'd booked a B&B for a couple of nights. It was a beautiful town which, like Nailsworth, had a pleasantly old-fashioned feel to it. The sort of place that still has a wool shop in the high street, with a lampshade shop nearby, as well as a haberdashery within easy reach.

It would have been enough to fill me with the joys of life, if only Bromley hadn't squandered a comfortable lead hours earlier.

Over breakfast the next morning, after Liz had made sandwiches and emergency sandwiches (just in case), we got talking to Steve, who ran the B&B. When we told him we were going to Coniston, which was a thirty-minute drive, he claimed that there were walks nearby that were just as good. One in particular that he recommended was Orrest Head, which he'd climbed the previous weekend. This was heartening news, as he looked as out of shape as I was, and around the same age.

We decided to trust his local knowledge, especially as the start of the walk was just a couple of minutes away. We left the car at the bottom of the trail, strapped the backpack on to my back and set off up a very steep path. This took us through some woods, with beams of sunlight breaking through the trees. It was another glorious day and we must have covered at least half a mile before our first stop, which came when we got our first glimpse of Lake Windermere, in between some pine trees. The water looked deep blue and perfectly still. My heart soared. This would look really good on Instagram. I took the photo and posted it. It felt like a good start to the day.

A little further up we came across a bench, and sat down. The first thing I did was remove the backpack and put it on the ground as it was starting to feel really heavy. The second thing I did was check Instagram. I had two likes already.

The stops became less frequent after that as we wanted to reach the summit in time for lunch. There would be plenty of opportunities for social media updates once we got there. We soon got into a walking rhythm, although I had to ask Liz to slow down a couple of times. On and on we went. The pathway seemed to be getting steeper and steeper and the backpack heavier and heavier. We seemed to have been walking for ever. I lost all track of time.

And then, just as Liz (who didn't seem to be struggling in the slightest) was explaining her fantasy about a St Bernard bringing her some emergency cans of chilled Dark Fruit (about the only thing that wasn't in the backpack), we saw a sight I had given up on ever seeing.

The summit was just ahead.

I was thankful that I was wearing mountain-climbing boots as they helped me keep my grip while clambering up the last twenty yards or so of the steepest, most treacherous terrain I'd ever encountered. My legs were aching and my breathing laboured. But it was worth it. As I stood atop the rugged peak, surveying the panoramic view of stone cottages dotted around the valleys, the rolling hills and the majestic lake, I got a small insight into how Edmund Hillary must have felt when he reached the top of Everest. I took a selfie that showed me smiling broadly and put it straight up on Twitter, thankful that I could still get a signal so far from civilization.

I was feeling a real sense of accomplishment, having satisfied the primal urge to conquer nature. I sat down on a piece of rock and Googled the climb I'd just done, to take a measure of what I'd achieved.

A few minutes later I was wishing I hadn't bothered.

'Many 3 and 4 year olds must have toiled through the woods to

Orrest Head and claimed their first "summit",' said one website. I didn't like the use of quote marks around the word 'summit'. And that wasn't the only site to diminish my efforts. 'Short walk' and 'lovely gentle climb' were phrases that popped up regularly. There was now an emerging suspicion that we were over-prepared for what appeared to be a stroll up a hill. The emergency sleeping bags, bandages, torches (with spare batteries) and so on might not, strictly speaking, have been necessary.

Feeling a bit deflated, I was suddenly eager to extend the climb into something the internet would be more impressed with. Unfortunately, we hadn't brought a map. Not of Orrest Head, anyway. There was one of Scafell Pike somewhere in the back-pack, but that would be about as useful as everything else in there.

And then Liz had a brilliant idea.

'We should just follow them,' she said, pointing at a group of four men and women who looked like experienced trekkers, com-plete with hiking boots and walking poles. Significantly, they were poring over a map as if discussing where to go.

So when they headed down into the valley, we followed at a safe distance. And when they stopped at a stile, we stopped about a hundred yards behind. Not long after that, they stopped again to look at something. We stopped, and I pretended to tie the laces on my mountain-climbing boots. But it wasn't enough. They'd defi-nitely noticed us and kept glancing behind. When they stopped again, a mile or two further on, and looked in our direction, we had no choice but to overtake them with a cheery 'Good afternoon'.

It wasn't that bad. Liz and I were pretty sure we were heading roughly in the direction we'd come from, so at least we'd get back to the B&B, even if it meant missing out on the longer walk we'd been hoping for.

The only drama came when we sat down for lunch on a fallen

tree, near where some sheep were feeding. A ram broke out from the pack and stared at us in a distinctly unfriendly manner.

'Can rams attack humans?' I asked Liz, trying to keep the panic out of my voice.

They could, she replied, but it was unlikely.

I didn't share her optimism, so got my phone out and started snapping pictures of the animal, just in case my fears were realized. That way, if someone found us, the authorities would be able to piece together what had happened.

But after a while he lost interest and we were left to enjoy our lunch.

Before long we saw the group of walkers we'd been following. As they went past, we decided to wait for a while before continuing our journey. We didn't want them to think we were following them again.

It was surprisingly easy to find our way back into Bowness-on-Windermere. The path we were on took us all the way back to where we started.

Sleep came easily that night, although getting out of bed the next morning was more challenging. My body ached and my legs were stiff. Liz, freakishly, seemed unaffected.

As we drove back to Leeds, my thoughts, predictably, returned to football. I was thinking about how much and how fast things changed. This was illustrated by the road signs we passed. The one directing traffic to Wigan's ground had the new name (DW Stadium) clearly painted over the previous name (the JJB Stadium). It was the same story in Huddersfield, where the sign showed John Smith's Stadium painted over the Alfred McAlpine Stadium.

That night, my mind was firmly on Barrow's Furness Building Society Stadium (previously the Holker Street Stadium) as I waited for the highlights on BT. My main areas of interest were to see if (a) Adam Cunnington's goal was as outstanding as it had

DAVE ROBERTS

seemed at the time, and (b) Barrow's penalty was in any way justified.

It soon became clear that the goal was indeed brilliant and the penalty was, as I'd thought, a terrible decision. But there was also a surprise in store. As the players shook hands and walked off, the commentator said, 'Bromley remain in the top half of the table in their first season at this level.' The picture then cut to a shot of the fans – including me – standing under Rich's hand-painted BROMLEY GEEZERS banner behind the goal, as the voiceover continued, 'Much to the delight of the travelling geezers.'

If speediej was watching – and listening – the hairs on the back of his neck must have been standing on end. As well as those on the back of his mate's neck. I know mine were. It meant that the Bromley Geezers were now known throughout the nation, and I was already looking forward to seeing them again.

It turned out to be a very long time before I next got the chance.

Twenty-two

I had to follow the next three games from my living room. I had
blown my football-watching budget. There was no positive way of
spinning it. The money had gone. The reason I'd only just found
out was that I had avoided checking my bank balance for about a
month.

The only saving grace was that I'd already booked, and paid for,
tickets for the Altrincham game on 9 April. I wasn't too bothered
about missing the fixtures before that: a trip to jinx team Braintree
on Good Friday, when rail works were scheduled, had almost no
appeal, and I'd already accepted that I wouldn't be going to Hayes
Lane to see Bromley play Forest Green and Lincoln, since I was
concentrating on away games.

As I listened to the build-up to the Braintree match, it became
obvious that The Iron (as they like to be known) had all sorts of
problems. They had several players out with flu and a few of the
starting eleven were also suffering from it. Three of the team had
just got back after playing for England C in Ukraine, and both
main strikers were out through injury. The replacement for one of
these had just been introduced to his team-mates, a few minutes
before kick-off.

This was depressing news, and my heart sank. Braintree

were bound to beat us like they always did – twice already this season, both times by a single goal. And this time it would be an even more humiliating defeat, since they were seriously under strength.

I don't want to dwell on the match, because everything about it turned out to be so predictable that there's no need to go into any detail. Suffice to say it was a miserable day for the travelling fans, who not only had to put up with lukewarm tea ('a diabolical liberty' according to Mickey) and half-cooked burgers, but also saw their team manage no shots on target whatsoever. Braintree won by a single goal, 1-0.

There was a Braintree link to the next game, at home to Forest Green Rovers on 28 March. It was the home town of referee Rob Whitton, who had endeared himself to me by sending off the Dover number 23 over the Christmas break. The game was being covered by BBC Radio Gloucestershire. 'Grounds like this,' said the hopelessly biased commentator in his preview, 'are places Rovers should win.'

The match got off to the worst possible start. As I was carrying a bowl of Waitrose chicken soup from the microwave to the dining table, it burned my fingers, causing me to drop it. At the same time as the bowl hit the floor and shattered, sending pieces of chicken, peas, potato and diced carrot all over the floor, the excited commentator was describing a very early goal by Forest Green's Kurtis Guthrie. He was not only describing it, he was also laughing about it. Apparently, it came from a Brett Williams shot that was 'bound for the corner flag' before smashing into Guthrie's leg and deflecting past a wrong-footed Alan Julian.

There are few things more likely to fill you with murderous rage than someone laughing at your misfortune when you're going through not just one disaster but two at the same time.

At least Jon Parkin, Forest Green's XXXXL substitute striker, provided some light relief for me as I mopped the floor. He was banned from his own dugout, which already had one of the other subs sitting on the ground 'like a naughty schoolboy', due to lack of space.

As the game drifted into first-half injury time, I absolutely knew Forest Green were going to score. And, of course, they did. It was in the fifth minute – despite the fact that only three had been added on – that Guthrie (who had blood on his shirt and therefore shouldn't have been on the pitch) added a second. At least this one sounded deliberate.

Pierre-Joseph Dubois, who had recently returned from injury, pulled one back on the hour, but with just minutes left on the clock Paul Rodgers was sent off, which perfectly set up Forest Green to snatch a goal in injury time.

Only it wasn't Forest Green that scored, it was Bromley. A Jack Holland header earned an incredible 2-2 draw against the second-best team in the Vanarama National League. Suddenly, life was full of hope again, and it took every fibre of self-control not to sell one of our possessions to fund a trip to Hayes Lane for the upcoming Lincoln game.

But I stuck to my original plan and followed the match on Twitter.

There was bad news before the game had even started. Louis Dennis, who had only just returned from injury, had hurt himself in the warm-up and was replaced by Bradley Goldberg. Fascinatingly, Bradley himself had been injured in the warm-up against Boreham Wood earlier in the season, and been replaced by Paul Rodgers. Who was now suspended.

The slight change in personnel didn't seem to affect Bromley who, judging by the Twitter feed, had three or four good chances before the first GOOOOAAAAL!!!!!!! This came from a Goldberg cross that was headed home by Adam Cunnington. If the score stayed like this, at the end of the game we would have the statistically interesting record of having won seventeen and lost seventeen, as well as scoring sixty-four and conceding sixty-four.

This glorious opportunity was squandered by Bradley Goldberg when he scored what sounded like an exceptional GOOOOAAAAL!!!!!!!, rounding the keeper after being put through by Cunnington.

It was a lead Bromley clung on to, largely thanks to Alan Julian, who seemed to be having a typically brilliant game. It was a huge relief when the tweet I was waiting for finally appeared on screen:

> FT. Final score here at Hayes Lane is Bromley 2
> Lincoln City 0.

We had done the double over Lincoln City. This was a thought I was barely able to process. How had it come to this? The fact that we were even *playing* Lincoln City in the League was bizarre enough, but beating them? Twice?

To complete my joy, we were now officially safe from relegation. I felt a huge sense of relief, as if a Jon Parkin-sized weight had been lifted from my shoulders. Even though we had technically been well clear of the bottom four for a while, there had still been a nagging worry in the back of my mind.

I had been impressed with the regularity of Twitter updates. This was something Bromley usually did well and it made me glad I wasn't a Sleaford Town fan. Their official Twitter updates for the afternoon had come to a sudden halt at 4.08 with the words 'Goal for Boston. Through ball from the midfield and the number 10 slots past McGann. 3-1.' And that was it. An hour later, after the final whistle, the mystery was finally cleared up with an apologetic follow-up. 'Sorry for break in tweets,' it said. 'I came on as a sub for Millard. Other subs were Anderson for Millington and Hollingsworth for Wright.' It seemed that Harrison Allen, one of the Sleaford subs, had volunteered to fill in for the absent social media manager.

But I wouldn't have to rely on Twitter again this season. Because I'd had an idea which meant I would be going to all four remaining games after all – I'd use the credit card, which I'd got for emergencies. Because if this wasn't an emergency, what was?

I got straight on to the Trainline website and booked tickets for Torquay (home, 16 April), Gateshead (away, 23 April) and Aldershot (home, 30 April), which Liz was coming to since it was the last game of the season. When I added cash advances for ground entry, programmes and miscellaneous foodstuffs, it took my credit card balance from zero to minus £327.

But that didn't matter. Not only would I be going to Altrincham, I'd also be going to all three games after that. I was proud of Bromley's recent form, even though I'd had to follow the games from a distance, and was pleased to see that Smudger had been given a two-year contract.

As Liz and I walked to Leeds station for my first Bromley game in nearly three weeks, I could feel the excitement building. Not just for the football – that was hours away – but for the new-look TransPennine Express. A week ago, the *Manchester Evening News* had carried a story about the massive improvements that were already under way. There was a long list that covered everything from fresh coffee and Manchester beer to cleaner carriages and faster trains.

A revolution was afoot, they said. A rail revolution.

It sounded too good to be true. Could the railway operator with one of the worst reputations in Britain change that dramatically? I'd seen it happen to my football team, so I knew it was possible. Then I noticed the date above the article: 1 April. Was this a cruel April Fool's prank? There had already been one train-related hoax on the same day, the North Yorkshire Moors Railway claiming it had created a carriage dedicated just to dogs.

But as we stood on the platform and the TransPennine Express pulled in, it was clear that something really had changed. Specifically, there was a brand-new logo painted along the side. Everything else was the same: standing room only, suitcases blocking the doors, rubbish on the floor and a trolley being bumped past frustrated travellers as a man in corporate uniform tried to flog them overpriced tea and crisps.

It was a relief to get to Manchester and board the tram to Altrincham. The original plan had been to get off at Timperley, to see a statue of Frank Sidebottom that Pete had tipped me off about. Frank was one of my musical heroes of the 1990s, a man in a 1950s suit who had a giant fibreglass head and sang songs, often about Timperley, in a high-pitched nasal twang. The statue had been made (in the Czech Republic) following the death of Chris Sievey, the man inside the huge head, who surely would have been delighted that TripAdvisor had it as number one of three attractions in Timperley. Since Liz and I were staying with our friends Andy and Kate who lived nearby, we decided to visit the next day instead, when we'd be able to spend more time with Frank.

After lunch in the outdoor market near the Altrincham tram station, we made our way to the ground. On the way we got talking to an Altrincham fan. He was around twenty and had a red and white scarf wrapped around his neck and a plastic carrier bag by his side. (These bags used to be free. By April they were 10p, which was symptomatic of the escalating cost of being a non-league football fan in 2016.) He was a big, friendly, cheerful young man who already had the ingrained pessimism of a seasoned veteran ('you'll win today, we've been rubbish'; 'we're definitely going down'). I instinctively knew that nothing much about him would change over the next seventy or so years.

Like his Cheltenham counterpart, our new friend showed us to where the away fans would be gathered before wearily shuffling off towards his own entrance.

Once inside the J. Davidson Stadium, which had a pleasantly

old-fashioned feel to it, I picked up a *Robins Review*, the official matchday programme. I was a bit wary about only buying one since rain was forecast for later in the afternoon, and I found myself wishing I'd brought a plastic carrier bag to keep it dry.

The programme touched upon the weather by mentioning the awful conditions the televised Hayes Lane game was played in back in November, saying, 'Let's hope this afternoon will be a shade drier!' But anyone wishing to learn about my home town from the *Robins Review* would have been disappointed. 'I fear there is little I can tell you about Bromley,' it read. 'Other than it takes 16 minutes to get there by train from Victoria.' This was accompanied by a picture of a Wetherspoon pub opposite Bromley South station.

When I saw Rockin Robin, the Altrincham mascot, walking past, I did something I'd managed to resist all season. I rushed down and had my photo taken with him. I had to. Rockin Robin was something of a local celebrity, having been involved in the switching on of the Altrincham Christmas lights, together with Elsa, Anna, Sven and Olaf from Frozen. I wondered what he was thinking as I draped my arm around him. And what sort of person dresses up as a giant bird on a Saturday afternoon anyway? It would be another week before these questions were answered . . .

When the players came out to warm up, I felt slightly alarmed – a natural reaction when failing to recognize all but one of the subs. The reserve goalkeeper looked about sixteen. I later found out that was because he was in fact sixteen.

Despite our minor injury crisis (no Chorley, Cunnington, Dennis, May or Wall), the feeling was that this was a game we should win. Altrincham were third from bottom and hadn't won for six games, while we were fresh off a scarcely believable draw with Forest Green and a brilliant win against Lincoln. Plus, we were in all yellow, which was generally lucky.

The home team, in purple shirts, probably had the better start and Sean Francis made a crucial last-ditch tackle to prevent the concession of an early goal. Bromley looked dangerous in patches but the lack of a big man up front was definitely working against us.

It was a game that had 0-0 written all over it, even with only about half an hour gone. Frustration was building among the away fans. There was only one thing for it. It had been a long time coming – many weeks since it had last been heard. And when it finally arrived, it felt like a giant release.

I think it was Rich who sang the first 'B-R-O', and after that almost everyone (apart from Jim from the club shop and his friend John, who both hated it) joined in, even Liz: 'B-R-O, B-R-O, B-R-O-M-L-E-Y, WITH A G-DOUBLE E-Z-E-R-S, BROMLEY GEEZERS ARE THE BEST!' On and on it went, over and over again. It was sung at least twenty times before the geezers seemed too exhausted to carry on. I know I was.

That was when one of the most magical moments of the season happened. The silence was broken by James, who I later found out was once in the world-famous Trinity Boys Choir, bursting into a soaring falsetto version of the 'Bromley Geezers' song. He'd slowed it down to about half its usual pace and his tone was pure and his intonation perfect. And when Mash (formerly of St Olave's Choir) gleefully joined in for the second rendition, with real depth of feeling, it was like listening to the voices of angels. Angels singing about Bromley Geezers being the best. It really was beautiful and I felt tears in my eyes. Tears of laughter. As far as songs sung at football matches was concerned, this was not entirely normal.

Then everyone else joined in again.

I'm not sure if it was some kind of sign, but at that point the heavens opened. As the rain pelted down, Mickey reached into a bag and produced a bunch of Unison-branded plastic ponchos, which he handed out, much to the delight of the rain-soaked fans who were even given a choice between purple and green.

A few minutes later I looked around, taking stock. Here I was, standing on an exposed piece of concrete somewhere in Cheshire, singing a terrible song in a high voice, alongside my wife and seventy-one borderline certifiable southerners wearing green and purple ponchos. In the pouring rain. Watching a dire game of football.

It's the simple pleasures that make life worth living.

Meanwhile, the game, which had been petering out from the moment it started, was showing no signs of improvement. A measure of the competence on show at Moss Lane came when the fourth official (David McNamara of Preston) was clearly struggling to work the electronic subs board, and the Altrincham kit man had to show him how to do it.

Fifteen minutes later, Jake Moult (number 4), the home captain, hobbled towards the tunnel having seemingly twisted his ankle. Mr McNamara held the board up, which notified the crowd that it was Ryan Crowther (number 19) coming off. Programmes can get ruined by this kind of misinformation, as it leads to crossing out the wrong names.

But it was typical of the whole game. Nothing was working the way it should. Shots were hit straight at goalkeepers or went wide, ball control was almost non-existent and passing was terrible.

When Steven Rushton (Staffordshire) mercifully blew his whistle to end a game almost completely devoid of quality, I felt both miserable and relieved. That morning I'd worked out that a draw would mean we could neither finish in the play-off places nor the relegation zone (which had already been established).

As we were leaving the Carol Nash and Family Terrace, I asked James what had prompted his choral reworking of the speediej classic. 'It just felt right,' he explained. I understood. His version of the song was still running through my head as I dropped off to sleep that night, at Andy and Kate's house just outside Macclesfield.

After breakfast on Sunday morning it was time for the pilgrimage to Frank Sidebottom's statue. We had picked the worst day possible to do it. The Manchester Marathon was on, but in spite of that our host Andy gamely volunteered to drive us to Timperley, continually coming up against roads closed, diversions and traffic at a standstill. When we arrived, he parked and we walked up to Stockport Road, where the highest-rated tourist attraction in Timperley could be found. We saw it as soon as we got there, right across from where we were standing. The only problem was, we couldn't get to it. The road was cordoned off because of the marathon. Which meant we could only admire it from afar – at least until a gap appeared between two groups of runners and we ducked under the rope and dashed across. The statue was smaller than I'd expected, but still a good size to pose alongside. A quick look around confirmed there were no obvious threats to its standing as the town's leading attraction.

Since we had a few hours before we had to get the train back, Liz and I decided to hang around and watch the marathon, shouting encouragement at the runners, even though we had no idea who they were. This was a very British thing to do. Alongside us, three Frank Sidebottoms in full Frank outfits were high-fiving the passing athletes, many of whom looked quite puzzled. A lot of them were in fancy dress, including, just like in every other marathon, a burly man with a beard dressed as a ballerina in a pink tutu. There was also a really convincing Gary Barlow lookalike, whom I told Liz about when she returned from getting a coffee from Costa.

'Are you sure he was a lookalike?'

'What do you mean?'

'Well, he comes from round here, doesn't he. Gary Barlow, I mean.'

My palm met my face at this revelation. It was possible I'd been a few feet away from Gary Barlow and not taken a photo. Hopefully it was just a lookalike – maybe one who'd come up from Lincoln for the day.

We stayed longer than we'd planned, getting caught up in the atmosphere. It was an unexpectedly brilliant way to spend a Sunday morning.

As I stood against the door on the TransPennine Express back to Leeds (Liz had somehow managed to find a seat), I thought about how exciting the last few games of the season were going to be, despite the previous day's uninspiring performance. We were stuck in a four-way fight with Macclesfield, Lincoln and Barrow for a top ten finish. And to add to the excitement, the next game was at home to Torquay, a fixture that brought back the most thrilling football memories it was possible to have.

Although if I'd known about the assault by a gang of six- and seven-year-olds that was awaiting me at Hayes Lane, I might well have stayed at home.

HOME
AND
AWAY

Twenty-three

I'd only been in the ground for fifteen minutes and had already lost count of the number of times I'd been punched in the belly by small children.

But that's the sort of thing you have to get used to when you're dressed as Ronin the Raven, Bromley's mascot.

It was Lloyd's fault. He'd alerted me to a tweet that had gone out for someone to step into the costume after the late withdrawal of the regular Ronin, and I'd jumped at the chance of representing Bromley in an official capacity, even though the hours weren't strictly to my liking: Cookie, the club's media manager and part-time commentator, wanted me at the ground by 1.30 p.m. at the latest which meant I had to eat my sandwiches on the way to Hayes Lane. The first thing I did was go online and visit a few mascot forums for tips.

As soon as I arrived, I went to the club office, a Portakabin situated between the turnstiles and the pitch, where Cookie helped me into the costume. It's a far more elaborate process than you'd imagine. A pair of footless white tights went over my jeans, followed by a pair of baggy Stanley Matthews-style shorts. I then slipped into some massive boots, which were almost impossible to walk in.

The body cage, strapped around my chest, was next, followed by an outsized Bromley shirt with the biggest Bromley badge I'd ever seen sewn on to the front. Once this was all in place, it was time for the head, which featured a massive black beak and big brown eyes. Attached to the interior was a baseball cap with a chinstrap which kept everything in place. Visibility from inside Ronin's head was poor. It was like looking at the world through a dark net curtain, and I could only see what was directly in front of me.

I waddled out to my position by the turnstiles, where my task was to wave and give high-fives to anyone who was interested. This went well for a while and I was quite enjoying myself.

But when one kid punched me in the belly and ran away giggling, others saw the entertainment value in this and followed suit. I started to panic. I didn't really fancy spending the next hour and a half getting assaulted by under-tens. I resisted the temptation to swat them with my giant wing – remaining professional at all times was a big thing in the mascot community – and, luckily, they soon lost interest.

By this stage I was beginning to feel the heat. Literally. What no one tells you is that it is hot inside these costumes. Really, really hot. I had to hurriedly invent a ventilation system by tilting the raven's head back slightly to allow fresh air in. And that wasn't the only downside I was discovering about mascot life. You don't realize how much you take for granted – when dressed as a mascot it's impossible to reach into your pocket for your phone, check your email, look at your watch or have a drink of water.

Despite the discomfort, there was real pride in wearing the badge, even though I wore it most of the time anyway, on replica shirts, T-shirts and polo shirts. But it wasn't long before the novelty began to wear off. Standing there giving high-fives felt a bit limited and time seemed to pass slowly.

That was when I remembered another tip: 'character

development', said an American website I had consulted, 'will provide motivation for the performer to create a unique persona'. I took the advice to heart, and introduced the 'Ronin Hop'. Unsurprisingly, this involved hopping on one foot then the other. To be honest, I felt really proud of this, especially when I saw a kid pointing and laughing. This was brilliant. All you had to do was hop and kids thought it was the funniest thing they'd ever seen.

Not so easily amused was the elderly Torquay fan who came up uncomfortably close to me and tried to peer inside my head. He was staring straight into my, or rather Ronin's, eyes.

'Why are you a raven?' he asked.

He would have heard a muffled voice shouting from inside: 'Bromley's badge.'

'What's that?'

'Ravens. They're on Bromley's badge.'

'Yes, I know that, but why?'

How was I meant to know? I was only a mascot. I tried charming him with a comedic Ronin mascot shrug, but it fell flat.

'You really should know that,' he said disapprovingly as he walked away.

The only positive thing to come from the exchange was the realization that the Torquay coach had arrived, judging by the steady stream of over-seventies in gold and blue scarves who followed him into the ground. I had lost all track of time, but this meant that kick-off couldn't be far away.

Most of the other Torquay fans had no interest in me. They were too busy complaining about the lack of programmes, which had sold out before they arrived. I could understand their frustration. It happened to me at Dover and I still hadn't come to terms with it.

One of the Bromley fans I vaguely recognized was next to approach me.

'Can my boy get a picture with you?'

'Of course. You don't have the time, do you, mate?'

He looked at his phone, as though this was a perfectly normal request to get from a raven.

'Two twenty-five.'

I felt invigorated by this. Only half an hour to go before I could get out of this sweltering costume. I was so relieved that I didn't even mind when a couple of hipsters, one so tall I could only see the bottom of his beard, wanted an ironic picture taken with Ronin the Raven. I suspected they were only there because Dulwich Hamlet didn't have an official mascot, so they'd had to make the short trip to Hayes Lane for their irony fix.

By now the crowd was pouring in and I was busy high-, mid- and low-fiving everyone, including the people I usually watched games with. I heard the teams being announced over the tannoy – another sign that my shift was just about over. I almost burst into a hop when I heard that Adam Cunnington was back. This would really help the balance of the side.

But as I made my way back to the office to meet up with Cookie, it was my own balance I was worrying about. Ronin's boots were not made for walking. They were huge, and didn't fit me properly, which meant movement was slow and ponderous, with an ever-present danger of toppling over. And if I did, what would happen? Would I just have to lie there hoping that someone would come along and pick me up?

Luckily, I got to the office safely, but felt a surge of panic when I found it locked, with Cookie nowhere to be seen. I leaned against the rail trying to stay in character, giving a few high-fives to latecomers.

Then a huge roar told me that the teams were running out. Not wanting to miss any of the action, I waddled up to the fence to watch the warm-ups. Not that I could see much through the mesh behind Ronin's eyes; I could just about make out Alan Julian catching the ball and rolling it out again.

I wished I could remove the head, but I couldn't, despite the sauna-like conditions. The first rule of mascot club is that you must never, ever do that in public. Kids don't want to see that there's a human inside the costume.

Instead, I rotated myself to face the goal Bromley were attacking; but I couldn't see that far due to the restricted vision. What I did see, however, was a glorious sight – Cookie scurrying towards me, arms waving apologetically.

He helped me into the office where I got out of the costume. The first thing I did was gulp down almost half a bottle of chilled water and check my emails before heading for the door to go and watch Bromley. My work was done.

Only it wasn't.

'Can you meet me here about five minutes before half-time?' said Cookie. 'You've got a presentation on the pitch, then you're finished.'

On the pitch? In an official capacity? This was brilliant!

I was still full of excitement when Torquay took the lead through a header by captain Angus MacDonald, direct from a corner. It was demoralizing, but I didn't feel as crushed as I had earlier in the season when Bromley conceded a goal. I think the fact that we couldn't possibly be relegated was at least partially responsible for this.

I was almost able to feel relaxed while watching a Bromley game in the Vanarama National League. Even when Lee Minshull, who had been playing well recently, went off injured it didn't feel like the disaster it would have been a few months ago. Bromley were losing to a team they'd beaten 7-3 in September and had lost one of their key players, and I wasn't filled with rage and gloom.

With five minutes to go in the first half, traditionally a time of danger for Bromley, I was once again being helped into the Ronin costume. Then, just after the whistle blew with, surprisingly, no change to the scoreline, it was time for my big moment. I wished the BT cameras could have been there as Cookie led me past the grandstand, through the gate and on to the pitch. A handful of people were even applauding. It was a moment I'd dreamed about my entire life, although in those dreams I walked out in full Bromley kit, not dressed as a giant bird holding hands with a thirty-year-old man.

I was told where to stand, but not what to do. So when the day's VIP stood beside me as a cheque was presented, I placed a wing lightly on his shoulder. Having looked at pictures of other mascots since, this seems to have been in keeping with mascot protocol.

Then came another presentation when half a dozen small kids arrived with one of their teachers. She lined them up then ordered everyone to jump around for the photo. I wasn't sure she was including me in this, but since she sounded pretty terrifying, I obeyed. Besides, it was one last chance to pull out the Ronin Hop.

After I'd lingered on the pitch a little too long, soaking up the glory, Cookie led me back to the office, where I removed the raven costume for the last time. I was going to miss it.

I joined a bunch of regulars behind the goal for the second half, hoping that no one had found out about me being Ronin. It was a bit of an embarrassing thing for a grown man to do and I felt that I'd be in for a bit of stick if anyone knew.

'It was you inside the mascot costume, wasn't it?' said Garvo.

'How do you know?'

He pointed out that my hair was completely flattened, plastered down with sweat, and my face was bright red. Plus, someone had seen me putting the costume on. I had to come clean. Surprisingly, after a few questions (the main one being 'But *why?*') they let the matter drop.

On the pitch the second half got off to a typical Bromley start when Ali Fuseini talked himself into getting a red card, but by that stage most people had lost interest. It was another terrible game. The biggest talking point came from Col, who complained that he'd had to wait twenty minutes for chips at half-time.

'But were the chips any good?' asked someone.

'No, mate, they were cold,' said a disgruntled Col.

While this was still sinking in, Torquay added a second. A superb curling free kick over the wall was too good even for Alan Julian. Again, I wasn't too upset. I wanted Torquay to stay up, as our 7-3 win would be even more impressive if it was against a side that wasn't relegated. Not only that, but it was looking increasingly likely that Liz and I would be staying in the UK – she'd had several interviews, while I'd got work writing about cat food – and we really fancied a trip to the English Riviera next season.

Predictably, all the noise was coming from the visiting fans, one of whom probably no longer cared why the Bromley mascot was a raven. 'We are staying up, we are staying up!' they sang.

After the game, which finished 2-0, I visited the Torquay forum. I don't usually go to forums of teams who beat us as the gloating is too painful, but I made an exception this time on the off chance that someone had words of praise for the Bromley mascot and his innovative hopping. No one did.

The following Saturday I was on my way to Gateshead and looking forward to seeing our last away game of the season – without Liz, who'd now had enough of these trips. There promised to be a huge turnout of Bromley Geezers. Mash had arranged a coach, while several people were flying to Newcastle from Gatwick. Others were driving, and quite a few, like me, were going by train.

The train, unfortunately, was the TransPennine Express. Which meant that it was so packed that passengers at Durham weren't able to get on board and were left on the platform, where they could admire the new logo on the side of the carriage. There was no way of knowing if the exciting new refreshment options were on board since a trolley couldn't possibly have found a way down the packed aisle.

It was a relief to get to Newcastle, where I met up with Harry Pearson, author of my joint favourite football book *The Far Corner*. I'd been hoping to persuade him to come and watch Bromley, but he had other priorities. The Northern League season was reaching its climax and Benfield, his team, needed at least a draw to be sure of safety.

After a city-centre lunch, he took me to The Back Page, a shop I'd always wanted to visit. It was packed with football programmes, memorabilia, T-shirts and books. Obviously the first thing I did was see if they had either of my books, *The Bromley Boys* and *32 Programmes*. Unbelievably they had both, which felt really good. Until Mike, the owner, told me that they stocked every football book published.

A short while later, after Harry had put me on the Metro, I was climbing up the hill to the away end at Gateshead International Stadium. Once inside it was obvious to me that it was the perfect stadium. For athletics. For football it was clearly rubbish. The pitch, right in the middle of the running track, was miles away.

At least the fans who had come by coach had arrived. They were eagerly awaiting a new set of Bromley fans, a group of about a dozen drunken Dutchmen, in town for the Sunderland v. Arsenal game the following day, who had been acquired in a Gateshead pub and kitted out with Bromley shirts. They were nowhere to be seen though.

And neither was Moses Emmanuel, who'd just had a season-ending hernia operation. News of his sidelining had coincided with news of a new job for his former boss Mark Goldberg, who had been appointed manager at freshly relegated Welling. Six months ago, the absence of these two would have caused untold misery at Hayes Lane. Having to start a game without September's

Manager of the Month and Player of the Month would have been unimaginable. Now it barely raised an eyebrow.

The game was borderline unwatchable. It was as if two pub teams had won a competition to play each other at an international stadium.

After ten minutes, Gateshead were a goal up. By the twenty-fifth minute, it was two. The travelling fans tried everything they knew to lift their team. There was a reprise of the falsetto version of the 'Bromley Geezers' song. A deep baritone male voice choir version of the 'Bromley Geezers' song. And a version of the 'Bromley Geezers' song seemingly influenced by the 1970s glam rock movement. These efforts led to no visible lifting of the team, and Mash was reduced to calling for an all-out defensive effort, imploring Bromley to 'Protect the two-nil defeat!' The players must have been listening because there were no further goals before the break.

At half-time, Mickey spotted the Dutchmen. It turned out that through a blend of alcohol and confusion (both teams normally played in white shirts and black shorts), they had ended up in the midst of hundreds of Gateshead supporters in the stand opposite. We found out afterwards that when they'd spotted the people they'd been drinking with earlier and finally realized they were in the wrong place, security staff wouldn't let them switch to the away end.

I felt sorry for them. Not only were they being deprived of the company of the people who had persuaded them to come to the match, they were also being forced to watch a truly awful game. This was not the total football of fellow Dutchman Rinus Michels, which they would have seen Bromley play earlier in the season. It was more like total rubbish.

The second half was as uninspiring as the first – until something happened that belonged in another, much better game. A lovely ball from someone called Higgs found Adam Coombes just outside the area and he rounded the keeper to finish confidently.

Of course, this brief burst of hope was soon snuffed out when the Heed (as Gateshead were known) added a third. It was well taken, true, but it was also predictable since Bromley had conceded more away goals in 2015/16 than anyone in the Vanarama National League. And thanks to my policy of concentrating on away games, I had witnessed most of them.

After Mickey pleaded with referee Tom Nield of Holmfirth several times to end the game, he finally blew his whistle.

I stood around afterwards, talking to a few people as they were boarding the coach, and couldn't help being impressed with Mash for organizing it. When he'd put on the coach to Southport a rumour had gone round that it had ended up losing £400, a sum he'd made up out of his own pocket. Which was a very non-league thing to do. I found out later that this Gateshead coach had also lost money, and this time someone else stepped in to plug the shortfall by donating £300. Club captain Rob Swaine. Again, a very non-league thing to do.

It was with mixed feelings that I made my way home from Newcastle on the crowded train. It had been a long season, and I was definitely feeling the effects of all the travelling and the stress of worrying about promotion and/or relegation. But I would definitely miss the closeness and camaraderie that had developed since my first away day in Grimsby back in August.

There was just one game left before the summer break, at home to Aldershot. To most, this would be a meaningless end-of-season affair between two very ordinary mid-table sides with nothing to play for.

To me, it was the most important game of the season. Yet again.

HOME
AND
AWAY

Twenty-four

The entire 2015/16 campaign hinged on Aldershot's visit to Hayes Lane. It all came down to this. Win, and we would more than likely finish in the top half of the Vanarama National League – a huge and unexpected success. Lose, and we'd end up with the disappointment of finishing in the bottom half of the table. How would the players react to the pressure of this? Would they even be aware of it?

Bromley were on the verge of minor glory, and on the 13.05 to King's Cross I was unable to hide my excitement. And Liz was unable to hide hers.

'So this is definitely the last game of the season?' she said, as though she'd just been told she'd won the lottery.

I promised it was. There wouldn't even be a Supporters v. Staff match, since Ian, who was supposed to be organizing it, had broken his leg in a five-a-side game.

Liz had agreed to come along for two reasons: we'd be going to the pub before the game, and the Ravens Bar after it. The pub was not far from the ground and was where most of the supporters congregated a couple of hours before kick-off.

Thanks to the Vanarama National League's unexplained decision to start all games at 5.30 p.m., we got there just after four. As we went in, I saw Sue sitting up at the bar. This was brilliant. She'd made it, which meant she was the only one, as far as I knew, to see every match of the season. And I mean every match. Friendlies against Sevenoaks Town and VCD Athletic? Sue was there. A meaningless Tuesday night Kent Senior Cup tie at Dover? Sue was there. The game at Whitstable that was called off at the last minute? Sue was there, too. As well as all forty-eight League and Cup games, at home and at grounds the length of the country, from Torquay to Barrow.

It would be fair to say that anticipation for today's game with Aldershot was fairly low key. Unbelievably, nobody was discussing the importance of three points for guaranteeing a finish in the top half of the table (as long as champions Cheltenham beat Lincoln at home). There was a real end-of-term feeling in the pub and, after three awful games on the trot, most seemed to be looking forward to the final whistle.

When we got to the ground and found out that the man who'd be blowing it was Adam Hopkins (Plymouth), I knew we were in for yet more disappointment. We'd never won a Vanarama National League game with him in charge – and that included the hopelessly unjust 2-1 defeat at Forest Green, and the 1-1 draw at Aldershot, today's opponents.

There was nothing unusual about the opening fifteen minutes of the last game of the season. Bromley's patched-together team was useless, conceding an embarrassingly easy goal and seemingly bereft of ideas. The big shock came after that, when Ali Fuseini hit a half volley from nearly thirty yards out which rocketed into the top corner, via the post. I was right behind the goal, obviously, and was amazed at how much it swerved and dipped. Suddenly, at 1-1 there was fresh hope for that all-important top-half-of-the-table finish.

This hope faded slowly and painfully over the next seventy-five minutes. The sole hint of excitement in that time came soon after the interval when Fuseini tried another long-range effort, which was our only shot on target for the whole of the second half. After that, a terrible attempted clearance by Rob Swaine led to a comical Sean Francis own goal, making it 2-1, and an equally bad attempted clearance by Alan Julian led to the unmarked Charlie Parker nodding home a third.

By then I was beyond caring, as was everyone else.

'If only I could find a wife,' said Mash, staring at the shambles taking place in front of him, 'you lot would never see me again.'

As it became obvious that Bromley weren't going to climb into the top half of the table, I once again managed to find comfort in an obscure statistic. 'At least we finished top of all the promoted sides,' I said to Liz, who was gazing longingly at the bar.

'That's nice,' she said.

It finished 3-1. The season had not ended in glory. The last four games had been virtually unwatchable. We'd won just one of the last nine. Moses Emmanuel hadn't scored, apart from a couple of penalties, all year.

Aldershot fans were doing a celebratory conga, which was slightly out of proportion to their team's achievement. A few home fans, sensing the chance to salvage something from an unexceptional day, tried to join them, but weren't allowed. Another victory for unnecessary segregation.

It was then that we were treated to the moving spectacle of Bromley players coming over to the end where we were gathered and applauding the fans, as we applauded them. Meanwhile, thirty yards to the left, the Aldershot players were also applauding their fans, who were returning the gesture. Everyone in the entire ground was clapping enthusiastically. It was, by far, the highlight of the day.

After that no one was in any hurry to leave. Liz disappeared into the bar with Garvo and Stu, but I preferred to stand and watch the early-evening sun setting over Hayes Lane. It would always be Hayes Lane to me, whatever short-term name the stadium was given.

Mash, Sue and young Mikey (Col and Emma's son) had climbed on to the pitch and were standing by a corner flag in deep conversation. Graeme, Heather and Donna stood by the side of the pitch, where Mark was talking to Col, Emma, Pete and Lloyd. Dozens of others were scattered around the ground. People whose names I didn't know but with whom I had stood on terraces up and down the country were drifting around, unwilling to end the season just yet.

It wouldn't just be the football I'd miss over the summer. It'd also be these fans. As Mickey put it, 'It's spending time with genuine nice people that's rewarding. No agendas. No pecking order. Just a glorious collection of rogues!'

I walked around from group to group, taking photos of some of the men and women who had made the season so memorable; and David, a photographer friend who had been there to cover the match, took a picture of me leaning against one of the barriers behind the goal, promising to send it later.

Both Liz and I were reluctant to leave the ground, but the time came when we had to catch the last train back to Leeds. When we got to King's Cross, with half an hour to spare I went into Waitrose for an egg roll, a packet of plain crisps and an apple. Which, for most, will not be the highlight of this book. Nor will the fact that I then went to WHSmith and got a notepad and pen, which I put in the Waitrose bag, together with the Bromley programme which had been sticking precariously out of my pocket.

The significance of all this didn't hit me until I caught sight of my reflection in the Leon Café window. Not only was I wearing a Bromley scarf, I was also clutching a plastic carrier bag with various possessions inside. I was unmistakably a non-league fan, and felt strangely proud of that.

Once on the train, Liz got stuck into a can of Dark Fruit that she had mysteriously acquired while I reached into the carrier bag and removed the pen and notebook. There was important work to do.

My plan was to use the journey to complete the annual *Two-Footed Tackle* fanzine end-of-season survey, which would give me a chance to reflect on the highlights and lowlights of a season during which I'd watched twenty-five games, travelled 7,545 miles (roughly the distance from England to Indonesia) and officially spent £2,400 (excluding use of the credit card, which doesn't count).

As we sped past the Emirates Stadium, Liz drained the last of her Dark Fruit, announced she was going to have a little nap and asked me to wake her when we were about fifteen minutes from Leeds. She then laid her head on my shoulder and was asleep within seconds.

Notepad and pen in hand, I also reached for the programme, which I'd need for the first question – Player of the Year. I'd narrowed this down to three names which I wrote on the page in front of me.

Alan Julian was first. He probably would have been an automatic choice had he not missed fifteen games (according to the programme) through injury. I don't think I've ever seen him play badly. There was also a case to be made for Moses Emmanuel, despite his poor scoring record in 2016. During September he was the best player in the League and it was mainly down to him that we finished clear of the relegation zone. But the winner for me was Jack Holland, who hadn't even been a starter in the first couple of games and still ended up as our best big number 9, as well as our best defender.

I stretched my legs out in front of me. Virgin trains were relatively comfortable, as well as sometimes being on time, and they weren't always massively overcrowded. If there was a best train category, that would be enough for them to win it.

But the next question wasn't about trains, it was about the best game of the season. This was another tough one, since basically every game we'd won was memorable. I thought back to some of the highlights: the opening day and a totally unexpected win against Wrexham, one of the biggest clubs we'd ever played; the 5-0 thrashing of Barrow, the biggest margin of victory of the season (even though I'd had to follow it on Twitter); that cold afternoon in Lincoln, when I witnessed a performance that finally convinced me we belonged at Vanarama National League level; and the win at Dover, which was mainly satisfying because it was a win at Dover.

But none of these was my final choice. Because for sheer awe and excitement, it was impossible to go past that day in the September sun at Torquay, when everything clicked and goals flew in. It's something I continue to think about (and rewatch) frequently.

As I was writing 'Torquay United v. Bromley 19/9/15' into my notepad, the catering trolley came past and I got Liz an apple juice for when she woke up. I then moved on to trying to pick the worst game of the season.

I wondered if I would be allowed to have ten joint winners. This was because when Bromley are bad, they're terrible. The last four games of the season were so dreadful that in my mind they'd already merged into one giant blob of awfulness. The away trips to Guiseley, Wrexham, Aldershot and Cheltenham were also nightmares, as was Altrincham on TV and Eastleigh in the Cup. Southport was so rubbish that some of our fans had started talking about steel corrosion rather than watch the game.

It came down to a toss of the coin between Wrexham (a) and Aldershot (a). I reached into my pocket, careful not to wake Liz, found a 20p piece and tossed it. Heads. Wrexham v. Bromley 13/2/16 was the winner.

Luckily I couldn't dwell on the horror of that day in North Wales because the next question was designed to bring back far happier memories: the best moment of the season. There were so many to choose from that I filled an entire page. Seeing John aka The Grubby at Hayes Lane again and conquering Orrest Head were magnificent. As was hearing the 'Bromley Geezers' song for the first time, at Halifax; and then witnessing it evolve into a moving choral masterpiece over the months. Watching Bromley on telly – the first half hour anyway, before it all went horribly wrong – was brilliant. Then there was the pride I felt at seeing Bromley take the field at places like Grimsby, Tranmere and Wrexham. Louis Dennis's goal against Barrow (even if I did only see it on the highlights, thanks to Jenny Eclair) was outstanding.

But none of these was my best moment of the season. That had come just a fortnight earlier when I walked through the gate and proudly stepped on to the Hayes Lane pitch as Ronin the Raven – finally, at the age of sixty-one, officially representing my club, Bromley FC. I still get emotional recalling it.

We pulled into Doncaster station – the perfect place to start thinking about the worst moment of the season, because that was where one of them had taken place. It was there, on a chilly August afternoon, that a group of Scunthorpe fans, seeing me writing something in a notepad, pointed at me and chanted, 'Train-spot-ter, train-spot-ter, train-spot-ter.' But there were plenty of other candidates. I felt my face turning red as I remembered being left dangling off the side of a horse before the Forest Green Rovers game, failing to book a taxi in Lincoln, and celebrating a goal that wasn't at Barrow. On the football front there was the injury-time disaster at Halifax, the highly illegal Forest Green goal being given, and Tranmere's goalkeeper not being sent off. These were all terrible injustices.

But none of them was my worst moment. The winner, the most soul-destroying thing that happened in 2015/16, was the ridiculous goal we conceded against moneybags Eastleigh on 24 October that knocked us out of the FA Cup.

By now I was tiring badly. It was coming up to midnight and I was feeling increasingly uncomfortable as Liz was trying to push me off my seat in her sleep, so that she could have more room. She had previous form for this – basically every time she fell asleep on a train home, which she did a lot.

Despite this I carried on, eager to finish by the time we got home. Best opposition fans was the next category. Most had been friendly, especially the plastic bag carriers at Cheltenham and Altrincham. I'd been impressed with the large numbers of Wrexham and Torquay fans that came to Bromley. But none were better than Guiseley, on whose coach I'm hoping to go to Hayes Lane again next season. I was delighted we'd be playing them again after they'd managed to stay up thanks to a nail-biting 4-3 win against Torquay that sounded like the exact opposite of our game against Aldershot. In other words, exciting.

Guiseley was also on the shortlist for best away ground, as were Barrow's Furness Building Society Stadium and Halifax's Shay Stadium, both of them a lot more pleasant than their surrounding areas. Some of the bigger, proper football grounds were breathtaking to the average Bromley fan. The Racecourse Ground in Wrexham and Blundell Park in Grimsby (which even had a giant TV screen) were in a different world to Hayes Lane. But the most impressive was the massive and well-maintained Prenton Park in Tranmere.

The worst away ground candidates included Boreham Wood's unrelentingly grim Meadow Park and the totally-unsuited-to-football Gateshead International Stadium. But the winner, in no way swayed by the fact that the club refused to supply me with a programme, was Dover Athletic's Crabble Athletic Ground.

The best food category required no thought whatsoever. For me, the magnificent award-winning cottage pie at Kidderminster beat Forest Green's surprisingly good vegan tofu pie. I'd bought a meat and potato pie at Old Trafford, but these were the only pies

I'd eaten at proper football grounds. The rest of the time I'd taken sandwiches.

Thinking about this made me hungry and I reached into my plastic carrier bag for some crisps, hoping that the munching wouldn't wake Liz. I was thirsty as well, so I helped myself to the apple juice I'd bought her earlier. What she didn't know wouldn't hurt her.

The best kit award was next, and this went to Altrincham's one-off purple ensemble, with Forest Green, once again, having to settle for second place.

Finally, it was time for my mini review of the season. 'Finishing 14th,' I wrote, 'was a spectacularly good result, showing that even the bookies, who'd had us down to finish 18th, had underestimated us.'

I breathed a sigh of relief. I'd finished, with time to spare. Or so I thought until I realized there'd been a scandalous omission in the survey.

Where was the best programme category?

Col probably hadn't included it because it was something no one but me cared about. I settled down to make my choice anyway.

Most of them were virtually identical, but *Heedlines* from Gateshead had been a surprising ray of sunshine on an otherwise dismal day. The (nameless) Bromley programme was up there, as good as most. But for me, Kidderminster's *The Harrier* was the best. It was well produced and the editor showed plenty of interest in the opposition, devoting six pages to us. This included the fact that 'David Bowie, Pixie Lott, Siouxsie Sue, Billy Idol, and spikey-haired 90s chef Gary Rhodes have all lived in Bromley. Possibly not together.'

Thinking about programmes reminded me of Dad, who had bought me my first one, at Craven Cottage on Saturday, 5 September 1964 for the game between Fulham and Manchester

301

United. I can still see him handing over sixpence to the programme seller. But then a lot of things remind me of him these days. I miss him enormously, and can't quite believe that I'll never see him again.

I started packing a few things away since we were almost in Wakefield, which was about fifteen minutes from Leeds. I woke Liz, as requested, and asked if I could borrow her phone, since mine was flat. She thrust it into my hand before going straight back to sleep.

I'd wake her again when we got to Leeds. Like I always did.

After checking the final Vanarama National League table on her phone, I went on to Facebook. David, the photographer, had posted the photo he'd taken after the game of me leaning on one of the barriers behind the goal on the now-deserted Hayes Lane terraces, staring out on to the pitch. The image seemed to have captured a moment, and I looked unusually contented. It took Heather, one of the many new friends I'd made while following Bromley this season, to recognize why. She'd left a one-word comment underneath the picture.

It simply said 'Home'.

Acknowledgements

Many thanks to Giles for all his support and for suffering two of the worst games of the season, Liz for not complaining too much about watching more non-league football than she would have liked, Dave Birrell for his superb thoughts and suggestions, Steve Garthwaite for all the encouragement and some brilliant ideas, Barrie for the Bromley shirt, Mickey for supplying T-shirts and ponchos, Warren Dudley for saying just the right things and finally, all the Bromley fans who have helped make the season so special, including Roy (the original Bromley Boy), Mash, Mickey, Sue, Garvo, Stu, Pete, Barrie, Nick, Pasty Pat, Simon, Paul, King Cobbler, Mike C, Mike H, Col, Emma, Club Shop Jim, John the Stick, Georgie, Ellie, Half Time John, Angie, Iona, Heather, Donna, Graeme, Ian, Tom, Lloyd, Will C, Manchester Will, Sunderland Sean, Howard T, Robin, Bob, DRFC Mike, Steve the Greek, James, Mark A, Tim W, Eddie, Richard, Rich, Jeff, David C, Louis, Matt, Dan, Uncle Gary, Stokesy, Edmund, Helen, Big Danny, Chris, Dingle Dangle, Ken, Alex, Mark C, Ingunn, Rob, Nigel, Geoff, Brian, Darren, Naughty Nigel, Jon, Steve B, Howard J, Lee, Mark, Tim H, Neil, Ben, Max, Martin, Rich R, Charlie, Geoff W and Paul.

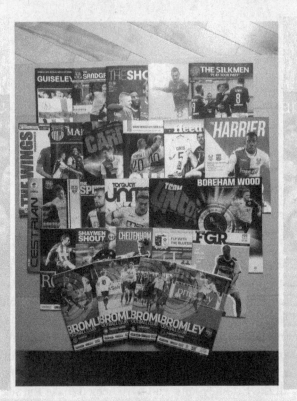

Author's Note

If you'd like to have a look at photos taken throughout the season, go to www.homeandawaybook.com, where you'll also be able to meet the fans.

If you'd like to subscribe to *Two-Footed Tackle*, the ace Bromley fanzine, write to Col here: wembley49@aol.com. And if you'd like to get the equally ace *In There!*, get in touch with Rich here: hayeslane22@gmail.com

And if you'd like to join the three other members of the Dave Roberts Fan Club contact Howard at htandm@btinternet.com

About the Author

Dave Roberts has been one of those annoying bike couriers, a security guard, a civil servant, a KFC chef who was fired for trying to steal a sample of the secret recipe, and a train driver – all before reaching the age of twenty. After that, he settled for a career in advertising, which was eventually cut short by illness, but not before accidentally winning a Silver Lion at Cannes. He now writes books, which all seem to have a theme in common: obsession . . .

Also by Dave Roberts

e-luv: an internet romance
The Bromley Boys
32 Programmes
Sad Men

For more information on Dave Roberts and his books,
see his website at www.daverobertsbooks.com
or contact him at dave@daverobertsbooks.com
You can also follow him on Twitter @thebromleyboys